CORNWALL COUNTY LIBRARY
3 8009 03096 1889

GW00578085

STEAMERS & FERRIES
OF THE
RIVER TAMAR
& THREE TOWNS DISTRICT

An Edward Chapman photograph, taken in the 1920s, with the paddle steamer PRINCE EDWARD *heading downstream after turning at Weir Head. The straight course of the Tamar Manure Navigation cut can be seen in the background.* ALAN KITTRIDGE COLLECTION.

STEAMERS & FERRIES
OF THE
RIVER TAMAR
& THREE TOWNS DISTRICT

BY
ALAN KITTRIDGE

TWELVEHEADS PRESS

TRURO 2003

CONTENTS

The Millbrook Steamboat & Trading Co Ltd's paddle steamer BRITANNIA *at Lower Pier, Millbrook in the 1930s.* CITY OF PLYMOUTH LOCAL & NAVAL STUDIES LIBRARY.

TWELVEHEADS PRESS

First published 2003 by Twelveheads Press.
Truro, Cornwall .
ISBN 0 906294 54 1
British Library Cataloguing-in-Publication Data.
A catalogue record for this book is available from the British Library.
Printed by The Amadeus Press Ltd., Cleckheaton, West Yorkshire.

INTRODUCTION

THE 'THREE TOWNS' OF THIS book's title comprised: the Borough of Plymouth – located in the south western corner of Devon at the mouth of the River Plym; the Borough of Devonport – which grew up around the naval dockyard on the banks of the River Tamar; and sandwiched in between, the Urban District of Stonehouse. Collectively these Three Towns were, as their conurbation – the City of Plymouth – still is, the largest centre of population west of Bristol and along the south coast of England. The 'district' in the title includes nearby communities in east Cornwall, the Tamar Valley and the South Hams of Devon, which were largely dependent upon the Three Towns but separated by the estuarine system that dominates the geography of the area. Six rivers and numerous navigable lakes (creeks) offered a water highway for the farming and industrial communities around their shores but, conversely, represented major obstacles to be crossed by travellers and locals alike.

Most of the district's ferries pre-dated passenger steamers, and the infrastructure of quays, roads and waterside communities which evolved at these crossings over the centuries served as a foundation for the new passenger steamer services of the early nineteenth century – which themselves pre-dated physical railway communication between Devon and Cornwall.

The opening of the Royal Albert Bridge in 1859 linked Cornwall and Devon by rail and initiated a network of suburban rail services in the district. Nevertheless, passenger steamers and ferries approached their zenith during the second half of the nineteenth century. The climax of their history was reached around 1900 and maintained until the Great War. Sixteen ferry crossings and 35 steamers served over 40 landings in the district during this period.

If the Great War brought the Victorian age to an end, then the industrial unrest of 1926 supplied the *coup de grâce* to its ageing paddle steamers in the Three Towns district. It is during this period that the steamboat fleets endured their nadir.

Twentieth century modernisation, meanwhile, seems to have been very slow in coming – in the case of the district's excursion boats, perhaps it didn't fully arrive until the 1950s when it was finally appreciated that the local population had largely turned their back on the 'steamers', and that the future of the passenger boats lay with visiting holiday makers and day trippers.

Road motor transport, particularly private motor cars after the Second World War, extended personal horizons as fundamentally as steamships and railways had over a century before. From the 1950s, few steamers or ferries

The Oreston & Turnchapel Steamboat Co Ltd's LIVELY *in 1935, heading up the Cattewater, off Turnchapel. A modest passenger steamer, but once a vital link with Plymouth for the villagers of Oreston and Turnchapel on the opposite shore of the River Plym.*
B. Y. WILLIAMS.

could still claim any importance as commuter carriers around the district's waterways and coastline. This history therefore chronicles the demise of some long serving steamers and ferries during the 1950s and 1960s and concludes with the closure of the Millbrook Steamboat & Trading Co Ltd in 1985 – the centennial year of its origins.

Today just one ancient ferry at Cremyll and the floating bridges at Torpoint survive, crossing the River Tamar between east Cornwall and the City of Plymouth. Excursion boats continue to ply in the summer season but now cater largely for visitors to the city, coach parties and charter trips.

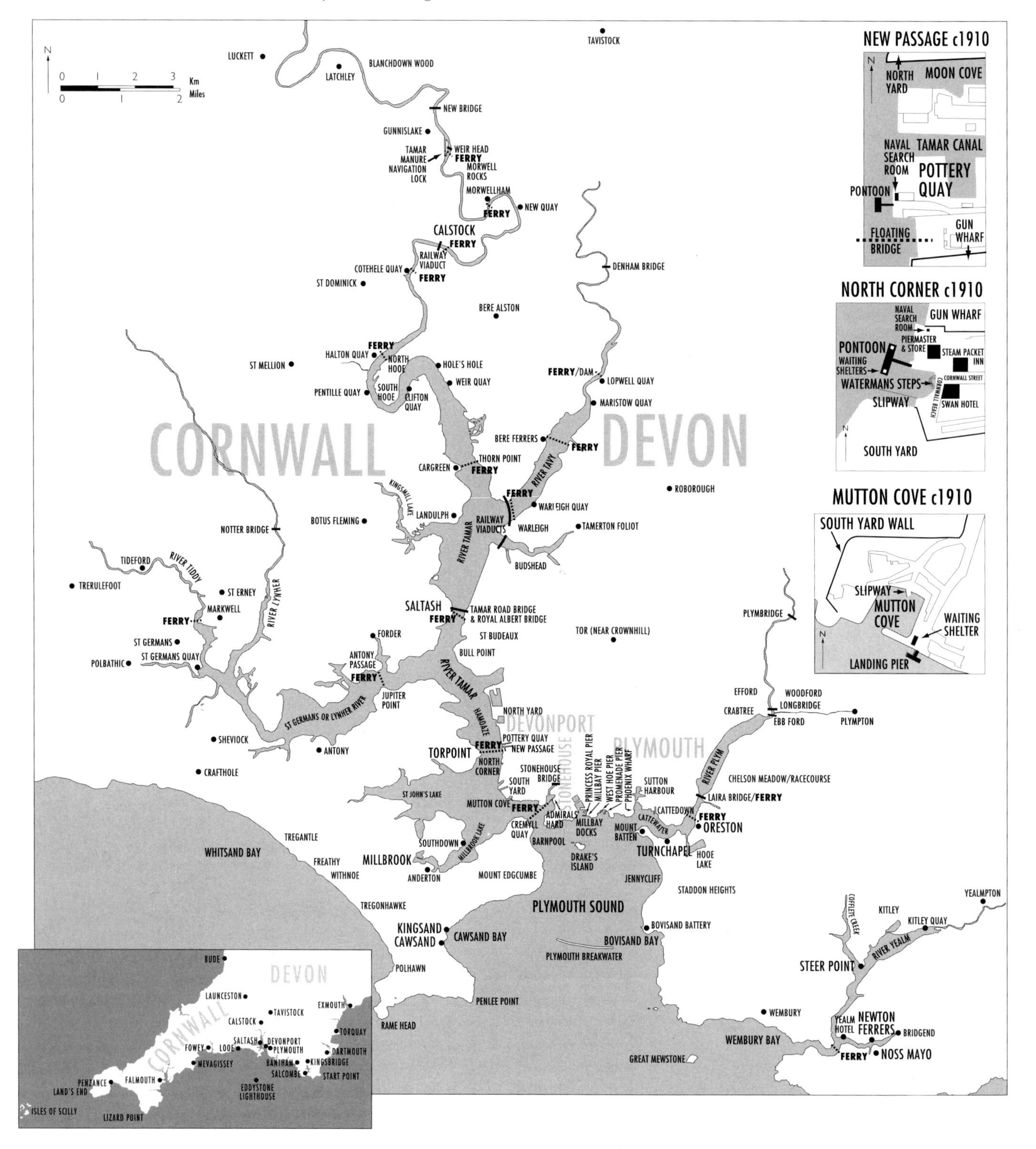

CHAPTER ONE

SINCE TIME IMMEMORIAL

Ancient passages and other ferries

ON THE EVE OF A POPULATION explosion which would result from major industrial developments around the Three Towns and in the Tamar Valley during the first quarter of the nineteenth century, a number of long established ferries existed in the area, most having evolved over centuries to serve the district's estuarine communities. Steam would power the imminent industrial expansion, and the adoption of steam engines to propel ferries and other passenger boats would transform navigation of the local waterways, but many of these ferries, especially those in sparsely populated areas, continued relatively unchanged until road motor transport eroded their use between the world wars.

THE CREMYLL FERRY

The conflicting and dangerous currents that swirl around the mouth of the River Tamar can be seen from the safe vantage of the rocky shore at Devil's Point, or experienced from the seemingly more vulnerable Cremyll Ferry which has crossed these waters relentlessly for hundreds of years. Contrary to the general rule of rivers becoming wider towards their mouth, Devon and Cornwall will not be as close again until Saltash is reached, over three miles upstream. In the absence of a more convenient passage place below Saltash, the Cremyll Ferry became established as a main route between the Plymouth district and south Cornwall.

Late in the fifteenth century Sir Piers Edgcumbe of Cotehele gained, by marriage, the old Valletort manors of East Stonehouse on the Devon shore and Maker (or West Stonehouse) on the 'Cornish' shore of Plymouth Sound, which included the Cremyll Ferry and ferry rights on the Tamar downstream of Saltash. He established his new manor house at the eponymously named Mount Edgcumbe, in Maker, overlooking Plymouth Sound. The Maker estate encompassed land between Kingsand and parts of Millbrook, all of which were a part of Devon until 1854.

The East Stonehouse landing of the Cremyll Ferry was a beach inside the mouth of the River Tamar, near the present basin of the Victualling Yard – Cremyll Street in Stonehouse still leads towards the former site of this landing place. The landing on the Mount Edgcumbe, or Cremyll, side was in Barnpool, a small bay just outside the mouth of the Tamar. By the end of the seventeenth century the ferry was an important part of the route into Cornwall *via* Crafthole, Looe and ferries at Bodinnick, Par and King Harry. Post horses carrying the south Cornwall mails, for Looe, St Austell, Truro and Penryn, had priority on the ferry.

At the start of the eighteenth century the Cremyll Ferry was still the only ferry crossing the Tamar below Saltash. But nearby, on the Devon shore of the Hamoaze (the estuary of the River Tamar) at Point Froward, the Admiralty was constructing a dockyard for the Royal Navy. The yard would expand south to Mutton Cove by the end of the century and later extend northwards to occupy most of the Devon shore of the Hamoaze. These developments were to transform the entire estuary and give rise to the dockyard towns of Devonport and Torpoint – facing each other on opposite shores of the Tamar.

The Cremyll Ferry landing on the Mount Edgcumbe side was moved from Barnpool to Cremyll Beach in 1730. It was suggested in *Brindley's Directory* of 1830 that it was '...from the annoyance it caused to the Lordly domain of Mount Edgcumbe...' that the landing had been relocated. While this may be have been a contributing factor during the landscaping of Mount Edgcumbe in the 1730s, the new landing place was better because it was inside the mouth of the river and nearer to the new dockyard.

Cremyll Passage pictured from Devil's Point – near the pre-1825 Stonehouse landing of the Cremyll Ferry. On the left is Cremyll Quay, in Cornwall, and in the distance to the right, Mutton Cove, which between 1741–1837 was the Devonport landing place of the Cremyll Ferry.
ALAN KITTRIDGE

John Smeaton's Stonehouse Bridge of 1773 (top left of picture) replaced the earlier Stonehouse Pool Ferry. This was a station for local watermen long before the bridge was built and remains a haven for Stonehouse boatmen to this day. In this 1970s view Plymouth Brewery can be seen (top centre) on the Stonehouse shore – the effluent from which often covered the creek in white froth. A public slipway between the brewery and the bridge served as a watermen's station. On the opposite side of the bridge are watermen's moorings and sheds. The creek beyond Stonehouse Bridge is now completely infilled and the 'bridge' now marks the tidal limit of Stonehouse Lake. King Street (top left) was the original route to the Stonehouse Pool Ferry from the Frankfort Gate of Plymouth. Edgcumbe Street (top centre) is part of Union Street which spanned the former marsh of Sourpool, 'uniting' Plymouth, Stonehouse and Devonport via Stonehouse Bridge. In the bottom left hand corner is the trackbed of the former L&SWR branch line to the passenger liner facility at Ocean Quay. The land in the top half of the picture is in Stonehouse, while that in the foreground is Richmond Walk, in Devonport, with Blagdon's boatyard in the centre
B. M. CARTWRIGHT COURTESY KEN BADGE.

James Swigg, the ferry lessee at the time, was granted permission to introduce two new boats in 1741 on an additional service between Cremyll and Mutton Cove, to serve the new community of Dock or Plymouth Dock (later Devonport) which was growing around the Naval dockyard.

Land in Stonehouse also attracted the attention of the Admiralty and on the banks of Stonehouse Lake (within the Port of Plymouth, creeks are known as 'lakes') the Royal Naval Hospital was completed in 1761, followed in 1784 by the Royal Marine Barracks, which dominated the skyline between Stonehouse Pool and Millbay. The Admiralty's programme of major developments in Stonehouse culminated with the building of the Royal William Victualling Yard near Devil's Point between 1823 and 1833 and the Stonehouse landing beach of the Cremyll Ferry vanished beneath its vast granite quays and storehouses. A new and far better paved landing for the ferry, named Admiral's Hard, was built by the Admiralty in Stonehouse Pool in 1826. This 100 yard long jetty, off Durnford Street, near the Royal Marine Barracks, offered landings at all states of the tide and has served as the Devon landing place of the Cremyll Ferry ever since.

Lord Mount Edgcumbe was elevated to Earldom in 1789. During the previous year he opened Mount Edgcumbe Park to the public on Mondays and the future of the Cremyll Ferry was thus secured, because in due course an increasing proportion of its passengers were visitors to the park. But any immediate gain was offset when, in 1791, the Torpoint Ferry won the contract to carry the Cornish mail. Partners in this new ferry venture were Reginald Pole Carew of Antony Estate and the Earl of Mount Edgcumbe.

Incursions by watermen on the Mount Edgcumbe Estate's ferry routes to Cremyll had long caused friction and the move to Admiral's Hard in 1826 increased confrontation. At Cremyll the ferry toll was collected from anyone landing on the beach – anyone the toll collector could catch that is – whether they used the official ferryboats or not. The collectors were sometimes subjected to physical abuse by watermen's passengers refusing to pay twice. The legality of this toll was challenged in court by the watermen but upheld for the Stonehouse route because it had been in use since time immemorial. The right to collect tolls from watermen's passengers from Mutton Cove, however, remained contentious because this ferry route had originally been started by the ferry lessee in 1741 and could not claim any ancient rights. Although the Mutton Cove route had become the busiest of the two passages, the three official boats were withdrawn in 1837, due to unprofitability caused by continuing competition from watermen. Admiral's Hard, therefore, became the only Three Towns landing place for the official Cremyll Ferry. At the same time the ferry landing on the Mount Edgcumbe side was improved by the construction of the surviving Cremyll Quay. The engineer in charge of this work was James Meadows Rendel – the principal figure in the ultimately successful introduction of steam to the Tamar's two most important ferry crossings at Torpoint and Saltash. The right to free landing on Cremyll Beach remained the subject of acrimonious debate between the watermen of Mutton Cove and agents of the Mount Edgcumbe Estate. The dispute dragged on until after the Great War, when the Mount Edgcumbe Estate railed off the entire Cremyll foreshore and erected turnstiles where the ferry fare was collected from all those passing through. This effectively ended a tradition of park visits from the Devonport shore, because watermen's passengers from Mutton Cove were left with no option but to pay twice each way – the waterman's fare and the Cremyll Ferry toll.

The Cremyll Ferry route that survives today between Cremyll Quay and Admiral's Hard was thus established but due to resistance from William, the fourth Earl of Mount Edgcumbe, steamboats were not to be introduced until late in the nineteenth century.

The Stonehouse Pool Ferry and the Halfpenny Bridge

Stonehouse Lake once reached inland as far as Pennycomequick, just below Plymouth's current North Road railway station. A part of what is now Victoria Park was a mill pool, from which water was sluiced through a mill on Sir Piers Edgcumbe's sixteenth century Millbridge. This bridge later carried a toll road between Stonehouse and Devonport, but until the second half of the eighteenth century the shortest route linking the Three Towns was *via* the Stonehouse Pool Ferry, located about a mile below Millbridge near the site of the present Stonehouse Bridge. Carriages, horses and foot passengers were conveyed across the lake in a boat drawn from side to side by a cable. In 1767 Lord Mount Edgcumbe and Sir John St Aubyn, seeking to promote the profitable development of their estates, upon which were growing the towns of Stonehouse and Plymouth Dock respectively, commissioned John Smeaton to design and build Stonehouse Bridge. Opened in 1773 it became known to generations as the Halfpenny Gate or Halfpenny Bridge, on account of the pedestrian toll, and has offered the most direct route between Stonehouse and Devonport ever since.

The Devonport landing stages at Mutton Cove and North Corner

Adjacent to the limestone wall of Devonport Dockyard's South Yard is Mutton Cove, a small harbour which once supported a community of watermen. The harbour basin is formed by a protective jetty which was built before 1790 – a map from that period shows it as New Wharf and standing in isolation with no buildings in Mutton Cove. A small community soon established itself in the cove and the harbour became a major watermen's station for licenced passenger boats running to Cremyll, Millbrook Lake and other places on the Hamoaze.

North Corner (i.e. the north corner of the original dockyard) and Cornwall Street grew up around a watermen's community at Cornwall Beach on the Hamoaze. Plymouth Dock originated here in the eighteenth century and

Watermen's boats at Mutton Cove, Devonport c1910 – a major watermen's station on the Hamoaze of the River Tamar. The small community nestled beneath the tall limestone walls of the Dockyard, which can be seen in the background. The volatile combination of watermen, garrison soldiers, sailors and dockyard workers, together with an abundance of public houses, earned Mutton Cove a notorious reputation.
ALAN KITTRIDGE COLLECTION.

North Corner (Cornwall Beach) c1910, a watermen's station on the Hamoaze which became Devonport's principal passenger steamer quay. The older name of Cornwall Beach and the generous provision of facilities for watermen, suggests that passage across the Tamar was available from the shore here before the beginning of Plymouth Dock. ALAN KITTRIDGE COLLECTION.

gradually extended up the hill alongside the north wall of the of the dockyard (now South Yard). The Gun Wharf (now Morice Yard) was built in the early eighteenth century by the Board of Ordnance on the opposite side of Cornwall Beach, establishing the narrow corridor of civic land that has existed ever since and forcing the future Devonport to expand inland, away from the Hamoaze. In common with Mutton Cove, North Corner was a major watermen's station, offering passage to Plymouth and Stonehouse, across to Cornwall, up the Tamar Valley, or to naval ships in the Hamoaze. It also became the landing place for market boats from St Germans and the Tamar Valley, which brought market produce (butter, cream, eggs, fruit, vegetables and meat) to sell in Devonport Market.

A waterman's boat, the EMMA, *in the Tamar Canal, Devonport 1989.* ALAN KITTRIDGE.

WATERMEN

Regulations controlling watermen's boats were issued jointly by the three local authorities and required every waterman to produce on demand a copy of the *Bye-laws & Table of Fares* which contained a list of fares from various watermen's stations in the district. The regulations also covered fares to ships moored offshore – defined as areas from No.1 (outside the Breakwater) to No. 22 (Saltash and above). Storm flags were flown at Teat's Hill (in Sutton Pool) and from Devonport Column. A red triangular flag denoted stormy weather and stipulated that there should be two watermen per boat in the Sound – but at twice the regular fare. Two red triangular flags denoted 'Tempestuous' weather and fares could be settled by agreement. *Nettleton's Guide* 1836 noted that visitors could hire boats at the Barbican (in Sutton Pool); at Sandy Cove (in Millbay); and that watermen were usually in waiting at the Royal Hotel, Plymouth. Not all were water*men*, women also worked the boats – the female water*persons* of Saltash in particular were noted rowers. Neither were the boats used solely for passengers – water, provisions and laundry were also delivered to vessels anchored in the Hamoaze, Cattewater and Sound.

The licence number of each boat was carried inside the transom and on the bows and each waterman wore a badge on his right arm. Watermen's boats had to measure above 15ft. long and were licenced to carry: 6 passengers (15ft.); 8 passengers (16ft.); 9 passengers (17ft.); and 10 passengers (18ft.). The traditional watermen's service faded away after the Great War but some watermen acquired open motor boats (usually licenced for twelve passengers – the maximum before Board of Trade regulations applied) and started running to the beaches at Cawsand and Kingsand, or offered trips around the dockyard to view the warships – as their successors still do.

Some watermen's boats survived as salmon seine net boats on the Tamar above Saltash and a few could still be found in the 1980s on the beach at Torpoint or in the Tamar Canal adjacent to the Torpoint Ferry slipway. Most were clinker built and carried a small unstayed sail. Builders of these boats included Kessel, Morris and Chant – all of Moon Cove in Devonport, Rogerman of Laira, and Blagdons of Richmond Walk who, from the 1860s, built watermen's boats and also hire boats for the Sea Front of Plymouth.

THE TORPOINT FERRY

Between St Johns Lake and the estuary of the River Lyhner a tongue of land slopes gently to the Tamar's edge at Torpoint. Until construction of the dockyard commenced on the opposite Devon shore both sides of the river were agricultural, with no important roads nearby. Torpoint was owned by the Carew family as part of the Antony Estate where, in the early eighteenth century, Antony House was built. By 1745 a small community at Torpoint (or Tar Point) was careening and ballasting naval and other ships. Passage was available between Torpoint and Cornwall Beach (North Corner) before an official ferry was introduced in 1791 and there is reference to this 'new ferry' charging 'the same rates as before'.

Horse drawn coaches were still a rare sight in Cornwall during the mid-eighteenth century, mainly because the roads were too poor for wheeled traffic, but from 1759 a number of turnpike developments in the county facilitated stage- and mail-coach services. The Liskeard Turnpike Act of 1761 authorised construction of

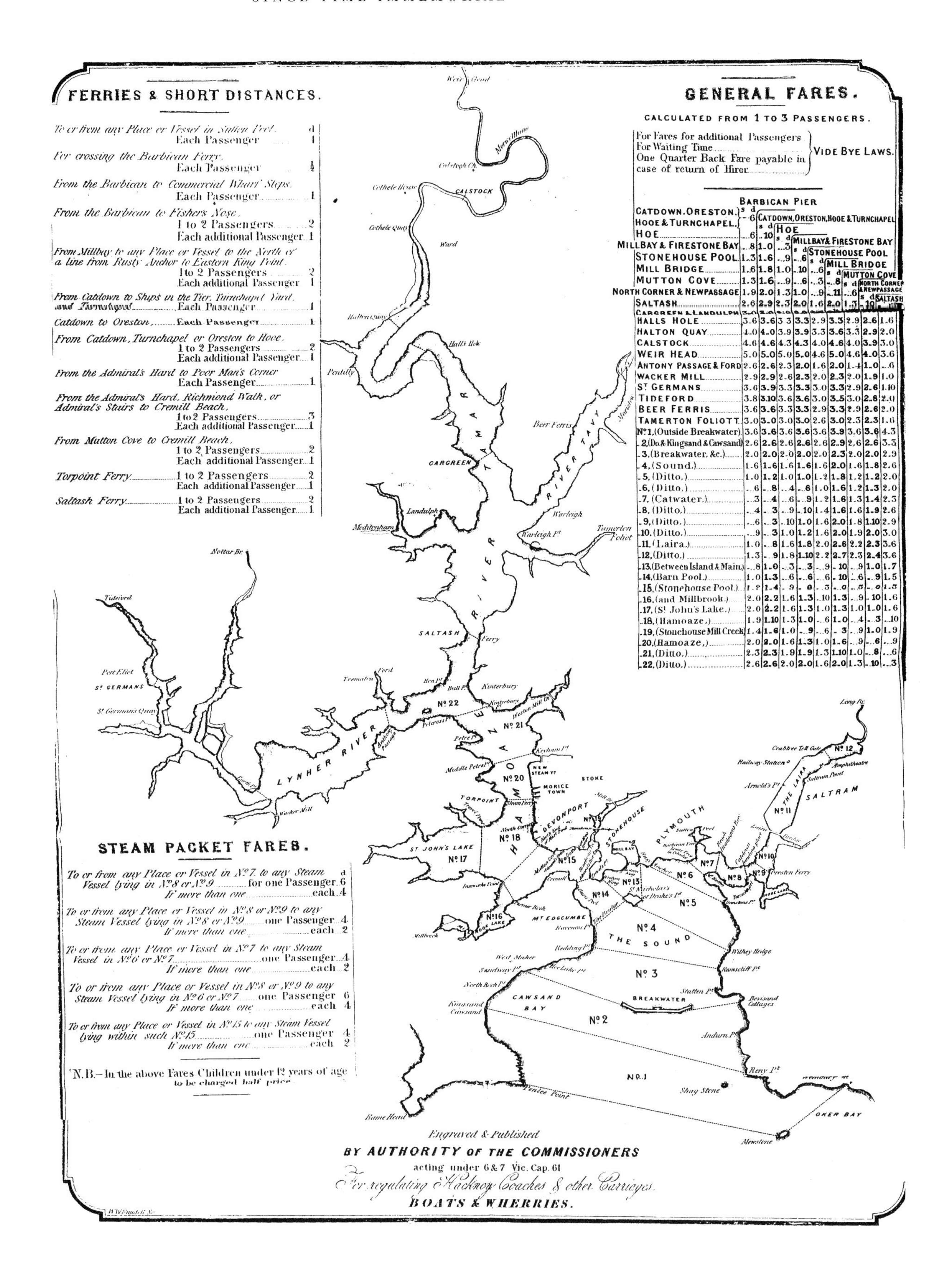

Watermen's fare structure and areas defined – taken from the The Plymouth, Devonport and Stonehouse Carriages and Boats, Regulation Act 1848. CITY OF PLYMOUTH MUSEUMS & ART GALLERY.

a road from Liskeard *via* Crafthole to Antony and Torpoint. Reginald Pole Carew inherited Antony Estate in 1771 and was the key figure in the creation of the town of Torpoint on his estate, with his plan of 1774 for its development as a satellite community of Plymouth Dock.

The Torpoint Ferry Act of 1790 empowered George, Earl of Mount Edgcumbe (who held exclusive ferry rights on the Tamar downstream of Saltash) and Reginald Pole Carew of Antony to establish and maintain a common ferry across the River Tamar between 'a certain place North of Plymouth Dock' (New Passage) and Torpoint. The ferry opened on Monday 4 July 1791 for the conveyance of foot passengers, carriages, horses and cattle. A handbill noted:

> It is, perhaps, unnecessary to add, that this passage opens a shorter and much easier communication between Plymouth Dock and the Western part of Cornwall, than any now in use…

Horse and carriage boats plied to 'New Canal' (a cut or basin, since infilled, at New Passage) from which a new road, New Passage Hill, was built leading to Marlborough Street in Plymouth Dock. An additional boat, for foot passengers only, continued the service to Cornwall Beach – which was nearer to the town and dockyard but not suitable for landing carriages. The ferry ran a shuttle service between 6am to 9pm in the summer and 7am to 8pm in the winter. Originally there were three footboats, each with two crewmen, and one horseboat crewed by three men. At least one more horseboat was introduced by 1825. In a letter dated 2 January 1826, to James Brown – the designer of a steam ferry at Dundee – Reginald Pole Carew described the boats:

> Our present boats are from stem to stern 28 feet 3 inches long, 8 feet 1 inch broad, from ceiling to the gunwhale 2 feet 4 inches deep. And they receive conveniently a coach of the largest dimensions and 4 horses, besides foot passengers.

Daily operation of the ferry was leased to innkeepers of the Passage House Inn or London Inn in Torpoint. Walter Cross was a notable lessee who in 1796 started a stage coach from Torpoint to Truro from the Passage House Inn. On 21 January 1799 Hooper & Co established another service with a coach for ten inside passengers, running from the Kings Arms in Torpoint to Liskeard, Lostwithiel, St Austell, Grampound, Truro and Falmouth. In 1794 the Torpoint Ferry won the contract to carry the Plymouth Dock, St Germans and Liskeard mails. The first Royal Mail-coach to run between Plymouth Dock and Falmouth *via* the Torpoint Ferry was introduced in 1806. New coaching ventures in the second decade of the nineteenth century included: the *Defence* from the London Inn to Falmouth; the *Lady Exmouth*, between Falmouth and Exeter *via* the Torpoint Ferry; the *Royal Eclipse* from Falmouth to Torpoint; and the *Bodmin & Torpoint Mail Diligence*. To help improve the route for these stage- and Mail-coach services an Act of 1826 authorised a deviation road which wound its way around Wacker, Sconner and Polbathic lakes (the present A374), superseding the hilly route through Crafthole. The new road prompted major improvements on the Torpoint Ferry and the adoption of steam propulsion.

TORPOINT FERRY.

NOTICE IS HEREBY GIVEN,

THAT THE FERRY

Eftablifhed by Act of Parliament for the CONVEYANCE of

Foot Paffengers, Carriages, Horfes, and Cattle,

BETWEEN

Plymouth-Dock and *Torpoint*,

WILL BE OPENED

On MONDAY the 4th Day of JULY next,

WHEN

Proper and convenient Boats, manned by able and careful Seamen,

Will be conftantly ready to accommodate all Travellers defirous of

Paffing TO and FROM the adjacent PARTS of the Counties of DEVON and CORNWALL.

It is, perhaps, unneceffary to add, that this Paffage opens a fhorter and much eafier Communication between Plymouth-Dock and the Weftern Part of Cornwall, than any now in Ufe; and the Proprietors are determined that no Attention or Expence fhall be wanting to render the Attendance punctual, and the Accommodation complete.

N.B. The HORSE and CARRIAGE-BOATS will ply only from the New Canal, North of the Gun-Wharf, to which a good public Road is lately made; the Boats for Foot Paffengers, both from thence and from North-Corner to Torpoint.

PLYMOUTH-DOCK, JUNE 30, 1791.

Announcing the inauguration of the Torpoint Ferry in 1791. CORNWALL RECORDS OFFICE

THE 'ST GERMANS OR LYNHER RIVER' AND THE ANTONY FERRY

The River Lynher rises on Cornwall's Bodmin Moor and joins the Tamar downstream of Saltash. It was navigable by river barges for about seven miles upstream to Notter Bridge. The tributary River Tiddy, which was navigable to Tideford, supported the important mineral and agricultural St Germans Quay, giving the estuary the unusual but once commonly used joint name 'St Germans or Lynher River'. The lakes of Polbathic, Sconner, Wacker, Tredown, Wivelscombe and Forder radiate off the densely wooded estuary. St Germans and its quay is situated on the western shore of the Tiddy and for locals going to Saltash the quickest route was by means of the Markwell Ferry which crossed the river from the shore near Higher Quay, upstream from St Germans, to Markwell Quay and a track on the Markwell or St Erney side. From there the track led to Landrake and Notter Bridge and the road to Saltash.

Antony (misspelled on the postcard) Passage with the Ferry House Inn on the left. The telegraph posts and fencing in the background mark the former route of the Great Western Railway before the line deviated further inland in 1908.
ALAN KITTRIDGE COLLECTION.

The Antony Ferry, near the mouth of the Lyhner, dates back to the fourteenth century and ran from Jupiter Point – on the Antony or Torpoint side, to Antony Passage – at the mouth of Forder Lake. Its value to those on the Saltash side wishing to communicate with the Antony or Maker districts can be gauged by comparing the alternative route around the Lynher and Tiddy rivers to St Germans. The ferry rights were owned by the Carew family (later the Pole Carews) of Antony Estate and the ferry was leased to the licensee of the Ferry House Inn at Antony Passage. Until the early years of last century a horse or livestock boat was provided but latterly a passenger only rowing-boat was used (a motor-boat was occasionally used on the ferry during the 1920s). A red flag was provided at Jupiter Point to hail the ferryman, who was always based on the opposite shore. The Crossley family, river pilots of Antony Passage, ran the ferry from the end of the nineteenth century until its closure in the 1950s. Until the Second World War it was popular with people from Torpoint who could walk down Ferry Lane to Jupiter Point and visit Apple Tree Cot Tea Garden on the opposite shore, or enjoy a circular excursion *via* the Saltash Ferry (with a stop at Little Ash Tea Garden – 'Devonport's Beauty Spot'), a tram ride through Devonport to New Passage and back across the Torpoint Ferry. Ferry Lane had replaced an earlier road to the ferry and passed very close to Antony House. Increased use of the lane and ferry by day trippers in the early twentieth century prompted the Antony Estate to investigate relocating the ferry. A public enquiry before the High Sheriff of Cornwall was held in 1920 regarding the changes to the ferry service and in 1921 a new route was suggested running from Wilcove Head, near Torpoint, to Wearde Quay, near Saltash – but it was never adopted. The Antony Estate sold its property on the Antony Passage side in 1951–2 and at the same time the Crossley's gave notice of quitting the ferry service. Although never officially closed (therefore still appearing on later maps) the ferry went out of use from that date.

THE SALTASH FERRY

For seven centuries, until closure in 1961, the Saltash Ferry was one of the most important ferry crossings on the River Tamar. Its origins date back beyond the Norman Conquest when it was known as the Ashe–Torre passage. Torre referred to Tor near the present day Crownhill in Plymouth, a major crossroads of ridgeways from Sutton (later Plymouth); the priory at Plympton (*via* Efford); the priory at Tavistock (across Dartmoor); and Cornwall (*via* Ashe or Saltash). In 1270 the ferry rights passed to Richard, Earl of Cornwall (later the Duke of Cornwall), who provided a boat but leased the operation to the Burgesses of Saltash. The ferry rights were granted to the Borough of Saltash in 1385 for 200 years. This was extended by Queen Elizabeth I and the Borough continued to hold the rights until 1961 but the passage was still subject to a rental charge by the Duchy of Cornwall.

The Saltash crossing earned some notoriety

Apple Tree Cot Tea Garden in Forder Lake, near Saltash, was a popular destination for strollers from Saltash – and from Torpoint via the Antony Ferry.
ALAN KITTRIDGE COLLECTION.

A Chapman & Son postcard, postally cancelled in Bere Alston on 7 November 1913, offers a rare view of the Lopwell Ferry. The boat ran from Lopwell Quay, in the right hand foreground, to the Bere peninsula and paths to Bere Alston and Bere Ferrers.
ALAN KITTRIDGE COLLECTION.

during its long history. When Daniel Defoe crossed in 1724 he described Saltash as 'a poor shattered little town' and the ferry boats so bad that '...I thought myself well escaped when I got safe on shore in Cornwall.' Nine years later twenty passengers drowned when the ferry capsized.

A new road from Trerulefoot to Saltash opened in 1761 and prompted improvements to the Saltash Ferry. The landlord of the Ferry House at Saltash, who leased the ferry from Saltash Corporation, announced that he had 'lately fitted up his house' and 'provided everything for the reception of travellers'. He assured good attendance at the ferry with 'carriages safely put in and out of the ferry boat'. The Corporation of Saltash fixed the rates at: carriage and six horses 7s 6d; carriage and four horses 5s; carriage and pair 2s 6d; one horse chaise 1s 6d. The improvements were appreciated by the traveller Dr W. G. Maton, who in the mid-1790s found 'a commodious ferry-boat, which wafted us and our horses across the Tamar'.

Gnatham Ford in 1989.
ALAN KITTRIDGE.

In the early nineteenth century there were at least two boats in service, one for carriages and a smaller boat for horses and foot passengers. There may have been an additional boat for foot passengers only. The horseboat was rowed by two men using long oars or sweeps. The 'Devon' landing – still a part of Cornwall until 1854 – was at the Inn immediately below the present Royal Albert Bridge. There was a steep climb up the hill to a halfway house – the Travellers Rest at Tamerton – and on to the crossroads at Tor.

The ferry continued unchanged until, in 1832, a private company leased the rights and established a steam ferry.

THE RIVER TAVY

One geographical feature, the Bere peninsula, which is formed by the meanderings and confluence of the rivers Tamar and Tavy, gave rise to almost all other ferries upstream from Saltash. There were at least nine regular ferries, each rural in nature and for foot passengers only. In addition there have been another four or five casual or workers ferries which served miners and others crossing the Tamar, usually at work times only.

The River Tavy rises on Dartmoor and before the construction of a dam at Lopwell the moorland river met tidal water just below Buckland Abbey at Terrace (or Terras) Meadows Hard, on the Bere peninsula side. Lopwell Quay was the highest quay on the Buckland side and served Buckland Abbey. From this quay the Lopwell Ferry ran to the opposite bank of the river where paths led to Bere Ferrers and Bere Alston. The nearest alternative crossing at high tide was two and a half miles upstream at

Another Chapman postcard, postally used in June 1905, depicting Bere Ferrers Quay near the turn of the last century – a scene little changed today. A lightly loaded Tamar barge approaches the quay. From here a ferry ran to Blaxton Quay on the shore in the background, thereby cutting a long detour via Maristow or Lopwell for Three Towns bound travellers. In the 1860s the Tamar & Tavy Steamship Co Ltd established a market day call at Bere Ferrers Quay and their paddle steamer AERIAL *called regularly.* ALAN KITTRIDGE COLLECTION.

Denham Bridge. The ferry was superseded by a ford running along a dam built at Lopwell by the water authority in 1954.

Below Lopwell, where the Tavy opens out into its wide estuary, is Maristow Quay which served the Maristow Estate of Lord Roborough – which was acquired by the Lopes family in 1798. Immediately upstream of the quay is Chucksford, a tidal ford at the end of a tidal track which runs along the shore to Bere Ferrers (*via* another ford at Gnatham). Once across the ford on the Maristow side, the traveller could continue to the Plymouth district *via* Tamerton Foliot. The paved ford is now covered in mud but still indicated with marker posts on the Maristow side.

Midway along the estuary is the quay and village of Bere Ferrers and from the end of Bere Ferrers Quay a ferry once crossed to Blaxton Quay, providing a quicker route to Plymouth *via* Tamerton Foliot. The ferry ran near high tide only, because Bere Ferrers Quay is dry at low tide. It closed after the Great War.

Yellowstone Quay, on the Bere Ferrers side, was located near the position of the current railway bridge (built in 1889), just inside the mouth of the Tavy, and a ferry crossed from there to Warleigh Woods. There seems also to have been a casual ferry across Tamerton Lake, immediately downstream from the River Tavy, to Budshead which would have been used in conjunction with the Warleigh crossing and bypassed Tamerton Foliot. Further along Tamerton Lake the creek could be forded at low tide, even though the village of Tamerton Foliot and the head of the creek is only half a mile further along. These Tamerton crossings were particularly local in nature, used by those who knew the tides and availability of boats.

The PD&SWJR bridge of 1889, across the mouth of the River Tavy, pictured from Warleigh Woods. ALAN KITTRIDGE

THE RIVER TAMAR ABOVE SALTASH

Returning to the River Tamar on the Cornish side, upstream from Kingsmill Lake lies Cargreen, once a ship owning village and an important market boat and agricultural quay – the village has grown alongside the road from the quay. A ferry, which dates back to Medieval times, crossed to the opposite Bere peninsula. The importance of the Cargreen Ferry once lay in linking the Landulph district of east Cornwall to Tavistock *via* the ridge road along the Bere peninsula. Its busiest period, however, occurred when the railway reached the Bere peninsula in 1890 and the ferry linked the market garden and flower growing districts of Landulph and

Cargreen in the 1980s with the Spaniards Inn – formerly the Royal Oak Inn – the lessee of which maintained the Cargreen Ferry ALAN KITTRIDGE

Pictured in 1998, Hole's Hole Quay (some nineteenth century maps spell it Hall's Hole) on the Bere peninsula shore of the River Tamar was once a distribution point for market garden produce and a major market boat quay. The house behind the quay is the former Tamar Hotel, which closed as a hotel in 1903. On the right of the quay is a limekiln – a feature of most Tamar quays above Saltash. Limestone from Plymouth quarries was burnt to produce lime for manuring the acid soil of the Tamar Valley. Lime becomes caustic when wet – so it was carried upriver as limestone and burnt at the quays on arrival. ALAN KITTRIDGE.

Botus Fleming to the railway station at Bere Ferrers. Fruit, vegetables and flowers were ferried across to the Plymouth, Devonport & South Western Junction Railway (PD&SWJR), the mainline of which was worked by the London & South Western Railway (L&SWR), bound for Covent Garden produce market in London. The ferry ran from steps below Cargreen's Royal Oak Inn (now the Spaniards Inn), the landlord of which held the ferry lease. At the opposite landing place at Thorn Point, on the Bere peninsula side, a red flag on a flagpole was hoisted to summon the ferry from Cargreen. A spit of land, or causeway, still runs out from the shore at Thorn Point, from which the ferry could be boarded at low tide. Use of the ferry declined after the Great War when the carriage of produce switched to motor transport for delivery to the Great Western Railway (GWR) at Saltash or the PD&SWJR (Southern Railway from 1923) at St Budeaux but it survived until the Second World War.

MARKET BOATS

Upstream, on the Bere peninsula, just before the River Tamar sweeps in a great meander around South Hooe, is the strangely named Hole's Hole and its quay. Farms in the fertile Tamar Valley grew food for the markets in Tavistock and Saltash and demand for their produce increased when a market was established at Plymouth Dock. Before the railways changed the nature of food distribution in the mid-nineteenth century, local agricultural communities produced most of the food for nearby towns and the Tamar Valley became the principal food producing district for Plymouth Dock (Devonport). The first community at Plymouth Dock was established in the early eighteenth century and by 1733 numbered around 3,000 residents. Daniel Defoe noted in 1724 that there was a good market at Saltash which was:

> ...very much increased since the number of the inhabitants are increased at the new town, as I mentioned as near the dock at the mouth of the Hamoaze, for those people choose rather to go to Saltash to market by water than to walk to Plymouth by land for their provisions. Because first, as they go in the town boat, the same boat brings home what they buy, so that it is much less trouble; second, because provisions are bought much cheaper at Saltash than at Plymouth.

Not until 1762 would there be a market at Plymouth Dock for market boats to ply to. However, there is evidence of market boats plying to Saltash from St Germans – in 1757 a man drowned when the 'barge' from St Germans sank. There was another market boat

Halton Quay, pictured in 1987, was an important agricultural distribution point for the St Mellion and St Dominick districts – a regular stopping place for market steamers until 1926. The white building on the right was the quay office of Messrs Perry & Spear (agricultural merchants) until 1918 when Plymouth Co-operative Society gained the lease of the quay. Further right, out of view, is a bank of four limekilns. ALAN KITTRIDGE.

accident in 1832, five people drowned when the boat foundered off Antony Passage. The St Germans market boat called at Saltash and in the second half of the eighteenth century at Plymouth Dock on Tuesdays, Thursdays and Saturdays – market days. With favourable weather and tides the voyages were evidently completed with some success but what occurred when the elements did not prevail is unclear. The estuary of the Lynher is wide but very shallow, and near St Germans Quay the River Tiddy virtually dries out at low tide. At such times voyages by heavily laden sailing barges must have been impossible.

The distance between North Corner and St Germans is about six miles but Calstock, the main village on the Tamar above Saltash, is almost twice as far and a sailing barge would have been be fortunate to complete the meandering journey to Plymouth Dock on one tide, leave alone arrive in time for the market at 9am. Boats of four or six oars may have completed the journey by rowing with the tide, but space for produce would have been limited. However, Hole's Hole Quay is only four miles upstream from Saltash. It was strategically positioned, in deep water, within reach of various ferry crossings in the district and both Saltash and North Corner could be reached at all states of the tide. Given also that Hole's Hole was a produce distribution point in the time of the market steamers it is possible that this quay, rather than Calstock, served as the Tamar Valley's principal market boat depot before the first market steamer was introduced in 1836.

From South Hooe to Weir Head

Nearly three miles upstream from Cargreen, at Clifton Quay, a ferry crossed to South Hooe on the Devon shore. This crossing, at the southern end of the horseshoe bend around North and South Hooe, probably survived until the second half of the nineteenth century, by which time nearby silver-lead mines on the Bere peninsula had fallen into decline. Hooe Passage (or Halton Ferry) at the northern end of the horse-shoe bend, dated back to the Middle Ages and crossed from a small quay below North Hooe Farm, on the Bere peninsula, either to Halton Quay or the nearby inlet of Greenbank. The ferry rights were leased to the tenant of North Hooe Farm. Latterly a Mr Down leased the farm and was required to maintain the crossing. He bought the farm around 1920 and the requirement to honour the ferry lease was quietly allowed to lapse. A road sign outside Bere Alston still points to Hoe Passage.

Cotehele Quay served Cotehele Estate and the surrounding district as a general agricultural quay and mineral dock. A ferry crossed from Cotehele Quay to Ward, on the Bere peninsula shore. Similar to the Cargreen Ferry, its peak years came after 1890 when the PD&SWJR arrived at Bere Alston providing access to London markets for market gardeners and flower growers of the St Dominick district. The ferry, which was always worked by rowing boats, closed in the 1930s.

Calstock was an important river port and ship owning community frequented by river barges and sea going trading vessels. The

A number of road signs on the Bere peninsula direct unsuspecting visitors along narrow roads and tracks leading to former river crossings and little used fords. At a fork in the road from Bere Alston a direction sign, pictured in 1990, indicates the one time market quay of Hole's Hole and the former ferry crossing from North Hooe (Hoe) to Halton Quay – out of use since the 1920s.
Alan Kittridge.

Cotehele Quay, pictured in the 1970s, was another market boat call. A ferry crossed from the quay to Ward, on the Bere side. The quay is now owned by the National Trust and the river's maritime history is remembered in a display by the National Maritime Museum on the ground floor of the quay warehouse. Behind the warehouse the Tamar barge Shamrock is pictured, covered in a tarpaulin. She was the subject of a preservation project which was completed in 1979. In the foreground are salmon seine boats.
B. Y. Williams.

Calstock Passage and the Calstock Ferry c1900. The ferry crossed from the inlet behind the ferryboat, to steps on Calstock Quay. On the right can be seen James Goss' shipyard. Formerly the yard was occupied by Edward Brooming, who built the Calstock & Devonport Steam Packet Company's paddle steamer QUEEN *there in 1845. Immediately behind the ferryboat is Passage Inn, with pleasure gardens laid out for passengers from visiting paddle steamers.* ALAN KITTRIDGE COLLECTION.

Calstock Ferry ran from Calstock Quay to Passage Inn (now Ferry Farm) on the Bere peninsula and is thought to date back to Saxon times. Its importance, whether just crossing to the Bere peninsula, or travelling further afield using any number of the district's other ferries, is evident by glancing at a map of the area. For a period before the Second World War it was worked by Lewis and Harry Goss of the adjacent boatyard at Calstock Passage. The ferry was owned by the Earl of Mount Edgcumbe and in October 1945 the new sixth Earl handed the rights over to the St Germans and Tavistock Rural District Councils. In October 1962 one hundred people from Calstock and Bere Alston met at Calstock in support of retaining the ferry

Passage Inn (including the ferry rights) was leased by a Mr James c1900 who developed it as a pleasure garden. Local photographer Fred. J. Paul (a bank manager by profession) was commissioned to create this postcard view. The two models are Fred. J. Paul's daughters – the smallest one, Marjorie, assisted my researches nearly eighty years later. ALAN KITTRIDGE COLLECTION.

which was threatened with closure. The Calstock–Bere Alston Ferry Committee reported that the ferry was carrying 6000 passengers a year but losing £200 per annum and that a new boat was needed. The ferry closed in 1967. At the time of writing the Tamar Passenger Ferry links Ferry Farm (formerly the Passage Inn), Calstock and Cotehele. The ferry is operated seasonally by the Calstock Steampacket & River Navigation Co Ltd.

A workmans ferry ran from Okel Tor, just outside Calstock, to Rumleigh Brickworks and Gawton Mine quay on the Bere peninsula. It was a casual service and was used by other locals, but fell out of use when the brickworks and mine closed between the world wars.

Since the twelfth century Morwellham Quay was a river port to the Stannary town of Tavistock, serving to export its blocks of coined tin. The Tavistock Canal to Morwellham was completed 1817 and was linked by a railway incline to the quay. Morwellham developed as an important mineral quay when, in 1844, rich copper deposits were discovered upstream in Blanchdown Woods. A ferry from Harewood offered a shorter journey between Calstock and Tavistock than the road *via* New Bridge, and passage to workers at Morwellham Quay. *Murray's Handbook for Devon and Cornwall* in 1859 recommended that visitors to the Morwell Rocks could proceed from Calstock '...through the grounds of Harewood and meet the boat ferry opposite Morwellham...' Jack Adams, a water bailiff and ex–bargeman living at Morwellham, was the last ferryman and worked the crossing with an 18ft boat until it broke from its moorings in 1963 and was wrecked.

The Tamar Manure Navigation was established by an Act of Parliament on 26 April 1796. The promoters were empowered to enable navigation between Morwellham and Blanchdown. A 5ft deep channel was dredged between Morwellham and Netstakes, where a lock measuring 70ft x 20ft was constructed to bypass the weir at Weir Head. For three quarters of a century this channel would help paddle steamers from the Three Towns to reach Weir Head. The fish-weir at Weir Head was enlarged to provide 5ft depth of water in the cut above the lock and along the river channel up to New Bridge, where the company built a quay. It was proposed to extend the navigation of the river to Blanchdown and build a tub-boat canal to Tamerton, above Launceston, where the navigation might have linked with the Bude Canal. But the Tamar Manure Navigation never extended beyond New Bridge. In its lifetime it served Tamar barges calling at Bealeswood Brickworks alongside the canal, or going further upstream to the Gunnislake gasworks (opened in 1872) and the quay at New Bridge.

From Netstakes Quay, which lies on the 'island' between the Tamar Manure Navigation and the River Tamar, just below Weir Head, a ferry crossed to the Devon shore, providing access to the Duke of Bedford's carriage road from Morwellham to his house at Endsleigh. It offered passage from Gunnislake to the Morwellham Quay area for dock workers and miners from the Gunnislake side and was also used by visitors to the local beauty spot of Morwell Rocks. The ferry was operated by the lock keeper from the surviving Ferry House. The last ferryman, Albert Teague, ran the ferry until 1948.

Above Weir Head was another casual or workers' ferry. *The West Briton* for 30 March 1849 reported that the bodies of two mine workers from Wheal Maria Mine, Lamerhooe, were recovered from the river. Together with thirteen other miners they got into a boat which was kept for the purpose of ferrying them across the river, the boat grounded and capsized and the two men drowned. The boat crossed below the Cornish village of Luckett to Lamerhooe on the Devon shore. Another, just downstream, crossed near Latchley to the Devon Great Consols mine, but it is possible that these 'two' ferries were the same boat. There was a ferryman working in this locality until at least the 1880s.

The River Plym

On the eastern side of Plymouth Sound the estuary of the River Plym separated the South Hams of Devon from Plymouth. The lowest bridged crossing on the Plym in the thirteenth century was Plym Bridge – about one and a half miles above the estuary. The only alternatives were a causeway across the marsh between

The flying bridge on the River Plym – forerunner of the Laira Bridge – viewed from the Prince Rock (Plymouth) side. Oreston can be seen on the South Hams side in the background. While James Meadows Rendel was working on the Laira Bridge of 1827, observation of the flying bridge inspired him to develop the steam floating bridges, which were later established at Saltash and Torpoint. COURTESY KEITH PERKINS.

Before the Dissolution, when Plymouth still owed vassalage to the priory at Plympton, the Oreston Passage offered the best route to the priory from Martyn's Gate of Plymouth, crossing the Plym from Passage House Inn at Cattedown. The community of Oreston grew up around the ferry landing on the South Hams side. Pictured here c1910 the Oreston & Turnchapel Steamboat Co Ltd's passenger steamer LIVELY *is seen at the company's Dummy Landing pier.* ALAN KITTRIDGE COLLECTION.

Efford and Woodford or a nearby 'ebb' ford off Crabtree, which as late as 1823 was described as a 'public highway across the sands'. As its name suggests, this latter crossing was only available at low tide. A long held theory suggests the name of nearby Efford is a corruption of 'ebb ford', but as this district is listed as 'Elforde' in the Domesday Survey of 1086, one wonders how long ago the supposed corruption took place. Until the higher Efford causeway was improved as the Longbridge (a combination of causeway and bridge) in 1758 to carry the turnpike into Plymouth, the ebb ford appears to have been the favoured route between Plymouth and Plympton, indeed, it was still used for some time after because it remained free of tolls.

In 1800 The Right Hon. Lord Boringdon (created Earl of Morley in 1815) of Saltram Estate, which lies on the South Hams side of the Laira (the estuary of the River Plym), engaged James Green to reclaim 75 acres of Chelson Bay on the Laira – which became Chelson Meadow. Seven years later Lord Boringdon gained an Act of Parliament to establish a flying bridge across the Plym from Pomphlett Point – downstream from Chelson Meadow, to Prince Rock on the opposite Plymouth shore. A letter to the *Mechanics Magazine* in 1839 described the Laira flying bridge:

The vessel was worked by two men with a chain stretched across the river and was fitted with lifting platforms or prows, to receive carriages, waggons, horses etc, similar to those at Torpoint.
The only difference between the two plans being that the one at Laira was a single vessel worked by a chain on one side only...I have crossed in the old Laira vessel in all seasons of the year and in all weathers. She was termed a flying bridge...

The bridge could carry up to four carriages and was built by Issac Blackburn at Turnchapel. It was established to bridge the route of the Modbury to Plymouth road of the Modbury Road Trustees. On the Plymouth side the bridge road linked with the toll road of the Plymouth Embankment Company which had embanked the Laira Marshes and helped establish a new route from Plympton Ridgeway across the Longbridge, along the Embankment and into Plymouth on the newly developed Exeter Street.

A little further downstream was the Oreston Passage running from the Passage House Inn, Cattedown to Oreston on the South Hams shore. It was an ancient ferry which had offered a route from Martyn's Gate of Plymouth to Plymstock and thence on to the priory at Plympton. A map of the late sixteenth century

shows it as 'Horestone Passage' and this once important crossing gave rise to the waterside community of Oreston. In 1732 two passage boats are recorded on the ferry, landing at two places on the South Hams side of the river: at 'Oreston Slip' and the 'Trott', possibly equivalent to the later Oreston Quay and Gutter. The ferry route was still shown on the Ordnance Survey map of 1915 but by the 1920s had gone out of use. The original Passage House Inn was demolished early in the twentieth century and replaced with a newer building – still named Passage House Inn.

There was a ferry across The Cut (the embanked entrance of Hooe Lake) until the early 1940s, running from Point Beach on the Turnchapel side to the opposite Oreston shore. It was a short cut ferry for workers and other locals, and saved a long walk around Hooe Lake. Another workers' ferry, or waterman's boat, took passengers across the Plym from Turnchapel to the industrial area of Cattedown. Passage was available from the nineteenth century until the Second World War.

Hooe Passage was an ancient ferry from Sutton to Hooe Lake, where the landing was probably near the present Hooe Quay and the Royal Oak public house, for the road leading to Plymstock. While the official ferry seems to have fallen out of use long before the introduction of steamers, a similar route was continued by watermen from Sutton Pool. Of all the ferries listed in this chapter Hooe Passage was the only one ever to run directly into the town of Sutton (Plymouth).

Within Sutton Harbour there was a short cut ferry between West and East Piers – which were built in the late eighteenth century. The ferry served fishermen, mariners, workers and other locals and saved a long walk around Sutton Harbour. Only licensed watermen could operate the service and the fares were regulated by the local authority (a halfpenny in 1848). The service died out after the Second World War. In 1994 work was completed on a lock between East and West Piers, making Sutton Harbour a floating harbour – and resulting in the destruction of much atmosphere around Plymouth's historic harbour. A particularly unsympathetic pedestrian crossing is intermittently available across the lock gates.

The River Yealm

Half a mile off the weather beaten cliffs of Wembury Bay the Great Mewstone stands sentinel at the mouth of the River Yealm, the

The West Pier of Sutton Harbour in the 1920s, from which a short-cut ferry crossed to East Pier – the vantage point for this picture. The service was mostly for the benefit of the Teats Hill, Coxside and Cattedown communities on the opposite shore. A motor boat is moored at Mayflower Steps. Besides being near the alleged departure place of the Pilgrim Fathers, Mayflower Steps was a station for beach boats running to Bovisand and Cawsand Bay and continues today as a station for Cawsand and other passenger boats. Contrary to popular belief that Plymouth's 'historic' Sutton Harbour is conserved – this scene, along with much of the area, has changed almost beyond recognition.
ALAN KITTRIDGE COLLECTION.

The ferry across the Pool of the River Yealm in the 1950s. Leaving from Wide Slip, on the Noss Mayo side, the boat is heading towards Warren Point on the Wembury shore. The ferry formerly crossed from Ferry Cottage, which can be seen on the shore in the background, behind the bow of the ferry. The track between Noss Mayo and this cottage is called Passage Road.
ALAN KITTRIDGE COLLECTION.

navigable waters of which lay within the Customs Port of Plymouth. The rugged and spectacular river mouth, between Season and Mouthstone Points, is further guarded by a sand bar which has restricted the commercial use of the river's natural harbour, the Pool, just inside the mouth. The densely wooded river banks were once virtually isolated, due in part to the geographical obstacle of the River Yealm itself. The fishing and farming communities of Newton Ferrers, Noss Mayo and Bridgend nestled along the banks of Newton Creek – a sheltered inlet off the eastern shore, near the river's mouth. The community was little known beyond its immediate neighbourhood and seldom visited owing to its remote position three miles south west of the largest nearby village of Yealmpton. Near the highest navigable point of the River Yealm, some five miles from the sea, Kitley Quay served Kitley Estate. Two miles downriver, on the eastern shore, is Shortaflete Creek from where a ferryman once offered passage to the opposite shore at Steer Point or Wembury Wood, the two being divided by Cofflete Creek. From Steer Point to the sea a channel permits navigation of shallow draught boats at most states of the tide.

A foss (causeway) links Newton Ferrers to Noss Mayo at low tide, and there is a similar crossing in Noss Creek. When the tide was in, locals of these waterside communities found little difficulty in gaining passage from family or neighbour. Newton Ferrers is pictured below in a W. R. Gay postcard c1900.
ALAN KITTRIDGE COLLECTION.

Near the mouth of the river, at Ferry Cottage, there was a ferry across the Pool of the River Yealm to the path for Wembury and beyond. The surrounding woods are called Ferry Woods. In the twentieth century the ferry moved upstream to provide a triangular service between Wide Slip, Warren Point and the Yealm Hotel. Both Newton and Noss Creeks could (and still can) be crossed at low tide by means of a foss – or causeway. In the nineteenth century this isolated but picturesque fishing and agricultural community was visited by regular steamer excursions from the Three Towns and, thus discovered, would develop as one of Plymouth's satellite suburbs.

These then were the estuarine ferry and passenger services of the Three Towns district in the early nineteenth century. The population in the area was already growing, particularly around the Hamoaze as a result of Admiralty developments. Turnpikes were creating regular carriage traffic for the major passages at Laira, Torpoint and Saltash, but ferry boats, little changed in centuries, were still coping with this increased traffic. The technology to mechanically power the ferries was not then available. When steam engines were introduced many of the ferries and landing places noted above provided the infrastructure upon which the steam ferry and river steamer services of the nineteenth and twentieth centuries were based.

CHAPTER TWO

THE EXCELLENT AND POWERFUL...

Steamboats before the railway 1823 – 1859

JAMES MEADOWS RENDEL

In 1822 a young engineer, James Meadows Rendel, moved into 7 Boons Place, Plymouth, and established a civil engineering business. J. M. Rendel was born in Drewsteignton in 1799 and in 1815 became a student surveyor on the staff of Thomas Telford. He worked under Telford and the engineer Captain Samuel Brown RN on proposals for a suspension bridge at Runcorn and also assisted on the construction of ferry landing slips at Dundee on the River Tay for the twin-hulled ferryboat *Union*. An acquaintance of Rendel, working in Scotland at the same time, was the Scottish engineer James Nasmyth who advocated a method of marine propulsion by which steamboats could engage laid chains over a sprocket wheel and warp themselves along a canal. These early engineering experiences and theories, to which the young Rendel was exposed, combined to influence his subsequent career and resulted in his surviving legacy – the Torpoint floating bridge.

A number of major developments in the Three Towns during the early nineteenth century attracted civil engineers and architects to the district. From 1812 John Rennie and Joseph Whidbey were building the Breakwater in Plymouth Sound. Completed in 1844, the Breakwater rendered the foreshore of Plymouth safe for development and Rendel was to be responsible for the construction of Millbay Pier, which was built on the sea front in 1841 to protect dock developments in Millbay. Between 1824 and 1835 John Rennie's son, also John, was designing and building the Royal William Victualling Yard at Stonehouse. Notable architects in the district at the same time included John Foulston and George Wightwick, both whom became involved in Rendel's projects – Foulston at Dartmouth's Higher Ferry and Wightwick who designed the octagonal customs office at the gates of Millbay Pier. A major attraction for Rendel in 1822 was the opportunity to present proposals for an iron suspension bridge across the Tamar at Saltash. Rendel submitted plans in competition with his former mentor Captain Samuel Brown. The prospectus of the bridge company stated:

> One of the most ancient ferries is established at Saltash, where the river is contracted to a width of 900 feet at high water, and here one of the principal roads into Cornwall has long existed; these circumstances render it the most desirable spot, for an iron bridge of suspension to be erected...

The Earl of Morley was Chairman of the Committee of Management of the Duchy of Cornwall for the project and in October 1822 suggested that Rendel might adapt his Saltash Bridge design for a similar bridge across the Plym at Laira to replace his flying bridge, which was proving unpopular with stage-coaches and other passengers, due in part to unreliability caused by contrary weather and tidal conditions. Rendel's eventual design for Laira was not a suspension bridge, but a 500 feet, five span iron bridge supported upon limestone and granite piers. Opened on 14 July 1827 the Laira Bridge – known to generations of Plymothians as the

James Meadows Rendel 1799–1856, civil engineer. COURTESY KEITH PERKINS.

An impression of Rendel's proposed suspension bridge across the Tamar at Saltash, looking upstream, with Saltash on the left and Saltash Passage on the right. The drawing was sent to the Duchy of Cornwall Office in Somerset House, London in September 1823, for their approval. COURTESY KEITH PERKINS.

View of the proposed Suspension Bridge at Saltash across the River Tamar.

An engraving of a Thomas Allom picture c1830 depicting Rendel's 'Iron Bridge' of 1827 across the Laira of the River Plym. A barge passing beneath the bridge demonstrates the need for a 'striking' mast. The height of Brunel's Royal Albert Bridge of 1859 was stipulated to obviate the need for ships to strike their masts. On the River Tavy, however, completion of the railway bridge of 1889 at the river's mouth forced subsequent vessels plying to the Tavy to fit or have striking masts. ALAN KITTRIDGE COLLECTION.

Advertisement for the SIR FRANCIS DRAKE'S *regular services later in her career between Plymouth and Falmouth and to the Channel Islands – while the South Devon Railway was advancing from Newton Abbot but 12 years before the Royal Albert Bridge linked Cornwall with the mainline from Paddington. From* William's Commercial Directory of Cornwall, 1847. ROYAL INSTITUTION OF CORNWALL

Iron Bridge – was the second largest iron structure in existence, surpassed only by John Rennie's Southwark Bridge in London. The Institution of Civil Engineers awarded Rendel the prestigious Telford Medal for his design. In the same year Rendel laid out Plymouth Racecourse at Chelson Meadow for the Earl of Morley – a source of revenue for the new toll bridge. The Earl also asked him to dispose of the redundant flying bridge – evidence that Rendel was familiar with its operation. Plans to build a bridge at Saltash, meanwhile, had been shelved.

STEAM COMMUNICATION BETWEEN
FALMOUTH, PLYMOUTH, GUERNSEY, JERSEY, FRANCE, &c. &c.

SEASON, 1847.

The Public are hereby informed, that the Favorite and Powerful STEAM-PACKET

SIR F.  **DRAKE,**

W. SADLER, Commander,

Will run during the Season as follows: (Weather Permitting), with liberty of Towing,

FALMOUTH FOR PLYMOUTH,

Every Monday & Thursday, at 7 in the Morning;

PLYMOUTH FOR FALMOUTH,

On Wednesday and Saturday, at 12 at noon;

She also Calls off MEVAGISSEY, on her trips between Falmouth and Plymouth, (weather permitting).

FREIGHT GOODS CARRIED ON VERY REASONABLE TERMS.

The advantages of this mode of conveyance are therefore obvious to every one, and more particularly to Consignees not residing in Falmouth as they may safely calculate on the time of her arrival, in order to send for their Goods. To ensure this regular mode, be particular to order Goods to the SIR F. DRAKE'S Company's Wharf, Old Victualling Office, near the Barbican, Plymouth.

SOUTH DEVON RAILWAY.

Coaches leave Plymouth, at 3 in the afternoon for the above Railway, at Newton, thereby enabling Passengers to join the Bristol and Exeter, and Great Western Railways, to proceed to London.

GUERNSEY AND JERSEY.

The SIR F. DRAKE leaves Plymouth for these Islands on Thursday Evenings, at 5 o'clock, taking on Passengers for ST. MALO and other parts of France; she leaves the Islands for Plymouth the following Evening. Steamers leave Jersey for St. Malo twice a week.

PLYMOUTH'S FIRST STEAM PACKET

While Rendel was drawing up his plans for the Laira bridge, a wooden ship was taking shape on the slipway of Alexander Brown's yard at Cattedown, less than a mile downstream from the bridge site. The ship was launched on 30 July 1823 (by which date Brown's yard had been taken over by Richard Hill). The hull belonged to the first steamer built in Plymouth, a 113 tons burthen, 103.8 feet long x 18.8 feet wide x 11 feet deep paddle steamer under construction for the Plymouth & Portsmouth Steam Packet Company (P&PSPCo). She was completed in August 1823 as the *Sir Francis Drake*, with two cylinder engines built by the Eagle Foundry, Birmingham. On 9 September she made her first voyage to Portsmouth *via* Dartmouth, Brixham, Torquay, Teignmouth, and Cowes. Subsidy for the carriage of mail was important to the success of the *Sir Francis Drake*, so a westward extension to the Post Office packet port of Falmouth was introduced. The Falmouth to Plymouth link was undertaken by the Bristol owned steamer *Royal Cambria* in 1824, and by her fleet sister the *St David* in the following year. Both the *St David* and the *Sir Francis Drake* moved to the new landing of Admiral's Hard, Stonehouse in 1826. The Bristol steamer was withdrawn in the same year when a new wooden paddle steamer, the Rotherhithe built *Brunswick*, entered service with the P&PSPCo. Initially she maintained the Cornish calls, linking with the *Sir Francis Drake* at Admiral's Hard. The P&PSPCo soon re-arranged their services with both steamers plying to Portsmouth but the *Sir Francis Drake* alone extending her western voyage to include Falmouth and other south Cornwall calls.

The significance of the *Sir Francis Drake* to our story, other than being the first steamer in the area, lay in the announcement that prior to her runs between Plymouth and Falmouth she would offer excursions to Cotehele and Calstock. '...on which occasions the company will be enlivened by a military band'. Open for engagement by private parties, who were urged to book a week in advance, these river trips were priced to attract 'select' (i.e. middle-class) passengers only and were the very first steamer excursions up the River Tamar. It would seem, from advertisements in the *Plymouth, Devonport & Stonehouse Herald*, that the steamer moored at Cotehele for about eight hours '...affording an abundance of time for visiting Cotehele House, the celebrated Morwell Rocks with their romantic scenery, Weir Head etc.' The *Brunswick* meanwhile inaugurated regular Tuesday afternoon steamer trips around Smeaton's Eddystone Lighthouse.

JEMIMA – THE FIRST STEAM FERRY IN THE DISTRICT

By 1800 the population of Plymouth Dock was outstripping that of Plymouth by a third – their respective populations being around 30,000 and 21,000. The townspeople of Plymouth Dock successfully petitioned for a change of name to Devonport in 1824 and twelve years later the expanding town became a Municipal Corporation. A combination of the growth of Devonport, the desire of Reginald Pole Carew to expand his new community at Torpoint, and imminent turnpike improvements between Sheviock and Antony, prompted measures to improve the efficiency of the Torpoint Ferry. On 2 January 1826 Reginald Pole Carew asked the advice of James Brown, the builder of the Dundee steam ferryboat *Union* – for which Rendel had helped design the landing piers:

> Sir having lately read a Pamphlet giving a Description of a Twin Steam Boat built by you for the Ferry at Dundee & conceiving that a Boat of smaller Dimensions built on the same Principles might be adapted to a Ferry in which I am interested, which is not above seven Hundred Yards in Breadth, I write to request that you will have the Goodness to inform Me, for what Sum you would engage to build a similar Twin Boat of a twelve Horse Power...
>
> As our present Sailing Boats answer very well, as to the Accommodation required you are also requested to advise whether a considerable Saving might not be made, & the Effect not be materially diminished, if the Steam Boat of a 12 Horse Power, were used only as a Tug for the present Ferry Boats...

The Torpoint Steamboat Company was formed and on 7 November 1826 a meeting of the subscribers, which included the Earl of St Germans, Henry Woolcombe, Sir John St Aubyn and Reginald Pole Carew, considered a favourable report by the engineer Henry Habberley Price regarding the establishment of a steam boat on the Torpoint Ferry. The meeting resolved that an offer from the proprietors of the Torpoint Ferry (namely the Earl of Mount Edgcumbe and Reginald Pole Carew) of a 21 year lease at £460 per annum should be accepted and that:

> ...the offer of Mr. H. H. Price to furnish the plans, and to give all the superintendence necessary for accomplishing the object, be acceded to...

Later the same month Rendel, armed with a letter of recommendation from the Earl of Morley, met with the Torpoint Steamboat Company, concerning construction of landing piers at Torpoint and New Passage.

The improvements to the turnpike from Sheviock were completed by December 1827 but two more years elapsed before the new twin hulled Torpoint ferry boat was launched from Richard Hocking's yard at Whitehall in Stonehouse on 29 September 1829. Measuring 70 feet long x 25 feet wide she was named *Jemima*, in honour of Lady Jemima Eliot, of St Germans and Miss Jemima Pole Carew. The vessel was to be fitted with two single-cylinder engines, each of twelve horse power driving a single paddle wheel located amidships, between the hulls, similar to the *Union*. For the first time, horse drawn vehicles could board the vehicle decks without unharnessing. There followed a long interval before the *Jemima* finally entered service between Torpoint and New Passage in February 1831. But the eagerly awaited new steam service proved a big disappointment. It was soon discovered that the engines were incapable of holding her on course against the tidal currents. Rendel observed that: 'The tides were found too strong, and the line of passage too direct across the current to enable the vessel to make her passage when there was either tide or wind to encounter'. By the middle of the year the steamer was withdrawn and the old foot- and horse-boats returned to service.

RENDEL'S FLOATING BRIDGES

Simultaneous to events on the Torpoint Ferry, Rendel was solving a similar problem at Dartmouth. Following opposition to Rendel's and Foulston's earlier plans for a suspension bridge to carry the Exeter to Plymouth turnpike across the River Dart at Greenway, the Dartmouth Floating Bridge Company was established by the Earl of Morley, Henry Woolcombe and others. This alternative solution to crossing the Dart was proposed by Rendel and Foulston and presented at the Castle Hotel, Dartmouth by Rendel on 3 October 1829. Their proposal recommended a floating bridge, guided by chains – being fixed at slipways on either side of the shore – drawn over a large diameter cog aboard the craft. The plan was accepted and, overcoming objections from the Duchy of Cornwall and other local interests, the steam floating bridge, located immediately upstream from Dartmouth at Lower Sandquay, was opened on 19 August 1831. The twin hulled vessel was built by Issac Blackburn at Turnchapel (builder of the Laira flying bridge). Her four horse power engine was built by John Mare of the Plymouth Foundry.

Meanwhile, the idea of a bridge at Saltash was revived and at midday on Wednesday 7 April 1830, a meeting was held at Elliot's Royal Hotel, Devonport:

> ...for the purpose of taking into

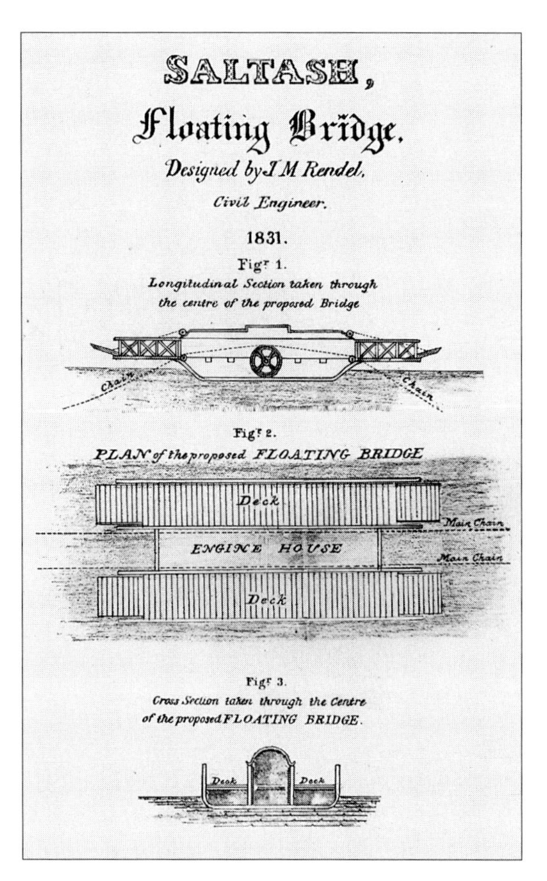

A general arrangement diagram of Rendel's proposals for a floating bridge at Saltash, presented as an alternative idea when plans for a Saltash Bridge were revived in 1830. COURTESY KEITH PERKINS.

consideration the Plan and Estimate that will be then laid before the Meeting, for erecting a Bridge across the Tamar...

> The importance of a safe, certain, and expeditious communication between the County of Cornwall and the Towns of Plymouth, Devonport, and Stonehouse, is so obvious as to require no statement...

Late in the following year Rendel produced alternative plans for a floating bridge at Saltash. These were accepted by the promoters and in March 1832 they notified the Officers of the Duchy of Cornwall that it was their intention:

> ...to apply to Parliament in the enduring Session, for leave to bring in a Bill, to establish a Floating Bridge across the River Tamar, as a substitute for the present inconvenient slow and dangerous boat now used at the Established Ferry at Saltash...

The Act was gained and the Saltash Floating Bridge Company claimed the ferry rights from Saltash Corporation, but a provision of the Act stipulated that the ferry rights would revert to the Corporation if the Company stopped working the floating bridge. In the same year they placed an order with John Pope – who had taken over the Turnchapel yard of Issac Blackburn – for a twin hulled ferry boat, her two decks each to measure 58 feet long x 10 feet wide, John Mare was to built the steam engine and machinery. The landing place on the Devon side was moved from the original ferry landing below the present Royal Albert Bridge, downstream to Little Ash, to provide an angled approach at the landings, rather than broadside on to the current. A fundamental improvement (to the Laira and Dartmouth floating bridges) in securing the chains ashore was to sink the chain ends, with counterweights attached, into pits, resulting in better tension and flexibility during passage. During trials on 21 December 1832 a crossing time of four and a half minutes was achieved. The Saltash floating bridge was opened in February 1833.

In 1832 the Torpoint Steamboat Company asked Rendel to design a floating bridge for the Torpoint Ferry. An order for a twin hulled vessel measuring 60 feet long x 50 feet wide was placed with Richard Hocking's yard in Stonehouse, while John Mare's Plymouth Foundry built two 11hp engines. An incident following the launching severely tested the strength of the new bridge. It was to be moored temporarily in the basin of the new Victualling Yard but due to a falling tide and the batter of the pier heads, the bridge became wedged in the entrance and suspended until the next high tide lifted it – undamaged. The Torpoint floating bridge opened on 1 April 1834. Meanwhile, in 1833, Rendel was invited to submit plans for a floating bridge across the River Itchen at Southampton. An Act of Parliament was obtained in the following year and orders for a vessel were placed, once again, with Hocking and Mare. The Southampton floating bridge was opened on 23 November 1836. Rendel was also invited to submit proposals for floating bridge across Portsmouth Harbour to Gosport but an iron vessel was specified and the contract for its construction was won by D. E. & A. Acraman of Bristol; it was to be the first iron vessel built in Bristol. When completed in 1839 the Portsmouth floating bridge was towed to Portsmouth by the Plymouth steam packet *Sir Francis Drake*. Recognition for Rendel's invention followed. A Silver Medal from the Institute of Civil Engineers for his Torpoint designs and acknowledgement from George Louis, Post Office Surveyor of Highways and Stage Coaches, who, whilst reporting on improvements to the passage of Royal Mail through South Wales in 1836 remarked:

> I should wish to say a word regarding the estuary bridges. Since Mr Telford's report on the Severn passages these bridges have been invented by Mr Rendel, of Plymouth; our mails pass over these bridges at three places. They are called floating steam-bridges; they are not expensive. The mail-coach from Dartmouth

goes in such an one. If such a bridge as that could be established across the Severn it would make the passage sure. It might be used again at Briton Ferry.

Rendel later surveyed an established ferry at Newnham, on the River Severn, for conversion to a floating bridge, and also surveyed sites for a bridge across the estuary at Aust and New Passage, where the two present Severn bridges now stand.

The Penny Magazine of 25 March 1843 carried an article on the principles of flying and floating bridges, describing Rendel's floating bridge at Torpoint:

> ...The bridge is a kind of large flat-bottomed vessel, nearly as wide as it is long, being fifty-five feet long by forty-five wide. It is divided lengthwise into three portions, the centre of which contains the machinery by which it is worked, while the sides form the two platforms on which the passengers and carriages are placed. At each end of these side platforms is attached a strong and commodious drawbridge, hung on hinges, which can be let down so that its extreme end may rest on the beach or shore, and thus form a convenient passage for passengers, horses and carriages to or from the beach and the vessel.
>
> The next point is to explain how this singular shaped structure is propelled. This is done by the aid of two strong chains, stretched side by side across the river, from one bank to the other. The length and weight of the chains are such that each chain, when the bridge is at one shore, lies along the bottom of the stream; and when the bridge is in the middle of its course the chain makes two curves, one between it and either shore. The chains are not permanently fixed at the ends, but are balanced by very heavy weights, so as to enable them to yield in a slight degree to any strain to which they might be exposed. The bridge or vessel is so connected with these two chains, that it cannot drift beyond the limits to which they extend...and as the chains are limited in their lateral deviation by the weights at their two ends, the bridge is rendered nearly independent of the current.

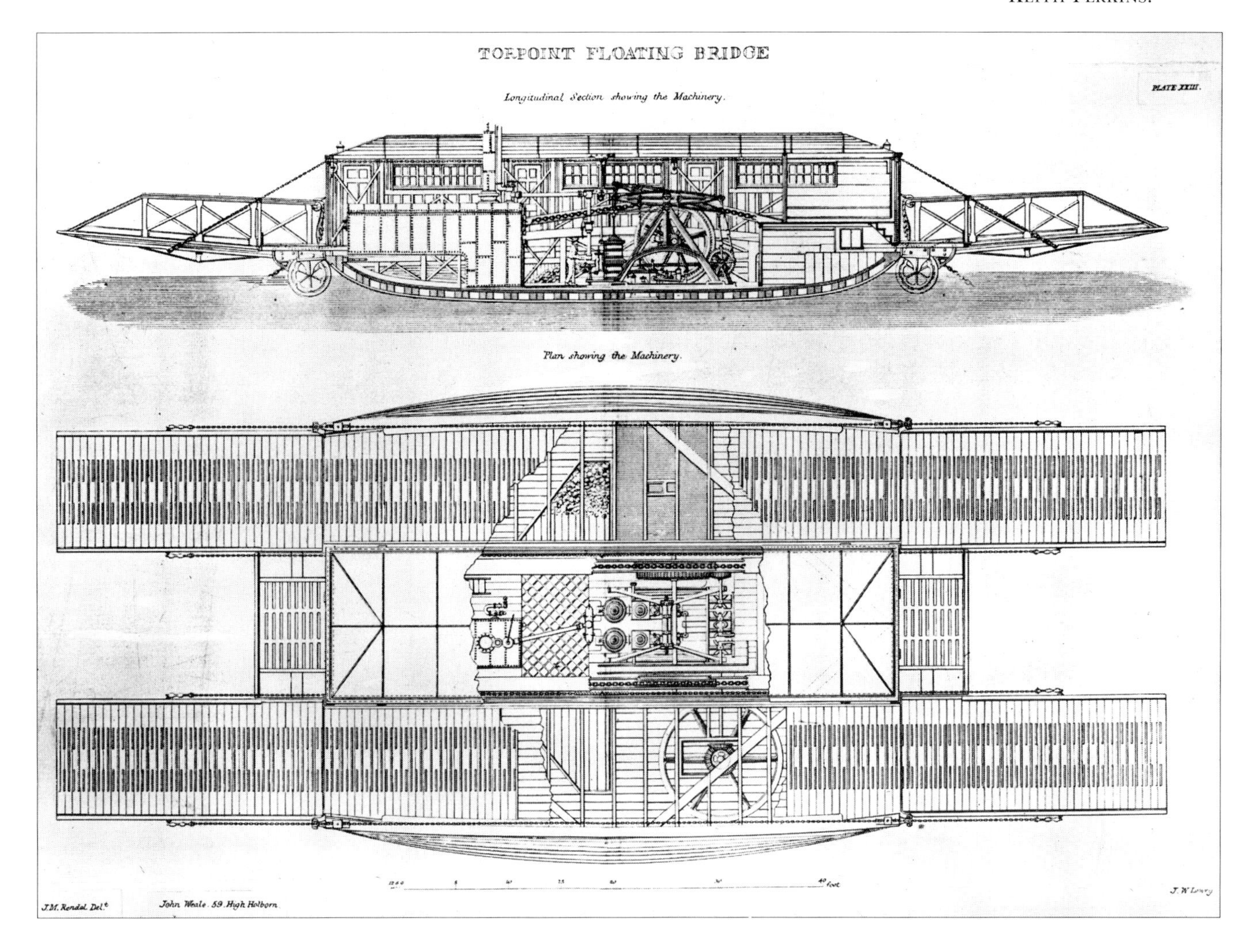

The first Torpoint floating bridge was designed by James Meadows Rendel and built by Richard Hocking, with machinery by John Mare's Plymouth Foundry. The two side lever engines can be seen, driving the large chain wheels. The steam feed is supplied by the boiler on the left. COURTESY KEITH PERKINS.

But the chains do more than guide the bridge on its passage; the links, by a very curious arrangement, are made to supply the place of paddles. In the middle of the vessel is a steam-engine, whose power is exerted in causing the rotation of two vertical wheels seven or eight feet in diameter. These wheels are parallel, about eleven feet apart, and lie in the direction of the length of the bridge. Round the periphery of each wheel is a series of cogs, exactly as far apart as the links of the great chains. The chains pass upwards from the water into one end of the bridge, over the cogs of the wheels, and down into the water again at the other end of the bridge; the cogs striking or catching into the links of the chain...The wheels rotate, and the cogs catch successively in all the links of the chain, thus causing the whole machine to be forcibly drawn onwards.

A second floating bridge was built for the Torpoint Ferry in 1835 by Hocking and Mare, the two vessels were to be used on alternate months (some accounts suggest there was an unsuccessful attempt at simultaneous operation). In the following year there was a setback when the Saltash floating bridge closed due to lack of funds for maintenance and repair. The Saltash Floating Bridge Company had been experiencing difficulties after only one year of operation and the bridge was withdrawn and replaced by horse-boats. Saltash Corporation considered the company was in breach of their Floating Bridge Act of 1832 and repossessed the ferry rights, re-instating their own horse-boats. Following protracted legal debate the Saltash Floating Bridge Company conceded defeat and the ferry rights officially reverted to the Corporation on 26 December 1839. The *Plymouth, Devonport & Stonehouse Herald* of Saturday 6 February 1840, carried an announcement regarding disposal of the floating bridge:

Floating Bridge, Steam Engines, Machinery etc. to be sold by Auction at Weakley's Hotel 21 February 1840. The Steam Floating Bridge lately worked across the River Tamar on the Saltash Ferry... steam engines, machinery and appurtenances belonging thereto, now lying on view at the yard of Messrs Hocking, Shipbuilders, Stonehouse.

This failure was followed by some uncompromising criticism of Rendel in the form of a letter to the *Mechanics Magazine*, 1839:

...I beg to state that Mr Rendel is not the

An early photograph of the Torpoint Ferry, showing the floating bridge of 1835 departing the Devonport shore c1860 – with a waterman grabbing a tow. COURTESY KEITH PERKINS.

inventor of the floating bridge now at work on the Tamar. The plan was copied from the vessel which was at work nearly 20 years since on the Laira river, near Plymouth, where now stands an iron bridge which was erected by Mr Rendel for the Earl of Morley.

The writer proceeds to describe the similarities between the Laira and Torpoint vessels concluding that the only difference was a second chain and the provision of steam engines on the Torpoint boat and that:

> The whole of the plan for those engines were furnished by Mr Mare, engineer in Plymouth, who designed them expressly for the purpose...I merely mention this in justice to Mr Mare, as it is now almost an every day occurrence that individuals who have attained a certain degree of eminence, still endeavour to extend their fame by publishing as their own, the result of the skill and ingenuity of others.
>
> ...The first copy Mr Rendel made from this vessel [the Laira boat] was for the Dart river, this one was worked by a steam engine which was designed and assembled by Mr Mare...The next was the Saltash Ferry on the Tamar, this one is altogether laid up for want of funds.
>
> The only person who can claim the merit of the invention of the present floating bridge in this part of the country is a Mr Parker who was in the employ of Mr Blackburn, a shipbuilder of Turnchapel, near Plymouth, where the Laira vessel was built, and who furnished Mr Rendel with the plan for the Dartmouth vessel, which was built at the same yard, now occupied by Messrs Pope. The Torpoint and Saltash bridges are merely an extension of the same plan.
>
> (signed) A Subscriber

There was also some suggestion that Rendel had plagiarised James Nasmyth's ideas on marine chain traction, but Nasmyth himself expressed admiration of Rendel's floating bridges when he visited the Torpoint Ferry after Rendel's death.

Tolls on the Torpoint floating bridge in 1834 were: 2d per horse; 1s 6d per horse and two wheeled chaise, or carts drawn by one or two horses; 2s 6d per coach and two horses; 5s per coach and four or heavy wagons. Fares included a day return but were doubled on Sundays. With regard to the capacity of the floating bridge, Rendel remarked that he had seen at one time on the bridge: three four-horse carriages, a two-horse carriage, seven saddle-horses and sixty foot-passengers.

The Royal Mail contracted out mail-coach services in 1835 and the *Royal Quicksilver Mail* (known locally as the *Devonport Mail*) won the contract for the carriage of mails between London, Devonport and Falmouth *via* the Torpoint Ferry. Other traffic using the ferry included fly wagons – slow moving conveyances carrying goods and passengers; carriers vans; horse omnibuses; and private carriages. The *Exquisite* stage coach (Elliot, Pearce & Co) started running from Devonport's Elliot Hotel to Penzance *via* the Torpoint Ferry in 1839, and a little later, the *Ruby* from Weakley's Hotel, Devonport *via* the Torpoint Ferry to Liskeard. The approach of the railway from London signalled an increase in stage- and mail-coach traffic using the ferry, as routes were adjusted to meet the advancing railhead. The *North Mail* from the Bodmin route switched to the Three Towns in 1846 because the railway was already at Exeter and progressing towards Plymouth. Two years later the South Devon Railway opened a station at Laira, followed one year later by the opening of their terminus at Millbay Station. From then, until the Royal Albert Bridge was opened at Saltash a decade later, Plymouth became the principal terminus for Cornwall's stage- and mail-coaches. The *Telegraph* met trains at Millbay and ran to Devonport, Torpoint, Liskeard, Bodmin, St Austell, Truro and Falmouth. The *Tally Ho*, which once ran between Plymouth and Exeter, switched to a Plymouth to Truro route, *via* Torpoint.

A closer view of the floating bridge on the Torpoint side, probably taken on the same day as the previous picture. Four or five wagons crowd the decks. COURTESY KEITH PERKINS.

Market steamers and river excursions

The Calstock & Devonport Steam Packet Company

On the morning of Wednesday 10 July 1850 the Calstock & Devonport Steam Packet Company's wooden paddle steamer *Queen* cast off from Saltash, heading for North Corner to pick up the Independent Dissenting Congregation, of Princess Street, Devonport, which had chartered her for a day out on the River Tamar. In command of the *Queen* was her designer and part owner David Mitchell, with James Smith as engineer and Thomas Lane as stoker. Also aboard was David Mitchell's nephew William Mitchell, who usually commanded the her fleet sister the *Alert* but had joined the *Queen* to help out for the day. Approaching North Corner the steamer was delayed by a trading ketch sailing upstream. James Smith mentioned to Thomas Lane that he was allowing the steam pressure to get too high but the stoker replied that the position of the safety valve indicated that all was well. Two minutes later the charter party's anticipation turned to horror when their steamer suddenly blew up – the boiler exploded throwing all four crewmen into the river. Three survivors were rescued and carried into the Steam Packet Inn at North Corner. William Mitchell and James Smith escaped serious injury but David Mitchell was badly scalded, although he subsequently recovered. Thomas Lane was killed and his body was still missing some days after the explosion. Fortunately this was the only such incident recorded in the history of passenger steamers in the Three Towns district, but it took a much happier event, involving the rescue of Queen Victoria six years later, before local confidence was fully restored.

The Steam Packet Inn, North Corner, pictured during the 1980s. In the foreground are the watermens' steps Alan Kittridge

The *Queen* and the *Alert* were amongst the earliest Tamar paddle steamers – but not the first. The impetus to introduce a market steamer linking the Tamar quays to Devonport came in 1836 when Devonport gained municipal corporation status and established a regular market under their own jurisdiction on Tuesdays, Thursdays and Saturdays. Previously a collection of stalls had congregated alongside the dockyard wall near the main gate in Fore Street and from 1762 in a market place which was provided nearby, but dues were paid to the landowner, Sir John St Aubyn. The Devonport Market building, with its landmark clock tower, was opened in 1852.

In 1836 Capt John Rickard of Calstock bought a small wooden paddle steamer from Falmouth. Named the *Alert*(1) – not to be confused with her later namesake mentioned above – she measured 24 tons burthen, 46.3 feet long x 10.1 feet wide x 6.5 feet deep and had a single cylinder engine. She inaugurated the first market steamer service from Calstock to Saltash and Devonport, calling at Cotehele Quay, Hole's Hole and Cargreen.

In April of the following year a group of Devonport businessmen trading as the Devonport Steam Navigation Company bought a larger, two masted, schooner rigged, wooden paddle steamer, with a man figurehead, from her Sunderland builders. She was named *Sir John St Aubyn* (41 tons burthen, 78 x 14.4 x 8.1 feet) and offered Tamar excursions from Devonport, but after just two years, in June 1839, she was sold to Portsmouth owners.

The *Alert*(1) was also 'sold' in 1839. Ownership passed to the Western District Banking Company and one year later to John Bowhay, an ironmonger of Devonport. It is uncertain how she was subsequently employed. She was scrapped in 1856.

From 1844, for ten years, the Keyham Steam Yard was under construction at Devonport – a major development to provide maintenance facilities for the Royal Navy's expanding steam powered fleet. The Tamar Valley meanwhile was also experiencing some industrial prosperity as lead and copper mines were being opened in the district, culminating in 1844 with the discovery of huge copper deposits in Blanchdown Woods, above Gunnislake, which became the Devon Great Consols Mine. The resulting increase in the population of the Three Towns and Tamar Valley districts gave rise to fresh attempts to establish river steamers on the Tamar.

In June 1845 William Elliot of Landulph bought from Yarmouth an iron paddle steamer, the *Alert*(2) – 43 tons gross [tg], 90 x 11.2 x 5.4

feet. She had been built at Bankside, Southwark in 1844. This second *Alert* maintained market services and excursions on the Tamar in the command of Captain Joseph Williams. During the same year Captain Williams and David Mitchell, both from Calstock, took delivery of the ill fated wooden paddle steamer *Queen* (52 tg, 68.5 x 13.5 x 7.0 feet) which was built by Edward Brooming in his yard adjacent to the Passage House Inn, opposite Calstock. Both the *Alert*(2) and the *Queen* were managed by a partnership of their respective shareholders trading as the Calstock & Devonport Steam Packet Company (C&DSPCo). The C&DSPCo faced immediate competition. On 15 March 1845 the *Plymouth, Devonport & Stonehouse Herald* carried the following announcement:

> PRINCE OF WALES
>
> The proprietors of the excellent and powerful *Prince of Wales* beg to inform the public that they have succeeded in engaging a steady and experienced master and pilot and trust by observing the strictest attention to the comfort and safety of passengers to ensure a share of their patronage.
>
> The proprietors of the above steamboat being desirous of arranging her hours for starting and to meet the conveyances and persons on the river, intend holding a meeting at Calstock in the course of this month for that purpose, of which due notice will be given.

The master of the *Prince of Wales* was Captain H. Huss. In advertisements the paddle steamer was described as 'the iron steamboat' and she called regularly at the newly completed Millbay Pier, Mutton Cove, North Corner and New Passage – where the company's office was located. She offered Tamar excursions similar to those made by the *Sir Francis Drake* – landing at Cotehele for the day. She also cruised further upstream, occasionally landing at Morwellham, returning to call at Calstock and Cotehele in the afternoon. Advertisements sought to attract middle-class passengers by advising: 'As it is intended to keep the company select the fare will be 2s, children half price'. This advice was notable for its omission on the market day services, when the steamboat owners packed as many Tamar Valley passengers aboard as possible. *The Strangers' Handbook* of 1847 lists both the *Prince of Wales* and the *Alert* as 'leaving Calstock every Tuesday, Thursday and Saturday morning, calling at several piers on the river for Devonport and Plymouth, returning each day'.

The *Prince of Wales* was not registered in Plymouth and no definite evidence has been discovered confirming either the steamer's identity or the company that was operating her. The principal contender, however, is the *Prince of Wales* of 1842, built at Neath Abbey in South Wales and owned by J. T. Price of Neath Abbey (father of H. H. Price), who was running coastal packets which called at Plymouth.

The *Queen* was repaired after her disastrous accident in 1850 and the *Prince of Wales* appears to have left the district soon after.

In 1854 the foundation of the later Devon & Cornwall Tamar Steam Packet Co Ltd was laid when a group of Calstock and Tavistock business men, including John Hornbrook Gill and Theophilus Hoskins, bought the iron paddle steamer *Princess* from Cosens of Weymouth. Built by Messrs Ditchburn and Mare at Orchard Yard, Blackwall in 1844, the *Princess* measured 25.86 tg, 110.5 x 14.05 x 7.55 feet and was fitted with a John Penn built 40hp, two cylinder oscillating engine (in oscillating engines the cylinders rocked on trunnions following the movement of the cranks on the paddle shaft – a space saving arrangement).

The Saltash floating bridge pictured above is the Routeliffe built vessel of 1851 (see below). In 1849 Brunel made his first trial bores for the Royal Albert Bridge. Work commenced on construction of the central pier in 1854. The steamers depicted during this four year period, therefore, could be the ALERT*(2), the* QUEEN*, or the* LORD YARBOROUGH*.*
ALAN KITTRIDGE COLLECTION.

William Gilbert and the Saltash & Devonport Steam Boat Company

The *Lord Yarborough* (79 tg, 86.2 x 12.3 x 9.3 feet) was an old wooden paddle steamer, complete with a man bust figurehead, which had been built at Fishbourne on the Isle of Wight in 1826 for the Portsmouth and Ryde Steam Packet Company. Purchased in 1852 by John Robins Vivian, a Stonehouse coal merchant, her shareholders soon included Thomas Willcocks of Plymouth and the man who would later monopolise the passenger steamer trade on the River Tamar – William Gilbert, a licenced victualler of Saltash.

In the same year ownership of the C&DSPCo's *Alert*(2) passed to Edmund Lakeman Elliot of Devonport (her master since 1850). He left the C&DSPCo to inaugurate a steamer service on the Hamoaze between Saltash and Devonport under the Tamer (*sic*) Steam Packet Company (TSPCo) banner. The

A view of the construction of the Royal Albert Bridge in 1857, with the first truss, on the Devon shore, ready for floating into position. The screw steamer pictured off Saltash could be Gilbert's VICTORIA *which in 1857 was running from Saltash to Devonport's North Corner. Just visible behind the buildings of Saltash's Waterside, is the Routeliffe built floating bridge of 1851.* CITY OF PLYMOUTH LOCAL & NAVAL STUDIES LIBRARY.

new service proved popular in Saltash, particularly with workers for the Dockyard and the growing commercial centre of Devonport. On his own account, two years later in 1854, William Gilbert bought a wooden, screw steamer, the *Victoria*, to compete for this Saltash–Devonport passenger trade. Gilbert kept the *Victoria* (and her successors on the Hamoaze service) separate from his other steamboat interests for nearly forty years, trading as the Saltash & Devonport Steam Boat Company (S&DSBCo).

In the winter of 1854-5 Gilbert and Willcocks bought a second paddle steamer for their Tamar excursion business. The *Gipsy* (46 tg, 76 x 12.2 x 6.5 feet) was an iron paddle steamer built in 1845 by Summers, Day and Baldock of Northam, Southampton. She drew only fourteen inches of water and was designed originally to maintain a ferry service to the shallow shore at Hythe, on Southampton Water. Her shallow draught would later prove particularly useful on the Tamar.

During the 1850s a number of major developments were in progress in the Three Towns district. In 1851 the total population of the Three Towns was nearly 100,000. A further increase in population was signalled by the opening of the Keyham Steam Yard (North Yard), north of New Passage, in 1854. Work had also started on the construction of Brunel's Royal Albert Bridge at Saltash, the final link in the railway between Paddington and Penzance. The Tamar Valley too was experiencing its own changes. A repeal of the tax on bricks in 1850 rendered the fireclay sources on Hingston Down, above Calstock, viable for exploitation. Tile and brickworks were established at Gawton, near Calstock and at Bealeswood, adjacent to the cut of the Tamar Manure Navigation at Weir Head. Bricks, including firebricks and engineering bricks for the Admiralty, were transported by the ubiquitous Tamar barges to the expanding Three Towns. The 1850s saw the peak of copper mining in the area, especially from the Devon Great Consols Mine. New Quay, downstream from Morwellham, was enlarged and improved to handle copper ore. In 1859 a new dock was completed at Morwellham, capable of berthing up to six 300 ton vessels and new paved ore floors were laid to handle copper and manganese ores and arsenic. A mineral railway was built, linking the new dock with the Devon Great Consols Mine. A special party was conveyed on this mineral railway, in an inaugural train, and one passenger thought it would add 'much to the enjoyment of excursionists up the Tamar if, after leaving their steamers at Morwellham, they could complete their trip on the Devon Great Consols Railway'.

Evidence that steamer excursions on the River Tamar were increasing in popularity is offered by growing condemnation of excursionists. Criticism of Tamar excursions was made, in the main, by middle-class Christians who objected to river trips on the Sabbath – the only full day-off that the working-class had. However, the steamboat operators of Saltash and Calstock experienced no moral dilemma in offering Sunday excursions – especially with 100,000 potential customers on the opposite shore. Detractors also objected to drunken behaviour – which, in fairness, is a misery that passengers sometimes have to endure to this day. The *Plymouth & Devonport Weekly Journal* reported the drunken behaviour of trippers from three steamers at Calstock in April 1854. The problem was caused, in part by the owners of the steamboats who sold as much alcohol as possible to increase the profits of a trip. While steamboat owners like William Gilbert would later be feted as doyens of their local churches and communities, and many shareholders of the steamboat companies undoubtedly shared the pious Victorian values of the critics, their social conscience fell well short of actually jeopardising their dividends by withdrawing the sale of alcohol aboard their steamers. Instead the steamboat owners arrived at the simplest and most profitable alternative, they doubled the ticket prices of some trips 'to keep the company select'. One can only admire their audacity, they created a social problem and then charged those they had offended twice the price to avoid it. Left to their own devices the working-class created their own remedies. Friendly societies, Methodists and other non-conformist congregations, chartered steamers and ensured that the bars remained closed throughout the day. Bands of Hope and temperance societies likewise chartered 'dry' steamers. The demand for abstentious excursions became so great that when William Gilbert introduced his new paddle steamer *Eleanor* in 1869 (see below), he designated her a teetotal boat to attract the patronage of temperance, chapel and church parties.

The Public Health Act of 1848 sought to address a national problem of insanitary conditions, particularly in the rapidly expanding industrial towns, and Medical Officers of Health conducted tours of inspection throughout the country. A Board of Health Report in 1851 stated that Plymouth (as opposed to the newer towns of Devonport and Stonehouse) ranked among the most unhealthy towns in Great Britain. The resulting heightened awareness about hygiene and health in general might be likened to the effects of similar government health propaganda today, except that instead of jogging, people in the nineteenth century took the sea airs and even took to the sea itself. This endorsement of the benefits of fresh air prompted greater demand for 'healthy' sea and river trips and further eroded the position taken by the 'anti Sunday desecration' lobby.

While these social matters were being addressed, an event in 1856 placed the Royal seal of approval on Tamar steamer excursions. On 15 August 1856 Queen Victoria, Prince Albert, the Princess Royal, Prince Arthur, Princess Helena and Princess Loiusa arrived at Barnpool aboard the Royal Yacht, to make an 'unexpected' visit to the Duke of Bedford at Endsleigh, in the Tamar Valley. The *Plymouth & Devonport Weekly Journal* reported:

> Yesterday the Queen, Prince Albert and the Royal children went up the Tamar to Cotehele and thence to visit the Duke of Bedford at Endsleigh. They left in the Fairy [Royal Yacht tender] at 11.15am, the Impregnable and Royal William firing a Royal Salute as they passed.
>
> On the Fairy nearing Calstock it was found that she drew too much water and could proceed no further. Here was a fix. However the Gipsy river steamer happened to be on the spot and without any reluctance on the part of Her Majesty she embarked on board of her and was then conveyed to Morwellham, where conveyance was procured and the Royal party thence proceeded to Endsleigh.

The effect of this Royal endorsement of Gilbert and Willcocks' steamer *Gipsy* appears to have been particularly rewarding as she suddenly became the most popular steamer on the river. They soon placed an order with a Stonehouse shipbuilder, for a new wooden paddle steamer, to be named *Fairy* in honour and gratitude for the opportunity the Royal Yacht tender had unwittingly offered them. Completed in September 1857, the *Fairy* (59.4 tg, 98.9 x 14.4 x 6 feet) replaced the *Lord Yarborough*, ownership of which passed to Devon Banking. She subsequently disappeared from the Shipping Register and local steamer programmes.

Meanwhile, in 1856, the TSPCo's *Alert*(2) was acquired by the Saltash Watermans Steam Packet Co Ltd (SWSPCo.Ltd). This new company was amongst the first in Britain to be incorporated as a Limited Liability Company – Company No. 10 – pursuant to the Joint Stock Companies Act of 1856. Registered on 31 July 1856, the principal promoter and shareholder was John Martyn of Saltash. There were a total of forty-eight shareholders in the new company, including: the Tamer Steam Packet Company; Richard Willcocks, an Innkeeper of Saltash and one time partner in the ill fated Saltash Floating Bridge Company, and six watermen of Saltash and Devonport, each with small shareholdings – a device perhaps to offer credibility to the Company's name or to secure landing rights at Saltash and Devonport. In the following year the *Alert*(2) was joined on her Hamoaze passenger service by a two masted, iron, screw steamer, the *Mystery* (36 tg, 79.5 x 11 x 7 feet), which had originally been built by W. Fairbairn & Co of Millwall in 1845. The SWSPCo.Ltd increased the frequency of their steamer services, making eight return trips between Saltash and North Corner daily, between 8am and 7.30pm, charging 3d return for the fore cabin and deck and 4d return for the after cabin. An acrimonious public argument ensued

The FAIRY at Town Quay, Saltash in the 1860s
COURTESY JOHN BINDING.

Above: *The Sea Front of Plymouth c1860. The D&CTSPCo.Ltd's* PRINCESS *anchored off West Hoe to view a regatta.*

Below: *The* PRINCESS *joined by the S&SGSPCo.Ltd's paddle steamer* FAIRY *(nearest) on the same day*
CITY OF PLYMOUTH MUSEUMS & ART GALLERY.

when William Gilbert, in his guise as the proprietor of the opposing S&DSBCo and the Hamoaze steamer *Victoria*, ran newspaper advertisements denigrating the financial stability of the new company and the poor condition of their steamers. He seems to have proved his point because within a year the SWSPCo.Ltd ceased trading. The *Alert*(2) was sold for breaking in Millbay and the *Mystery* was sold to a Sidmouth owner in 1858. In March 1859, in reply to a circular from the Joint Stock Company Registration Office, John Martyn, as Secretary of the SWSPCo.Ltd replied that the company no longer existed. A minor shareholder of the ill fated company was John Parson of Landrake, who held just one £5 share. It is tempting to speculate whether there was any connection with the John Parson who, by the end of the century, established the Millbrook Steamboat Company which became the principal rival of Gilbert's Saltash, Three Towns & District Steamboat Co Ltd.

New steamboat companies

Two other companies were incorporated in 1857. The Tamar Steam Navigation Co Ltd (TSNCo.Ltd) was established by William Truby Chafe of Devonport, James Joll of New Passage, Samuel Lang of Cotehele Quay and Richard Bowhay of Calstock to operate their newly acquired twin masted, iron, paddle steamer, the *Emperor* (45.8 tg, 89.1 x 14 x 6.9 feet) which had been built in Blackwall in 1842.

The other company was the Devon & Cornwall Tamar Steam Packet Co Ltd (D&CTSPCo.Ltd) which took over the management of the *Princess*. The same shareholders in the *Princess* and the D&CTSPCo.Ltd (Gill, Hoskins etc) also bought, from Newcastle, the twin masted, wooden, paddle steamer *Wellington* (75 tg, 84.3 x 17.2 x 9.2 feet), which had been built in Northumberland a year before.

In 1858 messrs Gilbert, Willcocks and others incorporated the Saltash & Saint Germans

Steam Packet Co Ltd (S&SGSPCo.Ltd). The objects of the new company were:

> ...to convey passengers, agricultural produce, goods, materials and merchandise, in steamers, vessels, boats and lighters, propelled by steam, sails or any other motive power, and to use such steamers, vessels, boats and lighters for the purpose of towing, tugging, or propelling any ships, vessels, boats or rafts in or on any of the rivers, waters or creeks in the counties of Devon and Cornwall or either of them and at sea within twenty miles of the coast of the said counties.

The nominal capital of the company was £8,000 and there was an immediate call on shares to raise almost £3,000 to buy the paddle steamers *Gipsy* and *Fairy* from Gilbert, Willcocks and their fellow shareholders.

In just three years since the visit of the Royal family, the passenger steamer trade on the River Tamar had been transformed and the foundations of future paddle steamer fleets were laid with the D&CTSPCo.Ltd at Calstock, and William Gilbert's ventures at Saltash. To summarise and help clarify the position in 1859, the steamers, companies and their principal areas of operation are listed below.

Calstock based steamboat companies:	
Calstock & Devonport Steam Packet Company	
Queen	Market service and excursions
Tamar Steam Navigation Co Ltd	
Emperor	River excursions
Devon & Cornwall Tamar Steam Packet Co Ltd	
Princess	River excursions
Wellington	Market service and excursions
Saltash based steamboat companies:	
Saltash & Devonport Steam Boat Company	
Victoria	Saltash–Devonport
Saltash & Saint Germans Steam Packet Co Ltd	
Gipsy	Market service and excursions.
Fairy	River excursions

Saltash Floating Bridge

On 31 May 1850 a new twenty-one years lease of the Saltash Ferry was granted to the partnership of: J. Hancock – the tenant of Ferry House Inn; F. W. P. Elverton – the Town Clerk of Saltash; and J. H. Cook. They planned to re-establish a floating bridge using Rendel's infrastructure of slipways and chain pits. A new bridge was ordered from Routeliffe of Mount Batten. The vessel measured 86 feet long x 26.5 feet wide and was designed by John Mare, who also supplied the engines and machinery. The new bridge entered service in the following year and differed from all previous floating bridges in that she had a central deck, 50 feet long x 11.5 feet wide, with two outer deck houses – one side housing machinery and two cylinder engines of 6hp each, the other housing the boiler and two passenger shelters. Up to 100 passengers and three carriage-and-pairs could be carried.

Another of Rendel's floating bridges, over the Itchen at Southampton, had been experiencing financial difficulties, as running and repair costs outstripped revenue. In August 1853 a delegation of directors from the Company of Proprietors of the Itchen Floating Bridge and Roads visited the both the Torpoint Ferry – which was experiencing similar financial disappointments, and the Saltash Ferry – which was at last achieving some success with the new John Mare designed floating bridge. First they visited the office of Henry Smith, solicitor and Secretary for the Torpoint floating bridge company, and reported:

> The earnings of the Company have, like our own, been overpowered by expense, and it seems their original Shareholders have never received any Dividend...
>
> Mr Smith admitted the superiority of the Bridge at Saltash to the heavy, costly bridges which they possessed at Torpoint.

At Saltash:

> The Deputation was at the very outset of their duty greatly struck with the remarkable celerity with which this bridge does her work – her general speed and the ease with which she took up her speed on quitting the Shore and the readiness with which she drops it on nearing the opposite side of the River ... with regard to structure and economy of working she is a vast improvement on any Floating Bridge hitherto seen by them, and is highly creditable to the skill of Messrs Mare of Plymouth by whom she was planned and built.

The delegation resolved unanimously that the Itchen company should buy a new bridge based upon the principles of that at Saltash.

Nearly all of the vessels which Rendel designed for his floating bridges proved unsatisfactory. The Dartmouth vessel had her steam engines removed in 1836. The first Saltash bridge had been withdrawn within a year. While the Torpoint and Southampton bridges were still working they were proving expensive to run. The Portsmouth bridge alone operated with some success but here the owners had specified the design. Contemporaries accused Rendel of plagiarism of the principles of flying bridges and chain traction, however, Rendel merely drew upon elements of his own engineering experience to invent a singular solution for the riverine passage of vehicular traffic, where bridges, for reason of cost or obstruction to navigation, could not be built.

A print published on completion of the Royal Albert Bridge. Unfortunately a number of things are out of scale – including the bridge. But the illustration does provide a view of the Routeliffe built floating bridge on the Little Ash (Devon) side. The Cornwall landing is immediately beside the main Cornwall pier of the bridge. COURTESY KEITH PERKINS

Each subsequent floating bridge was built upon Rendel's foundations and while new designs improved efficiency, the principles of Rendel's invention continued, and continue, to serve their purpose.

THE ROYAL ALBERT BRIDGE

The Royal Albert Bridge, which carries the mainline railway across the River Tamar and into Cornwall, stands today as a monument to its engineer – Isambard Kingdom Brunel. Devon and Cornwall had railways before the bridge was officially opened on 2 May 1859 and they were already effecting significant social changes. The railways assisted the migration of workers from the agricultural trades (where employment declined due to mechanisation) to the new industries in the Three Towns and also provided access to national markets for industrial and agricultural produce.

When alternative railway routes across the Tamar were being considered, Capt W. S. Moorsom proposed leasing the Torpoint floating bridge to ferry trains across the river. The idea was, surprisingly, supported by Brunel, but opposed as impractical by Rendel. The bridge at Saltash was eventually proposed by Brunel. Surveys and trial excavations were undertaken at Saltash as early as 1847 and construction work began in 1853. Most of the foreshore upstream of the ferry slipway at Saltash Passage was used as a construction site, where a huge cylindrical coffer-dam (for the construction of the central pier) and the two arched suspension tubes were built. These building yards proved a great attraction for steamer passengers and on 21 September 1857, when the first great truss was floated into position, thousands of sightseers from the Three Towns arrived by steamer to view the day's events. The first scheduled train crossed the bridge on 11 April 1859 and just over three weeks later thousands of spectators witnessed the official opening of the bridge by HRH Prince Albert.

Once the bridge was opened the stage- and mail-coach traffic ended abruptly – the *Quicksilver Mail* made its last journey on 15 May 1859. The completed railway route also spelt the end for some coastal packets, including the long serving *Sir Francis Drake,* which, although she was maintaining a service to the Channel Islands at the time, was sold out of the district. The bridge severed any future connection or dependence between the railway and local passenger steamers, but in the ensuing years it has provided a lasting spectacle for river excursionists – one of the highlights of a Tamar trip being to pass beneath the famous landmark.

CHAPTER THREE

'PROPER GRACEFUL BOATS'

Paddle steamer fleets of the River Tamar 1860 1893

MARKET STEAMER FLEETS

The Devon & Cornwall Tamar Steam Packet Co Ltd. During the second half of the nineteenth century a number of independent excursion agents and promoters appeared on the scene.

A. E. Rowe of Rowe's Pleasant Marine Excursions; Cole's Marine Excursions; McBryde's River & Sea Trips; and T. Sayers Marine Excursions. These agents either chartered steamers, or contracted to operate a programme of excursions on behalf of a steamboat company. Their bargaining position was enhanced dependent upon landing rights they had secured. The entire history of passenger boat operation in the Three Towns district is linked to the acquisition of landing rights. Only Mutton Cove, North Corner and Pottery Quay (New Passage) in Devonport, and from 1895, Phoenix Wharf in Plymouth, offered suitable local authority owned landing places for the larger steamers. The principal Plymouth landing places were privately owned: Millbay Pier and Princess Royal Pier by the Great Western Railway (GWR); and later West Hoe Pier and the Promenade Pier on the sea front by William Gilbert and the Plymouth Promenade Pier & Pavilion Co Ltd respectively. Above Saltash, however, it was the Calstock steamboat companies that had secured leases at nearly all the suitable quays.

In 1859 the four Calstock based paddle steamers: *Wellington*, *Princess*, *Queen* and *Emperor*,

An unidentified paddle steamer in the Hamoaze c1860, heading upstream from North Corner, with Torpoint on the left.
CITY OF PLYMOUTH MUSEUMS & ART GALLERY.

A paddle tug with a tow of three topsail schooners rounding Danescombe Bend into the Calstock reach of the River Tamar c1900. The masts of another ship can be seen in the background at Cotehele Quay. Both the Tamar & Tavy Steam Ship Co Ltd's VOLUNTEER *and the Devon & Cornwall Tamar Steam Packet Co Ltd's* EMPEROR *went 'seeking' tows during the winter months.* NATIONAL MARITIME MUSEUM.

were offering Tamar excursions. In September the *Emperor* was chartered by the Officers of the Lily of Devon Lodge of the Manchester Unity Independent Order of Oddfellows for an excursion up the River Tamar:

> ...giving parties ample time for visiting all the delightful scenes for which the river has been so justly praised, and which are rendered still more beautiful at this season of the year. An excellent Quadrille Band will attend to the dancing throughout the day.

Some excursion charters ran in the opposite direction, from the Tamar Valley to the Three Towns; the Gunnislake Wesleyan Chapel organised a day excursion, landing at Devonport. By 1861 the *Wellington* was unopposed on the market day services from Calstock because in that year the *Queen* (of the C&DSPCo) and the *Emperor* (of the TSNCo.Ltd) were both being managed by the D&CTSPCo.Ltd (operator of the *Wellington* and the *Princess*), effectively amalgamating all of the Calstock owned steamers into the same fleet. All four steamers were chartered during August 1864 to transport the Second Queens Own Regiment to Calstock for a 'day of sports and relaxation'.

The *Princess, Wellington, Queen* and *Emperor* became fully owned by the D&CTSPCo.Ltd in 1864 when that company bought the first two steamers from their private shareholders, acquired the assets of the C&DSPCo and gained financial control of the TSNCo.Ltd. The *Queen* was sold and converted to sail in 1874.

Mining in the Tamar Valley had peaked by the middle of the 1860s, followed by a slump due to a depression in the metal market in 1870 – subsequent unemployment brought hard times to the Calstock and Gunnislake districts. A branch of the South Devon Railway reached Tavistock in 1859, further reducing the importance of Morwellham Quay and eventually causing the Tavistock Canal to be abandoned as a navigation in 1873. In an attempt to counter competition from the railway, a new dock was opened at Morwellham in 1859, capable of docking six ships of 300 tons. Calstock, meanwhile, continued as an important river port and ship owning community, with its quays lining half a mile of the river bank.

The Tamar & Tavy Steam Ship Co Ltd.

In 1862 a general purpose passenger-tug paddle steamer was launched in Stonehouse. The new wooden paddle steamer, *Volunteer*, measured 59 tg, 86.2 x 16.3 x 7.1 feet. She was owned by Robinson Ridley, a shipowner of Stonehouse, skippered by Captain Ham and managed by Thomas Jones Stephens, a local tug operator. The *Volunteer* engaged in a variety of services including attending emigrant ships at Plymouth – chartered by the Emigration Depot at Elphinstone Wharf, in Sutton Pool. She similarly attended passenger liners of the P&O,

Union Steam Ship Company and New Zealand Shipping Company for Plymouth Great Western Docks at Millbay – until the dock company acquired its own tenders in the 1870s. Whilst engaged in ferrying mails to and from Millbay Pier the *Volunteer* flew the Royal Mail pennant from her mast and subsequent excursion advertisements for the steamer proudly described her as the 'Royal Mail steamer Volunteer'.

Both the *Volunteer* and the D&CTSPCo.Ltd's *Emperor* also sought work as tugs. Much of the estuarine cargo traffic was conducted by locally owned and crewed Tamar river barges – the lorries or trucks, as it were, of the local waterways – but the economics of their operation rarely extended to the cost of a tow up river. However, skippers of sea going schooners and ketches experienced difficulty navigating the river to Calstock and Morwellham and regularly negotiated a tow from Plymouth Sound. Tugs like the *Volunteer* and the *Emperor*, and non-passenger carrying paddle-tugs like Thomas Jones Stephens' *Secret* would 'seek' a tow well beyond the Eddystone, 'claiming' two or three vessels to share the cost of a tow up river.

The Tamar & Tavy Steam Ship Co Ltd (T&TSSCo.Ltd) was incorporated in 1865. Foremost amongst the subscribers were Thomas Jones Stephens, managing owner of the *Volunteer*, and George Johnson, a Glaswegian by birth, who was a 'gentleman of Plymouth' and a minister of the Scottish Universalist Church, with a chapel in Henry Street, Plymouth. Johnson's contribution to the new company was a new 43.4tg iron paddle steamer, measuring 115 x 14.1 x 4 feet. She was built by Hedderwick of Govan, on the Clyde, with 28hp, two cylinder, oscillating engines by J. Bennie of Glasgow. Launched on 4 May 1865 and named *Aerial*, she was by far the most luxurious and graceful steamer yet built for the Tamar passenger trade and set the standard for all future market and excursion vessels. She was destined to become a legend on the river and for long a thorn in the flesh of the D&CTSPCo.Ltd. The new paddler was fitted with feathering paddle floats (feathering floats had been around for a quarter of a century and were significantly more efficient than the earlier fixed floats – but at an increased initial cost) and, although she was the largest paddler on the river at that date, drew only 2ft 6ins of water. The most striking improvement were two main deck saloons extending to her full width and almost her full length – fitted with closely-set large windows instead of portholes. All outside passenger space was on top of these saloons. Inside, each saloon offered spacious accommodation with a headroom of seven feet and were provided with plush velvet seating and mahogany tables. A steam heated urn supplied hot water and space was reserved for a piano. The crowning glory, however, was the proudly announced toilet accommodation, novelty enough aboard a Tamar steamer at the time, but the *Aerial* boasted separate closets for men and women. Once fitting out was complete the next task was to get the steamer from the Clyde to the Three Towns. All the saloon windows were boarded up and coal for the voyage had to be stacked in her newly furnished saloons. In an article in the *Western Morning News* in 1961, George Johnson's son (also George) wrote:

> The voyage was a stormy one. Built as a river boat, with a flat bottom more or less, the scratch crew on occasions wondered if they would ever reach port. But after four days harbour was reached, and behold a boat the Plymouth people dubbed the Floating Greenhouse.

Her distinctive saloon windows prompted other similar nicknames such as the 'glasshouse' and the 'omnibus', but any derogatory intent was quickly supplanted with affection as the *Aerial* established herself as the most popular steamer on the river and was regularly packed to her 150 capacity. The T&TSSCo.Ltd timed the *Aerial's* arrival to perfection, because in the same month the Royal Yacht *Osborne* anchored in Barnpool, bringing the Prince and Princess of Wales for a visit to Plymouth and Mount Edgcumbe. *The Western Morning News* reported:

> Immediately the Osborne dropped anchor Mount Edgcumbe became the centre of attraction; and great was the bustle at the

An Illustrated London News *engraving of the Royal Yacht* OSBORNE, *with the Prince and Princess of Wales aboard, landing at Barnpool in 1865. Ahead of the Royal Yacht is the artists impression of the Tamar & Tavy Steam Ship Co Ltd's new paddle steamer* AERIAL *– her name is misspelled on her pennant and her funnel drawn too wide, but there's no mistaking her distinctive row of rectangular saloon ports.* ALAN KITTRIDGE COLLECTION.

The Aerial *c1870, wearing the funnel colours of the Tamar & Tavy Steam Ship Co Ltd. She is passing the incline of the East Cornwall Mineral Railway down to Calstock Quay. Note the lime kiln abutting the incline wall on the left, and the topsail schooner moored at the quay. Beyond the incline the fertile market garden slopes bear the distinctive vertical sowing pattern which is dictated by the severe gradient.* National Maritime Museum.

landing places on the Plymouth and Devonport side of the water. Stonehouse Hard was the most crowded, and the crush there was really dangerous. Every boat as it came in was filled with a rush; and oft-times would be passengers had to turn out again and wait for craft that were less overloaded. In their eagerness to secure a speedy transit ladies outdid the gentlemen, executing vaults from shore to boat, such as in calmer moments they would have shrunk from with horror.

The favourite passenger steamer on the day was the brand new *Aerial* which even managed to get herself included in an *Illustrated London News* engraving depicting the event. The *Aerial* was placed on market day services from Calstock, putting her in direct competition with the D&CTSPCo.Ltd's *Wellington*. Inevitably the *Aerial* proved popular with the market gardeners and their families making their way down to Devonport Market in the cold, early hours of the morning. Little further evidence of *Aerial's* success against the *Wellington* is needed than the following startling report in the *West Briton* on 25 April 1866:

> William Haynes was indicted for having wilfully and maliciously run into the steamer Aerial, with intent to destroy her. The prisoner was Captain of a steamer called the Wellington. ...The prosecutors who were the Tamar & Tavy Steam Packet Company had lately purchased the Aerial which they ran upon the Tamar in opposition to another company which were previously navigating the river, and looked upon the new company with a great deal of jealousy. The old company had a powerful steamer, called the Wellington and it was a curious fact that before the prisoner took command of that vessel there had been two or three collisions between he and the Aerial in which the Aerial received considerable damage. On 4th April the Aerial was proceeding up the Tamar, and when near Pentille the Wellington was seen approaching on the same side. The Captain of the Aerial fearing a collision ordered the helm to be ported, according to the rules of the river, so as to allow the Wellington to pass, but seeing that the Wellington came towards him he ordered the helm to be starboarded and ran the Aerial right across the river towards the Cornish side, but instead of the Wellington keeping her course she ran across the river in the direction of the Aerial, struck her amidships, cut her down to the waters edge and the Aerial had a very narrow escape from being totally destroyed.

After the court case the two companies seem to have settled to a quarter of a century of less belligerent competition.

The AERIAL *and the* EMPRESS

In 1877 the Plymouth Pier Co Ltd (PPCo.Ltd) was incorporated with the object to construct two limestone jetties protecting a boat basin and to build baths in an adjacent building. West Hoe Baths & Pier were duly completed in 1880 and Rowe's Pleasant Marine Excursions was successful in gaining the rights to operate excursions from the southern jetty, chartering steamers from all of the Tamar's excursion steamer fleets.

For the first time in the history of the district's passenger steamers Plymouth at last boasted a sea front steamer landing and the D&CTSPCo.Ltd responded in the same year by ordering a new paddle steamer, which was to successfully challenge the *Aerial* both operationally and in the fond memories of Tamar Valley inhabitants. This new steamer had been conceived some years earlier, in 1876, when the Plymouth Great Western Docks Company at Millbay took delivery of their second liner tender, the *Sir Walter Raleigh*, an iron paddle steamer built at William Allsup & Sons' Caledonian Works in Preston. It might have been on the occasion of her inaugural voyage, a once-only trip up the Tamar for invited guests, that an exchange related by George Johnson (jnr) occurred:

> The principal of an engineering firm boasted that he would build a boat that would carry twice as many passengers as the *Aerial* and beat her in speed – if not, he would 'eat his umbrella'.

A few years later William Allsup gained an order from the D&CTSPCo.Ltd to build the market steamer which he had boasted about. The result, in 1880, was the *Empress*, an iron paddle steamer destined to provide market services on the Tamar for nearly half a century. She measured 101tg, 115 x 16.2 x 4.9 feet and was fitted with 40hp, two cylinder compound, oscillating engines – also built by Allsup (compound engines were far more economic to run than non-compounding, or 'simple', engines because steam was used twice – in high pressure and low pressure cylinders). Similar to the *Aerial*, the *Empress* was provided with saloons fore and aft on the main deck, but they were fitted with portholes instead of rectangular windows. Following arrival of the new steamer both the *Wellington* (in 1882) and the *Emperor* were withdrawn from service and scrapped.

William Allsup's promise that the *Empress* would carry twice as many passengers as the *Aerial's* 150 was easily surpassed with her Class 5 (smooth water) certificate for 444 passengers. However, as George Johnson (jnr) recalled:

> In the matter of speed the Empress never

The AERIAL *in the funnel colours of the Saltash Three Towns & District Steamboat Co Ltd c1900, disembarking passengers at Calstock – as she had done every market day evening while still with the Tamar & Tavy Steam Ship Co Ltd. Note the 3ft 6ins gauge East Cornwall Mineral Railway, this quay section of which was worked by horses.* Below: *The* AERIAL *at Morwellham. The skipper pictured standing between the rails above and on the paddle box below is thought to be Capt Foot.* COURTESY JACK KINGSTON.

A steamer bill from the AERIAL'S *days with the Tamar & Tavy Steam Ship Co. Ltd.* COURTESY JOHN DYKE.

beat the Aerial and legend has it that it was the playful habit of the Aerial's crew to wave an umbrella as their own boat speeded past.

James Goss, the renowned Calstock shipbuilder, quoted in R. T. Paige's book *The Tamar Valley at Work*, also noted that 'The Empress was bigger than the Aerial but not quite so fast'. The rivalry between the *Aerial* and *Empress* became legendary. For one shilling return and sixpence per two hundredweight of market produce, passengers boarded for Devonport's North Corner landing stage, calling at Cotehele Quay, Halton Quay, Hole's Hole or Weir Quay, Cargreen and Saltash. Alfred Pengelly in his book *The Inside Story of Calstock* remembered:

ST. MATTHEW'S CHURCH,
STONEHOUSE.

THE ANNUAL
STEAMER EXCURSION
HAS BEEN FIXED FOR
WEDNESDAY, JUNE 10TH, 1885,
WHEN THE SALOON STEAMER
"AERIAL"
Will Leave North Corner, 10 a.m; Royal William Victualling Yard, 10-15 a.m.; The Promenade Pier, 10-30 a.m., for

THE BREAKWATER
To land and visit the LIGHTHOUSE, returning, to start from the Promenade Pier, 1 p.m.; Royal William Victualling Yard, 1-15 p.m.; North Corner, 1-30 p.m., for

THE RIVER TAMAR
TO
THE WEIR HEAD
(DIRECT), AND RETURNING TO
MORWELLHAM
To land, giving opportunity to walk on the MORWELL ROCKS, afterwards proceeding to

CALSTOCK FOR TEA,
Returning to North Corner, 9 p.m.; Royal William Victualling Yard, 9-15 p.m.; and the Promenade Pier, 9-30 p.m.

TICKETS—For the Morning Trip 6d; Children under 12 years of age 3d. Afternoon Excursion, or both Excursions 1/6d.; Children under 12 years of age 1/-.

WALTER A. PRIDEAUX, Incumbent.
E. A. H. BESLEY, Curate.
C. BULTEEL, H. D. STEAR, } Churchwardens.

At that time, the most well-known steamer was the 'Aerial', a glorious little market boat belonging to a Calstock company. Great consternation was caused when another company bought the 'Empress' to rival the 'Aerial's' trade and popularity.

Regularly, a representative of each of the two companies would stand together on the quay and shout respectively for the 'Aerial' and the 'Empress' in order to solicit the prospective passengers' sympathies.

At the appointed time of leaving, they would quickly let go the ropes and race to Cotehele Quay, where the rivalry would be resumed, and so on, until Devonport was reached. It is said that they even took pigeons to register the first arrival.

George Johnson (jnr):

Just below Calstock there was, and still is, a protruding rock – Kelly Rock. One morning, the Empress getting away first, struck the rock. There was a fearful crash and the paddle box of the Empress was shattered. The Aerial had to take over the passengers, mainly attending Plymouth and Devonport Markets.

The Aerial, too, once ran into trouble near the same place and actually sank. She was raised at low tide, but the ensuing cost for repairs was indeed heavy.

In 1882 the Calstock market steamer fleets comprised:

DEVON & CORNWALL TAMAR STEAM PACKET CO. LTD.	
Empress	Market service and excursions
Princess	River excursions and towage
THE TAMAR & TAVY STEAM SHIP CO.LTD.	
Aerial	Market service and excursions
Volunteer	River/sea excursions and towage.

Examples of their excursions can be gained from contemporary newspaper advertisements. On Monday 25 July 1881 Rowe's Pleasant Marine Excursions were running the *Empress* from West Hoe Pier to the Sound, Breakwater and Cawsand, landing to visit Penlee Point, the Grotto and Rame Head – tickets 9d. On the same day the *Volunteer* was plying from Millbay Pier and North Corner to Pentille Quay (on the Tamar below Halton Quay) for Pentille Flower Show, while the *Aerial* was chartered by the Presbyterian Church of Plymouth for their Annual River Excursion to the Breakwater in the morning and to Weir Head in the afternoon. In July 1883 Rowe was operating the *Aerial* from West Hoe Pier on River Tamar excursions, while the *Empress* was running from North Corner, Mutton Cove and Millbay Pier to Laira for the Races at Chelson Meadow.

The EMPRESS *in Plymouth Sound, from a Saltash Three Towns & District Steamboat Co Ltd official postcard c1900. Built by William Allsup's Caledonian Works in Preston for the Devon & Cornwall Tamar Steam Packet Co Ltd, the* EMPRESS *competed with the Tamar & Tavy Steam Ship Co Ltd's* AERIAL *for the market day trade between Calstock and Devonport.* CITY OF PLYMOUTH LOCAL & NAVAL STUDIES LIBRARY.

PLYMOUTH PROMENADE PIER

In 1883 the Plymouth Promenade Pier & Steam Packet Co Ltd (PPP&SPCo.Ltd) was incorporated to build a promenade pier on the sea front below Plymouth Hoe. The great pier builder Eugenius Birch was engaged to design the pier – his fourteenth and final pier contract. Already a sick man Birch died a few months after the pier was opened. Finished in 1883 at a cost of £45,000 the pier was 465 feet long with a pier head 190 feet wide, complete with a bandstand. On either side of the pier head landing steps and moorings were provided for steamers and a toll of one penny was charged for each passenger embarking or disembarking. In a district so well served by river paddlers it might be assumed that those steamers were encouraged to use the new pier but, surprisingly, in March 1884 only the Oreston & Turnchapel Steamboat Co Ltd (O&TSCo.Ltd – see Chapter Four) of the River Plym had arranged to run 'trips' from the pier. The O&TSCo.Ltd's steamers were small, utilitarian ferryboats, designed for short crossings of the Plym, they therefore lacked toilet facilities and were fitted with simple slatted seats and a covered cabin (as opposed to a saloon). The pier company soon realised that the O&TSCo.Ltd was only interested in establishing a steamer service between the pier and Mount Edgcumbe on park open days and the O&TSCo.Ltd minute books note: 'after only two Wednesdays the Promenade Pier owners granted a monopoly to Mr. Rowe – which shut us out'. A monopoly was indeed granted to A. E. Rowe in August 1884, however, instead of chartering the more suitable

DEVON AND CORNWALL
Steam Packet Company, Limited.

The "EMPRESS"
SALOON STEAMER,

Belonging to the above Company, Runs in the MARKET TRADE throughout the Year, on the DEVONPORT and PLYMOUTH MARKET DAYS, viz:—TUESDAYS, THURSDAYS & SATURDAYS.

The General time of leaving Calstock 7 a.m., and Devonport 4 p.m.

This Steamer has spacious Cabin and Deck accommodation and most suitable for

EXCURSION PARTIES.

Licensed to carry 446 Persons inside the Breakwater, and 211 Outside. Well adapted for the Water in all her appointments. For Terms, &c., apply to

STEPHEN PAUL, Manager, CALSTOCK.

Advertisement for the EMPRESS *in* Venning's Directory of East Cornwall *1887.*

Looking down river from the Bere peninsula, the EMPRESS *is pictured off Cotehele Quay c1910.* ALAN KITTRIDGE COLLECTION.

The Saltash Steam Boat Company's iron paddle steamer ELEANOR *approaching West Hoe Pier, with the Plymouth Promenade Pier and Plymouth Hoe in the background. The open bandstand on the pier head and Smeaton's Tower (ex-Eddystone Lighthouse) on the Hoe date this picture around 1890. Note the Camera Obscura, on the Hoe – behind the steps on West Hoe Pier.* ROYAL INSTITUTION OF CORNWALL.

Tamar steamers, Rowe employed steamers of the O&TSCo.Ltd. Meanwhile the Tamar steamers of the D&CTSPCo.Ltd, the T&TSSCo.Ltd and William Gilbert's Saltash fleet were all contracted to the management of Rowe's competitor – McBryde's River & Sea Trips – and ran from the adjacent West Hoe Pier. In 1889 the Plymouth Promenade Pier & Pavilion Co. Ltd (PPP&PCo.Ltd) was incorporated to take over the earlier pier company and raise a further £5000 to build a circular, glass domed pavilion and a marine lounge at the seaward end of the pier which was opened in 1891. The pavilion offered concerts, dances, bands, and later, rollerskating and boxing. Promenaders and excursionists could visit the 'frozen figures' of the Tableaux in the pavilion, or have their 'heads read' by the phrenologist at the end of the pier. Enamelled signs advised MAKE IT A HABIT WHEN YOU WANT A CUP OF TEA, OF CALLING AT THE CAFÉ WHICH OVERLOOKS THE SEA.

Interior of the new pavilion of 1891 on the Promenade Pier COURTESY JACK KINGSTON

By 1886 the T&TSSCo.Ltd was in financial trouble. As a result of a Judgement against the Company the *Aerial* passed to the ownership of John Rickard of Saltash, who sold half share in the steamer to Gideon Ebenezer Spear, the principal agricultural merchant in the Tamar Valley and owner of landing rights at numerous quays where his lime kilns were located. The *Aerial* continued much as before but the

The Devon & Cornwall Tamar Steam Packet Co Ltd's new flagship of 1888, the steel paddle steamer ALEXANDRA. *In this c1890 photograph she appears to be wearing the blue funnel colours of the D&CTSPCo.Ltd and is moored outside that company's office (the white building on the right) on Steamer Quay, Calstock. Her stern rests approximately where, nearly twenty years later, the railway viaduct would stand.*
ALAN KITTRIDGE COLLECTION.

Volunteer was sold to Thomas Emerson, a Plymouth shipowner. She was scrapped two years later. The T&TSSCo.Ltd subsequently ceased trading.

The D&CTSPCo.Ltd, meanwhile, had sold the *Princess* for scrap in 1884. Her belated replacement in 1888 was the D&CTSPCo.Ltd's new flagship, the *Alexandra* – the largest ever purpose built Tamar paddle steamer. Built by William Allsup's yard she was one of the earliest steel passenger steamers in the district and measured 127tg, 125.7 x 17.3 x 5.5 feet. She had 61hp, two cylinder compound, oscillating, condensing engines (condensers turned steam back to water, creating a self contained fresh water system which eliminated the need for descaling the boiler – more economic in operation, but a higher initial cost). The *Alexandra* – in appearance a larger version of the *Empress* – cost £4,808 and was built solely for excursion service and had a Class 5 (smooth water) certificate for 468.

This was the ultimate development of the Calstock paddle steamer fleets. Although the *Empress* and the *Alexandra* would continue to be based at the D&CTSPCo.Ltd's quay and stores in Calstock, the remaining 'Calstock' steamers were bought by William Gilbert of Saltash within four years of the *Alexandra's* arrival.

WILLIAM GILBERT'S SALTASH STEAMERS

There were three passenger steamers owned and operated from Saltash in 1860: the *Fairy* and the *Gipsy* of the Saltash & Saint Germans Steam Packet Co Ltd; and the *Victoria* of the Saltash & Devonport Steam Boat Company. But one person – William Gilbert – controlled both of the companies and their steamers. In 1861 the *Fairy* offered Tamar trips from Millbay Pier, calling at Mutton Cove and North Corner. Her day excursion for 13 August 1861 was 'for the benefit of the crew', an annual tradition whereby the crew shared the day's profits amongst themselves. Later in the same month the *Fairy* made two trips from North Corner and Mutton Cove, for the races at Chelson Meadow, on the River Plym. She was also running excursions to Jackson's Tea and Fruit Gardens (Clamoak Farm) landing at Bere Ferrers on the River Tavy. The *Victoria* was used exclusively on the S&DSBCo's steamer service between Saltash and North Corner, calling at Pottery Quay and periodically extending to Mutton Cove.

A newspaper report early in 1869 announced that the 'Saltash Company are after a large commodious steamer'. In the same year William Gilbert's S&DSBCo purchased the iron paddle steamer *Eleanor*, which arrived on 15 April. The *Eleanor* had been built three years earlier by Dudgeon of Cubitt Town, on the Thames at Poplar in Middlesex. She measured 73.9tg, 104.8 x 13.1 x 4.1 feet. and was fitted with two cylinder, oscillating steam engines. It appears that she was originally named *Elénore* (a spelling used at Plymouth in her early days) and had been built speculatively for an exhibition in Paris with a view to selling her to passenger steamer operators on the River Seine. At Saltash the *Eleanor* was fitted with a single mast, having none on arrival. She was a good looking steamer, being described by James Goss, the Calstock shipbuilder, as 'a proper graceful boat' and was distinctive at the time with her long line of deck saloon portholes.

The general public made no distinction between Gilbert's two Saltash companies, both the S&SGSPCo.Ltd and the S&DSBCo were referred to collectively as the 'Saltash Company'. Following the arrival of the S&DSBCo's *Eleanor*, the S&SGSPCo.Ltd's *Gipsy* was withdrawn and scrapped (in 1869 or 1870). Both concerns continued until 31 January 1877 when Gilbert wound up the S&SGSPCo.Ltd and purchased the *Fairy* on his own account for the S&DSBCo to replace the *Victoria* – which was withdrawn and sold or scrapped soon after. Ownership of the 'Saltash Company' was thus simplified but the Saltash fleet of passenger steamers was now reduced to two paddlers, the *Eleanor* and the *Fairy*. The *Fairy* maintained the Saltash and Devonport service, while the *Eleanor* was also used on excursions. In July the *Eleanor* was running for A. E. Rowe from Millbay Pier to Cotehele and Calstock, and on evening trips from North Corner and Millbay Pier to the Breakwater and Cawsand. On 10 July she was chartered for the day by the Church of England Temperance Society (St Stephens and Saltash Branch), for a morning excursion to the Breakwater, and in the afternoon to Pentille, Calstock and Weir Head. Both excursions started from Saltash, the morning trip costing 6d and the afternoon excursion up the Tamar 1s 6d, Children 1s. Tickets for the whole day were 1s 9d. The *Eleanor's* popularity with Church, Methodist and Temperance groups was assured by Gilbert's astute decision to run her as a 'dry' boat, i.e. no alcohol was carried aboard.

New competition on the Saltash-Devonport service.

The 'Saltash Company' advertised its timetable for services between Saltash and Devonport: 'Saltash 1st trip 6.10 am, 2nd 8 am, then hourly on the hour, last trip 6pm. North Corner 1st trip 7am, afterwards hourly on the half hour, last trip 6.30pm. Ordinary tickets each way 3d. Fish dealers 2d'.

The ELEANOR approaching Mutton Cove in 1896. Passengers are waiting on the landing pier of 1891 – an extension to the original jetty. The turret ironclad, HMS DEVASTATION, is moored in the Hamoaze – she was the Port Guardship in 1896. Behind her is an ex-ship of the line, the training ship HMS IMPREGNABLE. Note the waterman using his unstayed sail, holding the sheet by hand. CITY OF PLYMOUTH MUSEUMS & ART GALLERY.

Lopwell Quay, from a postcard, postally used in 1906. The steamer could either be John Parson's (or later the Saltash Three Towns & District Steamboat Co Ltd's) wooden screw steamer IOLANTHE, *or the Oreston & Turnchapel Steamboat Co Ltd's* SWIFT *(ex-*LILY*). The cottage in the background served teas at tables laid out in the garden. The message on the back of the card reads:* DEAR E. I HAVE SPENT MANY HAPPY TEA HOURS HERE EATING CHERRY CAKE… ALAN KITTRIDGE COLLECTION.

Within four months of Gilbert's reoganisation of 1877, the press announced 'Increased facilities for proceeding by water between Devonport and Saltash where there have been a large number of passengers'. Subsequently the *Lily*, a small, wooden hulled, screw steamer, introduced a service in competition to the S&DSBCo – the second time in twenty years that someone had the temerity to challenge William Gilbert. Later in the month the *Western Daily Mercury* reported that:

> Owners of the Lily, running in opposition to the boats of the Saltash & Devonport Steam Boat Co., are having another vessel built for the traffic, therefore they [the S&DSBCo] have it in contemplation to substitute two new, smaller steamers for the Eleanor and the Fairy, keeping those boats for excursion purposes.

Two new vessels duly appeared, the first of which was built for the S&DSBCo early in 1878. Named *Victoria* (41.44 tg, 77.4 x 13.1 x 6.9 feet) she was an iron, single screw steamer (a larger single screw was better for towage, being deeper in the water and directly forward of the rudder) built by Allsups of Preston, who also built her two cylinder, inverted, direct acting engine ('upside down' cylinders driving the propeller shaft cranks). Unlike the paddle steamers in Gilbert's fleet, the *Victoria* was a simple, no-frills, passenger-tug designed for use on the Devonport passenger service and for towage. The *Lily*, meanwhile, continued in solitary opposition – her trumpeted running partner never appeared. In his book *Around and About Saltash*, P. E. B. Porter recalls:

> …at one period in the seventies [there was] great rivalry with no regulation of this traffic, and as a result passengers were at times subjected to some amusing, if annoying, trips and adventures, for two steamers of equal speed would race down and reach a pontoon at the same moment, neither would allow the other to land her affrighted passengers, who were kept unwilling participators in cruises with turns and twists all over the harbour, until one captain could out-manoeuvre the other and rush back and land the passengers before his rival could molest them.

During 1881 Gilbert's Saltash & Devonport Steam Boat Company was renamed the Saltash Steam Boat Company (SSBCo) but continued the business as before, managed by William Gilbert's brother, Edwin P. Gilbert. Edwin Gilbert was a Saltash Solicitor who had also been manager and secretary of the earlier S&SGSPCo.Ltd, and would later become the largest shareholder of the Saltash, Three Towns & District Steamboat Co Ltd.

Gilbert's second new Hamoaze steamer appeared in 1882. She was the *Albert* (60tg, 82.8 x 14 x 8.5 feet), an iron, single screw steamer built by Willoughby Bros Ltd at their shipyard in Millbay Docks. The *Albert* was fitted with a 22hp, single cylinder, inverted, direct acting engine, also built by Willoughby. Initially the *Albert* joined the *Victoria* on the Devonport run – particularly when dockyard workers swelled the passenger numbers during the 'rush hours'. But three years later she was altered for river and coastal excursions and fitted with a new two cylinder compound engine by Willoughby Bros Ltd. A saloon was fitted out below her main

The Saltash Steam Boat Company's screw steamer ALBERT, *pictured off Cawsand, from a postcard postally used in 1913. Built by Willoughby Bros Ltd at Millbay in 1882, the* ALBERT *was initially used on the Saltash to Devonport steamer service. But soon after the* PRINCE *of 1885 took over as the main Hamoaze steamer, the* ALBERT *was altered and gained a certificate for excursions outside the Breakwater.* ALAN KITTRIDGE COLLECTION.

deck, aft. The conversion added 1.5ft to her overall length (due to alterations to her stern) and increased her gross tonnage to 61.

The opposing *Lily*, meanwhile, in addition to providing weekday services between Saltash and Devonport, was also offering excursions to Weir Head, St Germans and Maristow. A. E. Rowe was chartering the *Eleanor* and the *Fairy*, both of which were now available full time for excursions. On 22 August 1882 Rowe was running the *Eleanor* to the Breakwater and Cawsand from West Hoe Pier, landing passengers on the Breakwater for one hour. During the interval she proceeded to Cawsand and landed passengers wishing to walk from Cawsand through Mount Edgcumbe Park to Cremyll, returning by the *Fairy* which departed hourly for West Hoe Pier. Some of the *Eleanor's* evening excursions from West Hoe Pier and North Corner ran to Warleigh and Maristow...

> ...where by kind permission of Sir Massey Lopes the party will land to visit the gardens and grounds. Returning in the moonlight to North Corner at 9.20pm and West Hoe Pier at 9.35 pm. Tickets 1s.

The SSBCo took delivery of a third iron screw steamer in 1885. She was the *Prince* (44.94 tg, 78.3 x 13.4 x 7.5 feet), built by Willoughby Bros Ltd and fitted with an 18hp inverted compound, surface condensing, direct acting engine. The *Prince* became closely associated with the Hamoaze service until its demise in the 1920s.

In October of the same year the identity of both the *Lily* and her owner were revealed when the Oreston & Turnchapel Steamboat Co Ltd's minute books recorded the Company's inspection and valuation of the *Lily*, which was 'offered for sale by Mr Elford'. Henry E. Elford was a shareholder in the O&TSCo.Ltd and from 1889 the company's Managing Director. He had family connections in the Cargreen area, having married Elizabeth Grylles at St Dominick in 1861. His daughter Elizabeth was known in the family as 'Lily'. The *Lily* was purchased by the O&TSCo.Ltd in the following month. She was subsequently repaired, fitted with new engines and renamed the *Swift* – a steamer which would enjoy a long and extraordinary career, becoming one of the most familiar sights on the River Plym until the 1960s.

The PRINCESS ROYAL

In March 1888 the SSBCo took delivery of a

new flagship which was destined to become one of the best remembered of all the paddle steamers on the Tamar. Built by Willoughby Bros Ltd, she was the *Princess Royal*, the first steel passenger steamer in local service. Measuring 104.14tg, 117.6 x 16.6 x 4.7 feet, the *Princess Royal* was fitted with 45hp, oscillating, two cylinder compound, surface condensing engines, built by Willoughby's. A distinctive feature was the provision of an upper 'bridge' deck – roughly one third the length of the steamer – which was centred around the funnel with access by steps on the paddle boxes. Her passenger capacity for river excursions was 462. As built the *Princess Royal* resembled the *Eleanor*, with white (or light coloured) saloon sides lined with portholes. She also had the same rounded moulding at her saloon ends, picked out in a darker colour. Both steamers were fitted with a very distinctive large bell-like paddle-box motif. The *Princess Royal* was altered in 1891, her saloon top deck was extended to the bow and stern and the deck rails were plated-in. Her hull and superstructure were painted black, with gold lining and decorations, which made her livery more like the screw steamers of the fleet. She was also fitted with two masts, having only a fore mast when built. Some of her alterations were made with a view to gaining a Class 3 certificate for excursions along the south Cornwall and Devon coast and in subsequent years she would become a familiar sight at Salcombe, Fowey and Mevagissey. Her arrival spelt the end for the long serving *Fairy*, which was withdrawn and broken up in 1888.

The iron screw steamer PRINCE was built by Willoughby Bros Ltd in 1885 and was used exclusively on the Saltash Steam Boat Company's Saltash to Devonport service for forty years. She is pictured here, laden with 'Dockyardies', going astern from Town Pier, Saltash before turning to head down river.
COURTESY ERIC PAYNE.

SALTASH STEAM BOAT COMPANY FLEET IN 1890	
Eleanor	River excursions and Cawsand.
Victoria	Saltash-Devonport and towage.
Albert	Saltash-Devonport, river and coastal excursions.
Prince	Saltash-Devonport.
Princess Royal	Coastal and river excursions.

THE END OF THE CALSTOCK PADDLER FLEETS

Throughout the 1880s steamers from Calstock and Saltash had been chartered by A. E. Rowe to run from West Hoe Pier, but following Rowe's gaining of a monopoly to run steamers from the new Plymouth Promenade Pier in 1884, the Saltash and Calstock steamers remained at West Hoe Pier in the management of James McBryde. The reason for the split from

The steel paddle steamer PRINCESS ROYAL moored off Saltash. Built by Willoughby Bros Ltd in 1888, the PRINCESS ROYAL originally resembled the ELEANOR – from which the bell motif paddle box design was copied, but in 1891 she was altered, as pictured, to gain a coastal excursion certificate. In the background is the industrial training ship MOUNT EDGCUMBE.
CITY OF PLYMOUTH MUSEUMS & ART GALLERY.

Rowe and the seeming reluctance to leave the West Hoe landing laid with Gilbert's financial stake in West Hoe Pier, of which he was the sole owner by 1892. In March 1891 the D&CTSPCo.Ltd was wound up and its assets sold to William Gilbert. In the same year Messrs Rickard and Spear also sold the *Aerial* to Gilbert. The SSBCo fleet was thus substantially enlarged by the acquisition of the *Empress*, *Alexandra* and the *Aerial* and, importantly, Gilbert gained the market day trade and landing rights on the Tamar above Hole's Hole, including ownership of the D&CTSPCo.Ltd's quay and stores at Calstock. The *Victoria* was subsequently transferred to Gilbert's 'new' Calstock office where she was used as a tug. For the 1891 season, therefore, all of the Tamar's principal steamers were owned by William Gilbert and were running from his own West Hoe Pier. During the season the *Princess Royal* was offering coastal excursions to Looe and Salcombe; the *Alexandra* was running to the River Yealm and on the Tamar; the *Eleanor* and the *Aerial* were used on Tamar excursions; the *Empress* maintained market day and cargo services on the Tamar and river excursions; the *Albert* was running on the Breakwater and Cawsand service and coastal excursions; and the *Prince* was used exclusively on the Saltash-Devonport service. Most excursions and services also called at one or more of the Devonport Corporation landing stages at Mutton Cove, North Corner and Pottery Quay.

At around this time an additional pontoon landing at Dumpty Pier was inaugurated. The pier was at Bull Point, on the opposite shore to Saltash and downstream of the floating bridge landing. Steamers called at Dumpty Pier by request and it would appear to have been introduced to serve workers at the Admiralty's Bull Point Magazine and passengers from Saltash Passage and the St Budeaux district going downstream to Devonport. Due in part to the re-instatement and improvement of tram service No.14 to Saltash Passage in 1923 (which had been without a service for 8 years), steamer calls were discontinued and subsequent maps show the pier as disused.

Millbrook Steamers

Local folklore suggests that John Parson of Millbrook, returning late to Mutton Cove one night, could only obtain passage to Millbrook by paying a waterman the large sum of five shillings. This incident is cited as prompting Parson to consider providing a steamer service on the lake. John Parson was the owner of the tide mill at Insworke, just below Millbrook and, similar to Gilbert at Saltash, was a local entrepreneur, being a miller, an agricultural merchant and a coal merchant. The village of Millbrook lies at the head of Millbrook Lake – a creek immediately upstream of Cremyll and opposite Devonport's Mutton Cove. In the nineteenth century Millbrook and Southdown (near the mouth of the lake) supported

The four major units of the Saltash Three Towns & District Steamboat Co Ltd, moored at Calstock c1900. On the left the 'Calstock' paddlers ALEXANDRA *(outside) and* EMPRESS *are moored at the old Devon & Cornwall Tamar Steam Packet Co Ltd's Steamer Quay. Ahead lay the 'Saltash' steamers* PRINCESS ROYAL *and* ELEANOR. *Note the quay office and Bowdens Steam Packet Hotel behind.* ALAN KITTRIDGE COLLECTION.

agricultural, smelting and brickmaking industries, but Devonport Dockyard became the place of work for many in the Millbrook district, especially after the Keyham Steam Yard opened 1854. In the 1880s the lake's community was still dependent upon watermen's boats to provide passage across the Hamoaze. Jack Kingston, writing in the *Torpoint Parish Magazine* in the 1960s, noted that it was in consequence of a letter from Parson to the Earl of Mount Edgcumbe in 1884, that permission to start a service was granted. The Earl maintained ferry rights on the Tamar downstream of Saltash, and had himself only just introduced a steamer on the Cremyll Ferry – he declined, however, Parson's suggestion that he extend the Cremyll steamer's service to Millbrook Lake.

In 1885 Parson took delivery of his first steamer, the *Millbrook*, a wooden paddler measuring under 18 tons net, 56 x 10 x 2.2 feet. She was built by Waterman Brothers (John and James) of Cremyll. The *Millbrook's* engines were second hand, simple, high pressure, two cylinder, having been built by Sara & Burgess of Penryn, near Falmouth in 1875 (cheap to buy but very inefficient). She started running from Millbrook Lake to North Corner and in 1891 to Mutton Cove's newly opened landing pier. The fare was one penny each way. Landings on the lake were made at Millbrook when the tide served, or at Anderton, just below Millbrook, on lower tides. On the lowest tides the steamer could only reach Southdown at the mouth of the lake and passengers, having achieved the crossing of the Hamoaze, walked the rest of the way to Millbrook. A second steamer was built by Waterman Brothers in 1887, she was the *Iolanthe*, a twin screw (two small propellers – better than one for shallow working and cheaper than paddle machinery), clinker built wooden steamer measuring under 18 tons net, 60 x 11 x 2.2 feet. Her triple expansion, non-condensing engines and boiler were supplied by S. S. Welch of Millbay. A third steamer, the *Lady of the Lake*, was built by Waterman Brothers in 1890. Composite built (i.e. wood planking on an iron frame) she was a twin screw steamer measuring under 18 tons net, 62 x 12 x 2.2 feet. Her two cylinder, inverted, non-condensing engines were supplied by Willoughby Bros Ltd of Millbay.

For six years Parson operated his steamers on the Millbrook 'ferry' service and advertisements for 1891 state 'Steamer leaving Mutton Cove (new landing pier) for Cremyll, Southdown, Anderton and Millbrook'. Parson also offered occasional excursions aboard the *Lady of the Lake* to Lopwell Quay on the River Tavy but his steamers are remembered as being painfully slow. The rated speeds of the *Iolanthe* and the *Lady of the Lake* were 7 knots and 8 knots respectively – not unreasonable for small ferry steamers – it must be presumed therefore that they either failed to live up to these modest expectations, or struggled against adverse weather and tidal conditions.

The wooden screw steamer LADY OF THE LAKE *pictured at Cremyll Beach in 1898, during her time with the Saltash Three Towns & District Steamboat Co Ltd. She was built by Waterman Brothers at Cremyll in 1890, with engines by Willoughby Bros Ltd. Sold to George Hodge on the River Yealm c1905, she became well known as the* KITLEY GIRL. *This photograph was taken by Frederick James Johns, a shipwright in the Dockyard who lived near Millbrook and crossed to work on the steamers every day. He photographed Millbrook ferry steamers in 1898.* COURTESY JOHN DODDRIDGE.

THE SALTASH, THREE TOWNS & DISTRICT STEAMBOAT CO LTD.

On 19 January 1892 the Saltash, Three Towns & District Steamboat Co Ltd was incorporated with a nominal capital of £25,000 in 2,500 shares of £10 each. In the Memorandum of Association the Company's Objects were stated as:

> A. To purchase from Mr W. Gilbert of Saltash or owner or owners thereof for cash or paid up shares the steamships called the ALEXANDRA, the PRINCESS ROYAL, the ELEANOR, the EMPRESS, the AERIAL, the ALBERT, the PRINCE and the VICTORIA, their stores and equipment lately belonging to the Saltash Steam Boat Company. And the steamships called the MILLBROOK, the IOLANTHE, and the LADY OF THE LAKE with their stores and equipment lately belonging to Mr John Parson of Millbrook and the goodwill of the business of a steamboat owner lately carried on by the said John Parson.
>
> B. To purchase from William Gilbert or other owner or owners the pier, basin,

William Gilbert as Mayor of Saltash. A picture from the book Around and About Saltash *by P. E. B. Porter, published c1900. Porter described other ventures in which William Gilbert was involved: 'Into various other schemes he entered with heartiness, the old Brewery, the Ferry, and the Gas Company, all which showed his attachment to his native town'. William Gilbert served as Mayor of Saltash in 1880, 1881 and 1885.*

foreshore, wharves, stores and buildings known as West Hoe Baths and Pier. And also the land, dwelling house, workshops and buildings called The Battery at Saltash and the pier and floating pontoon at Saltash and the quays, stores, waiting rooms and piers at Calstock lately in the possession or occupation of the Saltash Steam Boat Company and also landing places in Millbrook Lake lately in the occupation of Mr John Parson.

William Gilbert received:

Steamers listed in schedule A	
Alexandra	£4,200
Princess Royal	£4,200
Eleanor	£3,100
Empress	£3,300
Aerial	£1,900
Albert	£1,500
Prince	£1,700
Victoria	£950
Total	£20,850

John Parson received

Steamers listed in schedule A	
Millbrook	£350
Iolanthe	£650
Lady of the Lake	£850
Total	£1,850
Grand total for schedule A	£22,700
Land listed in schedule B totalled	£7,000

Additional costs included the purchase from William Gilbert of moorings for steamers off Saltash, 36 hire rowing boats at West Hoe Pier, a 'prow' for beach landing, and various seats and fittings at West Hoe.

William Gilbert and John Parson took 200 shares each in the new company, being the largest amongst the 92 shareholders. Other shareholders of note included: William Dusting, Managing Director of the new Company; W. P. Vosper a leading shareholder and Director throughout the Company's history; Orlando J. H. Davis, the Company Secretary, and a shipping agent in Plymouth; and Gideon Ebenezer Spear of Halton Quay, an agricultural merchant, leaseholder of quays and limekilns in the Tamar Valley and former owner of the *Aerial*. There were also a selection of smaller shareholders, some probably with an eye to future business, including: James McBryde, the excursion agent; James Venning, a Callington printer (amongst other ventures) who produced many steamer bills and timetables; and Joseph Willoughby of Willoughby Bros Ltd.

The Saltash, Three Towns & District Steamboat Co Ltd (STT&DSCo.Ltd) virtually monopolised all of the passenger steamer business on the River Tamar, with landing rights at West Hoe, Cremyll, Millbrook Lake, St Germans Quay, Devonport, Saltash, Lopwell, and on the River Tamar at Cargreen, Hole's Hole, Halton Quay, Cotehele, Calstock and Morwellham. In 1892 the only other company with a foothold on the river was the O&TSCo.Ltd which called at Mutton Cove and had landing rights at Cremyll and Cargreen – the latter a legacy from the *Lily*. This foothold, overlooked by the STT&DSCo.Ltd, would be instrumental in it's eventual demise.

The *Millbrook* was immediately laid up by the new company and eventually hulked in Millbrook Lake. McBryde's River & Sea Trips continued as the agent at West Hoe Pier, but the steamers were now advertised as being the Saltash, Three Towns & District Steamboat Co Ltd fleet. 'Saltash' steamers from Mutton Cove were advertised for Cremyll, Southdown, Anderton and Millbrook for Whitsand Bay, Cawsand and Kingsand. These latter named beaches were reached by wagonettes which met the steamers at the Millbrook Lake landings. The increasing popularity with trippers from Devonport of a day at these beaches would culminate in the 1920s with the creation of three opposing motor omnibus companies on the Rame Peninsula, running in conjunction with the area's steamboat services.

For a period from 1892 the Saltash company gained access to the Promenade Pier and their steamers were advertised as running from the pier and Mutton Cove to Cremyll for Mount Edgcumbe Park on open days. The *Eleanor*, *Aerial* and *Albert* were also listed, running excursions from the pier to the River Tamar. The *Lady of the Lake* was advertised from the Promenade Pier calling at Mutton Cove and North Corner for excursions to Lopwell Quay. There was also a regular service from Saltash to the Promenade Pier. No sooner had William Gilbert achieved a monopoly of steamer services on the River Tamar than he died (in1892) and his shares passed to E. P. Gilbert.

The formation of the STT&DSCo.Ltd and the death of William Gilbert effectively concludes the history of passenger steamboat services which were primarily introduced to serve communities along the River Tamar and its tributaries. In future Plymouth's sea front would generate an increasing percentage of the Tamar passenger steamers' income. But the Saltash company's monopoly would be short lived, ended by a disenchanted John Parson who broke away from the STT&DSCo.Ltd and established a new fleet of steamers based at Millbrook.

CHAPTER FOUR

NOT A FERRY BUT A PASSENGER LINE

Steamboats on the River Plym 1869–1914

NOTICE TO THE PUBLIC

THE ORESTON STEAM-BOAT COMPANY

WILL COMMENCE RUNNING

ON MONDAY, THE 3rd OF MAY, 1869,

THEIR NEW

Steam-boat "Little Pet"

FROM

ORESTON

TO THE

BARBICAN PIER, PLYMOUTH

Calling at TURNCHAPEL each way.

Departure on Week Days.

	A.M.		A.M.
Oreston	5.30 -	Plymouth	5.45
,,	7.0 -	,,	7.30
,,	8.0 -	,,	8.30
,,	9.0 -	,,	9.30
,,	10.0 -	,,	10.30
,,	11.0 -	,,	11.30
,,	12.0 -	,,	12.30
	P.M.		P.M.
,,	1.0 -	,,	1.30
,,	2.0 -	,,	2.30
,,	3.0 -	,,	3.30
,,	4.0 -	,,	4.30
,,	5.0 -	,,	5.30
,,	6.0 -	,,	6.30
,,	7.0 -	,,	7.30
,,	8.0 -	,,	8.30
,,	9.0 -	,,	9.15

Departure on Sundays.

	A.M.		A.M.
Oreston	9.0 -	Plymouth	9.30
,,	10.0 -	,,	10.30
	P.M.		P.M.
,,	1.0 -	,,	1.30
,,	2 0 -	,,	2.30
,,	3.0 -	,,	3.30
,,	4.0 -	,,	4.30
,,	5.0 -	,,	5.30
,,	6.0 -	,,	6.30
,,	7.0 -	,,	7.30
,,	8.0 -	,,	8.30
,,	9.0 -	,,	9.15

FARE—ONE PENNY EACH WAY.

The Inhabitants of Plymouth and its vicinity will find the above arrangements a favourable opportunity for visiting the beautiful scenery at Radford, Hooe, Staddon Heights, &c., &c.

Persons going from the Country to Plymouth can be accommodated with good Stabling at Oreston.

Oreston, April 23rd, 1869.

Announcing the very first passenger steamboat on the Cattewater, calling at Oreston, Turnchapel and Plymouth's 'Barbican Pier' (West Pier).
ALAN KITTRIDGE COLLECTION.

THE FINAL STRETCH OF THE RIVER Plym below Laira Bridge is called the Cattewater, both banks of which, since the early nineteenth century, were lined with docks, shipyards, quarries and factories that offered employment to Plymothians and to residents of Turnchapel and Oreston on the South Hams shore. In the mid-nineteenth century Lord Palmerston advocated the fortification of the south coast of England, resulting in a ring of defence positions around Plymouth. The location of three of these: Stamford Fort – immediately behind Turnchapel; Staddon Fort; and a battery at Bovisand; provided additional passengers for watermen on the Cattewater. While Rendel's 'Iron Bridge' at Laira served through traffic from the larger South Hams district, a faster journey from Oreston, Hooe and Turnchapel across the Plym to Plymouth could still be gained by water – this would remain the case even after the railway arrived in Turnchapel in 1897.

The *Little Pet* inaugurated a steamer service between Oreston, Turnchapel and Sutton Harbour's West Pier on 3 May 1869. She was owned by the Oreston Steamboat Company (OSCo) and ran sixteen round trips on weekdays and eleven round trips on Sundays. Writing in 1943 Walter Stephens could remember when the *Little Pet* first started running:

> There were no steamers to Oreston and Turnchapel in those days. The people from those villages came to Plymouth to do their shopping by boat. Then I think it was Mr. Popplestone and Mr. Elford who started the Oreston Steam Boat Co. and the first steamer they had was called the Little Pet; you sat in the stern under an awning. I went up many times.

The OSCo introduced a second steamer, the *Favorite*, on 2 August 1869 and extended their service to include calls at Hooe, Cattedown and Mount Batten, increasing the frequency to a half hourly service. Nine days later, on 11 August, the Oreston Steamboat Co Ltd (OSCo.Ltd) was incorporated by John Goad, Edmund A. Jones, Thomas Balhatchet, S. Popplestone and Henry Emmanuel Elford, to take over the assets of the OSCo. The Board of the new company immediately sent a letter to the Duke of Bedford, the owner of the foreshore at Oreston, requesting sole landing rights at Oreston. The letter, from his 'humble petitioners' who had 'set themselves to work with untiring zeal and energy', complained of another steamboat – with a second in preparation – running in opposition. The proprietors of these opposing boats had apparently declined the opportunity to join the new company. The opposition in question was the Turnchapel Steamboat Company (TSCo), a partnership between William Kelly, shipbuilder and Alfred Burlace, boat builder, both of Turnchapel, and Captain A. V. Usborne RN. According to the OSCo.Ltd this company did not maintain a timetabled service but picked up passengers when and where they saw them – mainly just before the OSCo.Ltd steamer reached the pier. By 1871 the TSCo fleet included the steamers: *Beagle*, *Greyhound* and *Lightning*.

An unidentified Oreston & Turnchapel Steamboat Co Ltd steamer backing out from Turnchapel – the helmsman in the bows can only gain a rough impression of his position. Soldiers aboard the steamer are probably Volunteer Artillery Corps from Stamford or Staddon forts. In the background a big ocean going sailing ship, her waterline very high, appears to be loading cargo or ballast from local barges. ALAN KITTRIDGE COLLECTION.

In July 1870 the OSCo.Ltd added a third steamer, the *Eclipse*, which assisted at peak times and additionally inaugurated a Monday afternoon service between Millbay Pier and Mount Edgcumbe (park open day). On 4 April 1871 a joint committee of the OSCo.Ltd and the TSCo rationalised their timetables by running joint services on the Cattewater. Two boats would maintain the service with a third boat, the *Lightning*, added at peak times to increase the frequency. Two other steamers were allocated to maintain half-hourly Sutton Harbour–Millbay Pier–Mount Edgcumbe runs on summer Mondays. However, during the winter season (November to February inclusive) only two boats were required on the Cattewater and in 1872 the joint committee sought to reduce the size of the combined fleet by offering steamers for sale. In October the *Greyhound* was sold, followed in the new year by the *Eclipse*. The committee also served notice that after 12 August 1871 the Oreston Ferry to Cattedown would in future be operated half hourly by 'Oreston & Turnchapel Steamboats', with their Cattewater steamers calling at Cattedown Ferry Beach each way between Turnchapel and Oreston.

THE ORESTON & TURNCHAPEL STEAMBOAT CO LTD.

Early in 1873 the Oreston & Turnchapel Steamboat Co Ltd (O&TSCo.Ltd) was incorporated to take over the landing rights and property of both the OSCo.Ltd and the TSCo, including their remaining boats: the *Beagle*, *Lightning*, *Favorite* and *Little Pet*. Leading shareholders and directors of the new company were H. E. Elford, Captain A. V. Usborne and T. Balhatchet. The manager of the O&TSCo.Ltd until 1889 was Edmund Jones, while John Goad served as Chairman of the Board and Captain Usborne as Secretary.

A new steamer was built in 1873 to maintain the Mount Edgcumbe run. Built by F. Darton at Turnchapel she was named the *Greyhound* (16tg, 48.5 x 11.4 x 4.6 feet) and Captain Lugger was employed as her skipper. So familiar did Lugger become at Cremyll that when the Earl of Mount Edgcumbe introduced steamers on the Cremyll Ferry in 1884, Lugger accepted the offer to skipper one of them. The *Favorite* was sold in September 1874 to be replaced by a new boat built by Alfred Burlace, also named *Favorite*.

A 6d weekly ticket was available for schoolchildren and apprentices in 1876, while pilots returning to Turnchapel were only charged half fare (Turnchapel was a base for pilot cutters of the Port of Plymouth). A late return steamer for the benefit of concert goers was also introduced.

The *Little Pet* was sold in 1877, reducing the fleet once again to four steamers: the *Beagle*, *Lightning*, *Greyhound* and *Favorite*.

The landing stage at Oreston was known as the Dummy Landing, a wooden pier which extended from the quay wall in front of the Kings Arms public house, to the low water channel. At low tide, however, steamers had difficulty navigating this channel to the end of the pier and the company applied to the Cattewater Commissioners regarding dredging a channel, not less than four feet deep, to the landing stage. Instead, the Harbour Master and Edmund Jones surveyed the Oreston foreshore for an alternative low water landing place. A long running legal debate ensued, involving the Admiralty, Duchy of Cornwall and the Duke of Bedford's agent, until the agreement of all parties was eventually reached in 1891, resulting in a second Oreston landing at Gutter, on Oreston Quay, upstream from the Dummy Landing. A lease was also signed in 1881 for a landing place at Mount Batten, in front of the Castle Inn. In the same year the company ordered a new steamer from Darton's yard at Mount Batten, with engines and boiler from Tangye of Birmingham. The new boat was launched in September and named *Express*. She was the company's first boat to be fitted with an upper deck and had a Class 5 'ferry' certificate to carry 110 passengers. Her arrival signalled the end for the *Lightning* which was sold.

Having failed to agree terms with the Great Western Docks at Millbay Pier to continue steamer landings on their Mount Edgcumbe Park open day service, which had now changed to Wednesdays, the O&TSCo.Ltd secured an alternative, better landing at the new Promenade Pier on the Sea Front. The first call was made by the *Express* on 16 July 1884, but after just two weeks the pier company granted a monopoly for excursions to the excursion agent A. E. Rowe and the *Express* had to run from Sutton Harbour, without any sea front landing.

A letter from the Post Office in 1885, regarding the carriage of post and telegraph personnel, mistakenly addressed the O&TSCo.Ltd as a ferry. Jones indignantly replied:

> I am directed to say that this company is not a ferry company but a passenger line, calling at four stations on both sides of the Cattewater. There are several ferries on both sides – to landings we have nothing to do with...there is no obligation on us to carry post and telegraph officials without payment.

Perhaps it was this insistence that the O&TSCo.Ltd was a passenger line rather than a ferry that gave rise to their local 'P&O Liners' nickname – in allusion to the termini at Plymouth and Oreston. They also sported a similar black hull (originally red) and light brown superstructure livery to liners of the Peninsular & Oriental Steam Navigation Co Ltd, a likeness realised, no doubt, when ships of that line started regular calls at Plymouth in the 1880s.

Throughout the O&TSCo.Ltd's history it seems to have had a surplus of steamers and was always looking for additional employment for the boats. Edmund Jones applied to lease the Cremyll Ferry in 1882 and operate it with O&TSCo.Ltd steamers. In 1883 the company offered to run a late steamer service on the Torpoint Ferry for £10 per day inclusive of boat, crew and coal – neither offer was taken up. O&TSCo.Ltd steamers could be hired for excursions for between 30s to £3.10s and the company also advertised itself as 'the best and cheapest excursions out of Plymouth – visit Mount Batten, Staddon Heights and Radford Grounds Tea Gardens' – the latter named being adjacent to Hooe Lake. Nevertheless, yet another steamer was ordered in March 1885. Built by William Kelly of Turnchapel with engines by Tangye, the new steamer was named the *Despatch*.

Since 1880 the O&TSCo.Ltd had also been chartering the *Lily* from one of its directors, H. E. Elford. Seemingly having given up the unequal competition with William Gilbert's iron screw steamers on the Hamoaze service between Saltash and Devonport (see Chapter Three), the *Lily* had been advertised on excursions to the Lynher and Tavy rivers during the early 1880s. Although not listed as O&TSCo.Ltd trips the company had chartered her to run these excursions. In November 1885 the Company bought the *Lily* from Elford and she was subsequently reconditioned, with new engines and boiler. When she entered service as an O&TSCo.Ltd steamer in the following year she was renamed the *Swift*. Rowe's Pleasant Marine Excursions invited the company to run the *Swift* from the Promenade Pier in 1886. The invitation was accepted but the O&TSCo.Ltd would never run steamers on Sunday excursions – H. E. Elford, the company's largest

The DESPATCH *of 1885, from an engraving which accompanied an article about the Cattewater steamers in the November 1888 edition of* The Engineer. *The* DESPATCH *was built by William Kelly of Turnchapel, with machinery by Tangye's of Birmingham. All boat building and maintenance work was put out to tender to at least three parties. A detailed specification was provided by the Oreston & Turnchapel Steamboat Co Ltd and regardless of occasional, sometimes justified, variation from the brief, the cheapest bid was always selected.* ALAN KITTRIDGE COLLECTION.

The GREYHOUND *(1873) pictured on the Flushing Ferry in Falmouth Harbour after 1888.* ROYAL INSTITUTION OF CORNWALL

The FAVORITE *(1874) pictured as a houseboat at Lopwell on the River Tavy after use by the contractors Relf and Pethick during construction of the railway viaduct over the Tavy* ALAN KITTRIDGE COLLECTION.

Main picture: *The* RAPID *is moored adjacent to Turnchapel Pier c1905, alongside the Oreston & Turnchapel Steamboat Co Ltd's unsightly coal hulk – about which the company received many complaints. At the end of the pier is the attractive little waiting shelter and piermaster's office. Moored off the pier is a group of coaling barges and lighters. On the opposite shore is the bewildering industrial landscape of Cattedown, which grew up in the former limestone quarries.* COURTESY TONY KINGDOM.

shareholder, was a staunch Methodist. Following the purchase of the *Lily/Swift*, the *Beagle* was withdrawn and repaired and subsequently seems to have been sold. By the end of 1885 the fleet comprised of five steamers: the *Greyhound*, *Favorite*, *Express*, *Swift* and *Despatch*. The *Despatch* was the subject of an article in *The Engineer* in November 1888, which offered an account of the mechanical running of the Cattewater passenger service:

> ... The material of the boat is of pitch pine in two thicknesses copper fastened–a fairly strong oak frame and steamed elm timbers at close intervals–the whole forming a very strong job, that stands the rough work very well. They are partly metalled to protect against the marine worm, and are calculated to last eighteen to twenty years. An upper deck surrounded with tubular rails, tapered tubular stanchions, threaded with wire rope, gives safety to passengers. They are kept inboard about a foot partly for the same reason and to avoid catching projections when going alongside piers, or vessels ... The general dimensions are 60ft to 65ft long by 12ft beam and 4ft draught ... They are steered by a wheel about 4ft from the stem ... The propelling power consists of pairs of 9in. cylinders by 9in. stroke using 80lb. steam, exhausting through an annular feed-water heater into a steam trap, from whence the steam passes to the funnel in a dry state and nearly silent. No cold feed reaches the boiler, an automatic Gresham and Craven injector and the engine pump being the only supplies used when steam is up. ...simple engines are preferred to compound for their certainty of action when approaching landings end on, as is often necessary. Stoppages are so frequent that the saving of coal by compound engines would be very small indeed and hardly worth the seeking.

The fleet was reduced to three in 1888 when the *Greyhound* and the *Favourite* were sold. The *Greyhound* went to Falmouth where she worked the Flushing Ferry until broken up in 1904. The *Favorite* was sold to Messrs Relf and Pethick, civil and railway contractors who in 1888 were engaged in constructing the PD&SWJR line from Lydford to Devonport and in particular the railway bridge across the mouth of the River Tavy. It is possible that the *Favorite* was purchased as a site workboat and tender to their accommodation ship ex-HMS *Bittern*.

Henry Emmanuel Elford became the Manager of the O&TSCo.Ltd in 1889, His principal task was to oversee construction of a pier at Turnchapel for the sole use of the O&TSCo.Ltd. For years the company had been using the public landing steps adjacent to the Dockyard at Turnchapel. However, the new pier was not owned by the O&TSCo.Ltd, but by the Elford family and remained so until they finally sold it to the company in 1955. A newspaper report describes the opening day on 24 July 1889:

> A new pier, erected at a cost of £1000 by Mr H. Elford, of Oreston, was formally opened yesterday. ...The structure is a substantial work, the piles being of greenheart with iron clamps. It is 182 feet long by 8 feet 6 inches wide, and is protected on the top by strong iron rods. At the end a pretty waiting room has been erected, and benches are provided here and there for the benefit of passengers. ...The sole right of landing and accommodation belongs to the Oreston and Turnchapel Steamboat Company, whose steamers have plied between the Barbican

The Dummy Landing at Oreston c1905, with the RAPID *alongside, viewed downstream from Oreston Quay. The low tide landing at Gutter is behind the photographer.* ALAN KITTRIDGE COLLECTION.

and Turnchapel for many years. ...The Oreston and Turnchapel Company has made rapid progress recently, and, within a few days, will add to their present fleet a magnificent steamboat with all the latest improvements.

The 'magnificent' new steamer mentioned in the report was the rather unremarkable *Rapid*, which was subsequently delivered from the Mount Batten yard of Issac Darton. Once again engines were supplied by Tangye of Birmingham.

GREANEYS' STEAMERS

All of the changes and improvements noted above were undertaken amidst a period of competition from a new line of steamboats, the conclusion of which resulted with the Elford family's financial control of the O&TSCo.Ltd for the rest of its history.

The first suggestion of imminent competition comes from a note in the O&TSCo.Ltd's minute book for August 1884, threatening that if John Greaney's boat was run in opposition, two other members of the Greaney family working for the O&TSCo.Ltd would be discharged. John Greaney's boat, the *Teaser*, duly commenced to 'run on our line' – as the O&TSCo.Ltd put it – on Good Friday 1885 and the *Express* was put on 'to attend to him'. John Greaney soon withdrew the *Teaser* in return for employment by the O&TSCo.Ltd.

Peace prevailed until John and James Greaney gave notice to quit in April 1888 and started running the steamer *Odd Trick* in opposition. By January 1889 the Greaneys were making their presence felt and the O&TSCo.Ltd was complaining to Mr Sparrow, the owner of Cattedown Quay, about the *Odd Trick's* alleged trespass at Cattedown Steps. Sparrow evidently sympathised with the Greaneys and replied that they had permission to land there. Competition increased when the Greaneys introduced two additional steamers in the same year, the *Wide Awake* and the *Nick-o-Time*. A clue to the builder of the Greaney boats was given in the O&TSCo.Ltd minutes for January 1890, when the company 'considered that it would be indiscreet to let Darton audit at present as giving our enemies important and to them valuable news of our doings'. Issac Darton was never again asked to tender for work on O&TSCo.Ltd boats. The argument regarding the Cattedown landing continued. In February 1890 Sparrow complained that the O&TSCo.Ltd was not calling at Cattedown Steps and threatened to withdraw their landing rights altogether and to dismiss them from Mount Batten – where he also held landing rights. The O&TSCo.Ltd replied that they had leased the Mount Batten landing directly from the Earl of Morley and it was therefore nothing to do with him. In March 1891 an offer of peace arrived from the Greaneys and was discussed by the Board of the O&TSCo.Ltd. The resulting deal was a payment of £2,300 for the purchase of the Greaneys' boats and business. This large sum of

The ex-Greaney steamer DART *approaching Turnchapel Pier c1905.* CITY OF PLYMOUTH MUSEUMS & ART GALLERY.

The Oreston & Turnchapel Steamboat Co Ltd's excursion steamer COUNTESS OF MORLEY *at Morwellham c1900. Her passengers would appear to be a charter party, possibly Methodists judging from the sashes worn by some of the men.*
To ensure that the majority of steamers' passengers, in a group photograph like this, looked directly at the camera, photographers sometimes blew a whistle at the opportune moment – more faces, more sales.
MORWELLHAM QUAY MUSEUM.

money indicates that the Greaneys were inflicting some serious damage to the O&TSCo.Ltd. The brothers made their final trip on Saturday night 11 April 1891.

THE ELFORDS IN CONTROL

The net result of the buy-out of the Greaneys was the acquisition by the O&TSCo.Ltd of three additional steamers the *Odd Trick*, *Wide Awake* and *Nick-o-Time* and effective financial control of the O&TSCo.Ltd by H. E. Elford, who had financed the deal. Miss L. E. Elford was installed as Company Treasurer. The 'Greaney' boats cost £100 to put in order. By 1892 the *Wide Awake* and the *Nick-o-Time* had been renamed the *Dart* and the *Lively* – unfortunately the allocation of the names remains unclear. The *Odd Trick* was not renamed but some employment was found by chartering her to the 'Dockyard' in 1892. However, following some repairs to her boiler in July of the same year the *Odd Trick* vanished from the records.

The company still held landing rights at Cremyll Beach and in April 1894 put the *Despatch* on a new ferry service between Mutton Cove and Cremyll. In September of the same year John Parson of Millbrook approached the O&TSCo.Ltd with an offer to buy both the *Despatch* and their Mutton Cove–Cremyll service. The offer of £650 was accepted and Parson took over in November, thus laying the foundation of the Millbrook Steamboat Company and sparking a long, acrimonious and almost ruinous period of competition with the STT&DSCo.Ltd.

In the same year the O&TSCo.Ltd sought tenders for the construction of a major new excursion steamer, quite different to any vessel they had operated before. Built by Allsups of Preston the Company obtained permission to name her the *Countess of Morley* – flattering the local landowner perhaps, but also an attempt to raise the steamer's profile from the utilitarian nature of the rest of the fleet. Charles Elford, one of H. E. Elford's sons, and a delivery crew went to Preston to collect the new boat. She was a flush decked, steel, screw steamer measuring 63tg, 87.1 x 15.1 x 6.5 feet. The flush deck was specified to enable her to run trips outside the Sound to the River Yealm. She had a capacity of 300 passengers. Refreshments in her two saloons were provided by Plymouth Coffee House. The new steamer was due to enter service early in June 1895 but arrived too late to honour a charter contract with the Devonport Branch of the Early Closing Association on the 26th of that month. The association subsequently took the O&TSCo.Ltd to court for breach of contract and a fine of £13. 0s. 10d was imposed. However the new boat was soon offering: Yealm trips – landing at Newton Ferrers; Four River excursions on the Plym, Lynher, Tavy and Tamar; and longer Tamar

Henry Emmanuel Elford
COURTESY
MARY ANTHONY

Phoenix Wharf in Sutton Pool was opened by Plymouth Corporation in 1895 and served as the Oreston & Turnchapel Steamboat Co Ltd's Plymouth landing place for the rest of the company's history. An unidentified O&TSCo.Ltd steamer approaches the landing steps. Cattedown is in the background. ALAN KITTRIDGE COLLECTION.

excursions. On her Tamar trips the *Countess of Morley* picked up passengers at North Corner and Pottery Quay, calling at Cargreen, Calstock, Weir Head, and back to Morwellham to land. Other trips featured: thirty-minute landings at Cargreen; trips up the Plym to the Iron Bridge; landings at Cawsands; and landings at St Germans Quay.

Another event in 1895 was the opening of Phoenix Wharf in Sutton Pool by William Law, the Mayor of Plymouth. The occasion, on 10 September, was attended by the Board of Directors of the O&TSCo.Ltd, as Phoenix Wharf offered a free landing place for their steamers. Built by Plymouth Corporation with iron work supplied by Willoughby Bros Ltd, the landing stage was available at all states of the tide. It had steps on two sides, a waiting room and seats on the passenger deck. Phoenix Wharf survives today as the major excursion boat pier in Plymouth. The O&TSCo.Ltd was granted free access provided they left the West Pier (Mayflower Steps) for the sole use of watermen. Plymouth Corporation also asked if the O&TSCo.Ltd would reciprocate their improved Plymouth landing by offering free landing to watermen at their Mount Batten pontoon. The company duly asked the Earl of Morley's agent who responded with a demand of £3 per annum from each waterman – in truth, neither the Earl's agent nor the O&TSCo.Ltd wanted the watermen there.

At the turn of the century the fleet comprised: the *Swift, Express, Rapid, Lively, Dart* and *Countess of Morley*. The Cattewater steamer landing places were: the company's own Oreston landings at Gutter, where a pontoon was proposed and the Dummy Landing; Cattedown Steps – rented on an annual basis; Turnchapel Pier – leased from H. E. Elford; Mount Batten – leased from the Earl of Morley and greatly improved in 1908 by the provision of a pontoon; and Phoenix Wharf – a free landing owned by Plymouth Corporation. The O&TSCo.Ltd's excursion ambitions are harder to ascertain. The company had landing rights at St Germans Quay, Cargreen, Hole's Hole, Steamer Quay at Calstock and Morwellham. However, the O&TSCo.Ltd were resisting payment of dues at Cargreen and Calstock and in 1901 put the *Countess of Morley* up for sale – seemingly unhappy either with the steamer or their lack of success in operating her (their refusal to run Sunday trips couldn't have helped). Her machinery would appear to have been satisfactory because the company bought new engines from Allsup to fit in a 70 feet long steamer they were building themselves – supervised by H. E. Elford and designed by his son Sidney. The new steamer was launched on 8 May 1902, thus her name – *May Queen*. Her design was a return to the tried and tested Cattewater ferry steamers and during the summer season she offered Three Rivers excursions (Plym, Sound, Tamar [Hamoaze], Lynher); Four Rivers excursions (as above but additionally viewing the Tavy); and landings at St Germans. The *Express,* meanwhile, had been sold in the previous year to Jack Angel of Falmouth, where she replaced the *Greyhound* and was used on the Flushing Ferry until scrapped in 1919. In 1901 the first of a number of major accidents befell the *Swift* when she was burnt 'almost to the water's edge' and was out of service for a considerable time. The *Countess of Morley* was sold out of the district in April 1903 for £2,650 – a profit of over £300 on her original price.

The opening of the L&SWR's Turnchapel branch on 1 July 1897 posed a threat to the Cattewater steamer service, however, due to the geography of the area it was still quicker to travel to Plymouth by steamer from Turnchapel – although trade was lost from other 'inland' areas of Oreston and Plymstock where the train was more convenient. Fortunately for O&TSCo.Ltd the L&SWR's station at Friary was a similar distance from Plymouth's town centre as Phoenix Wharf.

H. E. Elford died in November 1916, ending an association with the O&TSCo.Ltd that had spanned nearly half a century. At the start of the Great War the fleet comprised of five steamers, the names of which would long be associated with ferry services on the Plym: the *Swift, Rapid, Lively, Dart* and *May Queen*. William Henry Elford succeeded his father as Chairman of the company, while Charles Clarence Elford became a director.

CHAPTER FIVE

THE ONLY WAY TO CROSS

Ferries and steamer services on the Tamar and Yealm rivers 1860–1914

AFTER THE OPENING OF THE ROYAL Albert Bridge the ferries on the Hamoaze lost their mail- and stage-coach traffic, which the railway had made redundant. The Saltash Ferry also lost some local passengers to the railway, but any immediate decline was soon recouped with the resulting growth in the district's population. The Borough of Saltash emerged as a desirable 'satellite' of the Three Towns – the choice of many, who built their homes there and commuted to work in Plymouth, Devonport or Stonehouse.

The Royal Dockyard was enlarged yet again with the development of the enormous North Yard Extension between 1895 and 1907. When complete, Admiralty establishments dominated the Devon shoreline of the Hamoaze for six miles, from the Royal William Victualling Yard at Devil's Point to Bull Point Magazine near Saltash Passage. Naval ships crowded the basins of the dockyard and were also moored in trots in the Hamoaze and on the River Lynher. Before the Great War Devonport's population had increased to around 84,000, mostly as a direct result of the growth of the dockyard.

Torpoint also grew up as a dockyard town, with the ferry transporting hundreds of 'dockyardies' at work times. The Torpoint Ferry remained as the best passage for road vehicles travelling to and from the area of south east Cornwall. In addition to the floating bridges and the Cremyll Ferry, three steamer lines from Saltash, Torpoint and Millbrook also linked the Cornish communities of the Hamoaze to the Devonport landing stages. Discounting illegal moonlight crossings of the Royal Albert Bridge on foot, the only alternative to the railway at Saltash, indeed, the only way to cross the Tamar downstream of Saltash, were the ferries, steamers and watermen's boats which plied the Hamoaze.

THE CREMYLL FERRY

Having lost its importance as a principal route into Cornwall the Cremyll Ferry continued to serve communities on the Rame Peninsula as their main link to the Three Towns. But the Earl of Mount Edgcumbe stubbornly refused to introduce steamers, leaving daily passengers and park visitors no option but to endure the open rowboats, in all weather conditions.

Cremyll Beach c1900. The Mount Edgcumbe Estate never conceded their right to collect tolls from any passengers landing on Cremyll Beach (although steamers from the Sea Front and Hamoaze seem to have negotiated landing arrangements and included the toll in their ticket price). This picture serves to illustrate how difficult the toll collectors' job must have been. Watermen from Mutton Cove were finally defeated when the Mount Edgcumbe Estate railed off the entire foreshore, forcing Mutton Cove arrivals through turnstiles on Cremyll Beach and at Cremyll Quay, which can be seen at the far end of the beach with the ferry steamer SHUTTLECOCK *alongside.*
ALAN KITTRIDGE COLLECTION.

In 1870, answering mounting criticism of his failure to introduce steamers on the Cremyll Ferry, the Earl of Mount Edgcumbe considered that a steamboat was unnecessary because only on park open days was there sufficient traffic to warrant the cost, and besides, he didn't want to encourage even more visitors. Over a decade later the Earl still refused to introduce steamers, claiming that the increased cost of operation would result in fare increases, for which he would need to apply to Parliament – a procedure upon which he was unwilling to embark. He even suggested that ferry passengers preferred the rowboats to steamers. The O&TSCo.Ltd was running between Plymouth and Cremyll on park open days and in May 1882 the company's manager, E. R. Jones, offered to run steamboats on the Cremyll Ferry. The Earl rejected the proposal but two years later bowed to the inevitable and bought his own steamboats.

In 1884 a passenger steam launch, the *Dodo*, was introduced, crossing every fifteen minutes. To overcome the requirement of a Parliamentary Act to alter the fare structure the Earl kept a rowboat ferry in operation at the old fare but charged extra in the steamer due to the superior accommodation. The ploy immediately attracted criticism and protests, but the Earl weathered the storm until a second steamer soon replaced the rowboats altogether and the higher fares were grudgingly accepted.

Cremyll Quay from a postcard postally used in 1905. The bows and helm of an unidentified Cremyll ferryboat are in the bottom right. Two wagonettes await passengers. Note the 'wooden walls' in the background, forming the training school HMS IMPREGNABLE. ALAN KITTRIDGE COLLECTION.

There is some confusion regarding the identity of the first steamboats used on the Ferry. Unfortunately the Mount Edgcumbe Estate is unable to help because many estate documents were burnt when the house was reduced to a ruin early in the Second World War. Likewise the Town Clerk of the City of Plymouth – the passenger boat licensing authority – stated that '...records relating to boats and vessels prior to 1939 were destroyed through enemy action.' Furthermore, Shipping Registers fail to help because the steamers were too small to require registration. The following chronological list of the early Cremyll Ferry steamers, therefore, is compiled from previously published sources, enhanced by more recent researches by Brian Hillsdon.

In his book *The History of the Cremyll Ferry*, Hull notes the first two steamers as the *Dodo*, which was purchased for £600 in 1884 and had a covered cabin, and the *Ferryboat*, which was purchased from Yarmouth, having been built some years earlier.

The decorative clock on Cremyll Quay which the Earl of Mount Edgcumbe erected in 1885 to mark the introduction of steamboats. ALAN KITTRIDGE.

An unexpected benefit of the researches of Brian Hillsdon of the Steamboat Association, into the records of Plenty & Son Ltd marine engineers of Newbury, was his discovery of engine specifications and orders from the Mount Edgcumbe Estate for their ferry steamers in the 1880s and 1920s. A double, high pressure engine, No. 673, and a boiler were ordered in July 1884 and delivered in the following October for a ferry steamer named *Shuttlecock*. The *Shuttlecock* had a well deck forward and the helm located in the bow (similar to the O&TSCo.Ltd's steamers). She had a cabin but no top seating deck – none of the Cremyll steamers were fitted with seating on top of the cabin. The *Shuttlecock* had one mast and a black funnel. In view of the engine delivery date it might be safe to presume the steamer entered service late in 1884 or early in 1885.

A second set of two cylinder, high pressure machinery (engine No. 713) was ordered from Plenty & Son Ltd in March 1886 for another ferry steamer, the *Armadillo*. She could carry 108 passengers and had a crew of three: skipper, engineer and deckhand. The *Armadillo* had an upright funnel, one mast stepped against the forward bulkhead and, similar to the *Shuttlecock*, was steered from a helm located in the bow. Her engines were delivered in June 1886, indicating that her completion date was in the second half of 1886.

Another steamer mentioned by Hull was the *Carrier*. She was either built or acquired in 1889 and was distinctive in having two raked masts, the mainmast being stepped on the after part of the cabin. She was larger than any of the other steamers with a capacity of 150 passengers. Her funnel was raked in line with the masts and she had fore and aft well decks. The *Carrier* was distinctive in having a private cabin for the use of the Earl, his family and guests. Since 1855 his father, Ernest Augustus, had owned a two masted, wooden, paddle steamer, the *Earl of Malmesbury*, a former Solent ferry (49.1tg, 107.4 x 17.2 x 9.7 feet) for his private use. By the time his son William introduced steamers on the Cremyll Ferry a note in the *Earl of Malmesbury*'s register states that she could not be traced. It appears that William reserved the *Carrier* for use in a similar capacity – trips to Cotehele, excursions for guests etc, thus resulting in her infrequent public use, initially, but nevertheless appearing on the ferry's accounts.

While there is no doubt surrounding the existence of the *Shuttlecock*, *Armadillo* and *Carrier*, further evidence regarding the identities of the *Dodo* and *Ferryboat* has yet to be discovered. It seems unlikely that having held out against the introduction of steamers for so long the Earl suddenly introduced five in as many years. However, in the absence of primary recorded sources, details of the earliest years of steam on the Cremyll Ferry are subject to conjecture.

The Cremyll crossing from Admiral's Hard to Cremyll Quay was far less dangerous than the old route between Devil's Point and Barnpool, but steamboat passengers still endured some frightening moments. P. L. Hull recorded one incident during a gale when Captain Lugger handed his only passenger a life belt saying, 'You had better put this on, I doubt if we will reach the other side'. The open well decks of the steamers appear to have been the principal cause for concern. They shipped a lot of water in heavy seas – the *Shuttlecock* almost sank on one crossing. However, despite all the safety alterations inflicted upon the Cremyll ferryboats over the years, the well deck remains – unscathed.

The Earl marked the introduction of steamers by erecting a clock on the piermaster's house on Cremyll Quay. Inscribed amidst the decoration are two rather patronising maxims: 'Time and tide tarry for none', and 'Dost thou love life then do not squander time'.

Whilst the steamers supplanted the old passenger 'footboats' there was still occasional horse traffic and a horse boat was maintained and towed by the ferry steamers as required. In 1903 a new horse-boat was ordered measuring 36ft x 10ft 2ins x 3ft 9ins. It was fitted with a stern ramp and could carry two four wheeled carts and their horses. On Cremyll beach, adjacent to the tollhouse is a winch made by the Moir Foundry of Stonehouse, which was used for hauling the horse-boat up onto the beach. Between the world wars the horse boat was regularly used by the Co-operative bread delivery van, coal carts and the Plymouth Breweries dray. It also carried livestock to the slaughter house in Stonehouse. The vessel was continually breaking from its moorings and once drifted to Barnpool before rescue. Believed to have broken its moorings one last time, the horse boat disappeared during the Second World War

The steamboats were moored off Cremyll Yard when out of service. In 1910 the *Shuttlecock* broke from her moorings and was wrecked at Mount Wise, on the opposite shore. The *Armadillo* and the *Carrier* continued to maintain the ferry service until replaced by two new steamers in the mid 1920s.

THE SALTASH FERRY

The John Mare designed floating bridge of 1851 was moored off Saltash Passage at night. In 1865 she was moored too near the shore and grounded, slipping into the foreshore mud where she was partially submerged as the tide rose again. During the subsequent attempt to lift her off, her back was broken and she was wrecked beyond repair. A new floating bridge was built and fitted with the salvaged machinery from the 1851 vessel. The new vessel was built at John Mare's old premises, re-styled as the Plymouth Foundry & Engine Works (later Ellacott & Son), for £770 and had an iron hull with wooden deckhouses.

Six years later the 21 year lease of the ferry was due for renewal and Saltash Council expressed an interest in running the ferry themselves once again. Enquiries were made to Messrs Sara & Burgess of Penryn regarding building a new iron floating bridge, but in the event the ferry company negotiated a new 21 year lease and continued the service. When this lease expired Saltash Council finally took over the ferry. A new steel bridge was designed by A. M. Brummage C.E., R.N. and built by Willoughby Bros Ltd. The new vessel was 2 feet wider and 4 feet longer in the carriageway and could carry six horse-carts or carriages. Two 24 feet long prows at each end gave an overall

The Cremyll Ferry horse-boat winch beside Cremyll Quay (on the park side). The winch, made by the Moir Foundry of Stonehouse, was used to haul the horse-boat onto the beach. ALAN KITTRIDGE.

Admiral's Hard c1905 with the ARMADILLO *(of 1886) and a rare picture of the Cremyll Ferry horse-boat. The horse-boat could carry two four wheeled carts and their horses, which were embarked and disembarked over a stern ramp. The two paddle wheels in the bows are puzzling, they could be to help manoeuvre the craft at Admiral's Hard and Cremyll Quay. Ocean Quay is in the background.* CITY OF PLYMOUTH MUSEUMS & ART GALLERY.

The third Saltash floating bridge was built by the Plymouth Foundry & Engine Works in 1865, utilising the John Mare designed machinery of her predecessor. She is pictured here at Saltash Passage (Little Ash). The ferry was still leased to commercial operators at the time of this picture – one of the partners being William Gilbert. The Royal Albert Bridge stands as built – without any of the later strengthening additions. CITY OF PLYMOUTH LOCAL & NAVAL STUDIES LIBRARY.

length of 103 x 26 feet wide. Trouble had been experienced with the old bridge from chain breaks, when the bridge would drift out of control. To help in similar circumstances a chain was added to the side of the bridge for a steamer to bring her ashore. The new bridge was installed in December 1892. Photographic evidence suggests that the old bridge was tried on Dartmouth's Higher Ferry, but in 1896 a new Philip built floating bridge was installed on the Dart crossing.

To maintain the ferry during the floating bridge's annual inspections or other repairs, the council acquired a barge from W. J. Reynolds of Torpoint and fitted it out to be used as a pontoon, propelled by a steamer – similar to the pontoons of the Lower Ferry at Dartmouth, from where the idea had come. In 1896 this reserve ferry replaced the last of the old horse-boats and was subsequently known as the 'Horse-boat'.

In 1901 a tram route was opened by the Devonport and District Tramway Company, running between Saltash Passage and Devonport – albeit until 1903 a broken line, with a wooden bridge connection across Weston Mill

The fourth Saltash floating bridge, built by Willoughby Bros Ltd of Millbay in 1892. She is pictured approaching Saltash, with Saltash Passage in the background and the Calstock owned Tamar barge SILVER SPRAY, *making her way up river.* ALAN KITTRIDGE COLLECTION.

The fifth floating bridge (SALTASH FLOATING BRIDGE NO. 2) at Saltash Passage c1912. She was designed by Bickle & Co Ltd of Millbay and built by Willoughby Bros Ltd. The Willoughby floating bridge of 1892 became SALTASH FLOATING BRIDGE NO. 1 – the reserve vessel. Note the passenger decks on both sides of the bridge.
CITY OF PLYMOUTH LOCAL & NAVAL STUDIES LIBRARY.

Lake at Camel's Head. This resulted in even more commuter traffic on the ferry. Furthermore, the Saltash Ferry was still one of the main routes into Cornwall and by 1910 a larger ferry bridge was needed to cope with increasing traffic. The floating bridge at Cowes was inspected with a view to purchase but turned down in favour of a new, larger bridge. Built in 1911 by Willoughby's from plans drawn up by J. Bickle of the neighbouring Bickle & Co Ltd in Millbay, the new bridge could carry two rows of four vehicles with their horses and had passenger decks above the deck housings on each side. The 1892 bridge became the reserve, used in winter months, replacing the 'Horse-boat' which was sold in 1913 for £2. 10s. 0d. In 1914 the destiny of both the Saltash and Torpoint floating bridges was indicated when the Saltash Ferry introduced weekly tickets for motor car users.

THE TORPOINT FERRY

Despite Henry Smith's criticism of the 'heavy, costly bridges which they possessed at Torpoint' (see Chapter Two), Rendel's first bridge, of 1834, was not replaced until 1871. Willoughby Bros Ltd built the new bridge but the old arrangement of a central superstructure and two outside carriage decks was retained. The dimensions of the new bridge, excluding the landing ramps, was 58 feet long x 48 feet wide. She was powered by two 10hp, high pressure, condensing engines. Bridge No. 2, of 1835, was kept as the reserve ferry until she too was replaced in 1878 by No. 4, another larger Willoughby built vessel – prefabricated in workshops and assembled in Stonehouse Pool.

Gantries were erected at the top of the landing slips to give the chain weights a longer drop in their shafts, thereby increasing tension and improving the angle of approach as the floating bridge drew near the shore. Single ferry operation was maintained but increasing traffic prompted the ferry company to investigate running two ferries in 1905. The proposal met with opposition from Devonport Corporation and the Admiralty as the ferry company needed to expand the Devonport landing beach. An experiment was conducted in running two ferries with the existing shore installations but the strain on the equipment caused the trials to be abandoned.

In 1910 a destroyer collided with one of the Torpoint floating bridges, due in part to

This postcard view is titled 'The 12.30 p.m. Ferry' and shows the Willoughby built Torpoint floating bridge No 3 of 1871 with a load of Dockyardies arriving at Torpoint, going home for their midday meal.
ALAN KITTRIDGE COLLECTION.

The Willoughby built floating bridge No. 4 of 1878 at New Passage c1910, with Pottery Quay in the background. Note the red flag and red spectacle glasses in the sides of the lanterns. ALAN KITTRIDGE COLLECTION.

uncertainty as to the direction in which the ferry was travelling. The Admiralty directed that in future the floating bridges at both Torpoint and Saltash should hoist red flags and show red lights at night, to indicate their direction of travel.

In 1912 the Torpoint ferry company acquired and operated the floating bridge on the Higher Ferry on the River Dart but sold it to Philip & Son Ltd, six years later.

TORPOINT STEAMER SERVICE AND EXCURSIONS

The floating bridge at Torpoint closed at 9pm each night after which passengers had to obtain passage from watermen. Answering appeals for the introduction of a nightime passenger steamer service W. J. Reynolds, the Torpoint tug boat operator, announced plans to run a passenger service between Torpoint and Pottery Quay. In 1895 he introduced two small screw steamers, the *Dainty* and the *Link*.

Floating bridge No.3 at Torpoint, well loaded with troops, possibly going to Tregantle or Scraesdon Forts. CITY OF PLYMOUTH LOCAL & NAVAL STUDIES LIBRARY.

To create daytime employment for his steamers Reynolds offered short excursions aboard the *Link*, visiting Forder Lake and Apple Tree Cot Tea Garden on the nearby River Lynher. The *Link* was also used for running to special events such as the 'Primrose Fete' at Mount Edgcumbe in June 1897, when she offered an hourly service from Torpoint, Pottery Quay and North Corner. In 1898 Reynolds bought an ex-Thames paddle steamer, the *Marguerite* (23tg, 68.1 x 10.1 x 4.5 feet) which had originally been operated by the Metropolitan Asylums Board as a river ambulance – for carrying patients with infectious diseases from a clearing house at Rotherhithe to the isolation hospital at Dartford. From 1890 she was owned by a succession of passenger operators on the Thames in London and Oxford until purchased by W. J. Reynolds. At Torpoint the *Marguerite* was employed as a full time excursion steamer, managed by T. Sayers. She ran trips to Lopwell on the River Tavy, landing for one hour at the 'Tea House, Fruit and Flower Gardens' near the quay, and offered longer excursions on the Tamar to Calstock and Weir Head. She also took over the Apple Tree Cot trips from the *Link*, departing from Phoenix Wharf, the Promenade Pier, North Corner and Pottery Quay. In some advertisements she was described as the 'Torpoint Steamboat – Marguerite', but it is unclear whether Reynolds ever adopted a fleet name for his steamboats.

Faced with an increase in landing dues at Torpoint that he claimed would make continued operation of his steamers unprofitable (levied by the ferry company – who coincidentally were considering running their own passenger steamer service), Reynolds withdrew the *Dainty* and *Link* in February 1901, ending the late night steamer service. The hull of the *Link* survived, hulked for many years on the mud of St Johns Lake at Torpoint. The *Marguerite* was another casualty of Reynolds disenchantment with the passenger steamer business and she failed to reappear for the 1901 excursion season.

Late night passengers were once again dependent upon watermens boats but the Torpoint Ferry company promised to revive the passenger steamer service themselves. Their first steamer, the *Volta*, arrived from Portsmouth, where she had operated passenger services between Portsmouth and Gosport for the Port of Portsmouth Steam Launch & Towing Company. The *Volta* was built by Edwards & Symes of London in 1884, with a compound engine by A. Wilson & Co of Vauxhall, London. She carried 70 passengers and measured 53 feet

This photograph is thought to illustrate W. J. Reynolds' two steamers: the LINK, *in the foreground; and the* DAINTY, *alongside the ferry slip – just visible on the right.*
ALAN KITTRIDGE COLLECTION.

W. J. Reynold's ex-Thames paddle steamer, the MARGUERITE, *pictured en-route to Weir Head, passing Tuckermarsh Quay, above Calstock c1898.*
ALAN KITTRIDGE COLLECTION.

The landing pier on the right awaits its pontoon and therefore dates this picture around 1905. The pier and pontoon were to be part of the new daily supplementary steamer service of the Torpoint Ferry and moored off the pier is their first passenger steamer the VOLTA. ALAN KITTRIDGE COLLECTION.

long x 15 feet wide. The *Volta* started running in 1902 and was joined two years later by the specially built steamer *Lady Beatrice* (named after Lady Beatrice Pole Carew). She was a wooden, screw steamer built in Watermans' Yard at Cremyll and measured 52tg, 60.7 x 16.2 x 6.4 feet. Her 15hp two cylinder, compound engine gave her a 10 knot speed. Her Class 5 passenger capacity was 191.

The two steamers initially maintained a similar evening service to that offered by Reynold's steamers but in March 1905 the ferry company and Torpoint Urban Council reached an agreement with the Devonport Landing Stage Committee to allow regular landings throughout the day at the pontoon landing stages at North Corner and Pottery Quay. In the following month the new triangular route began running daily and a new pontoon landing stage was constructed for the passenger service north of the ferry beach at Torpoint.

YEALM STEAMER SERVICES

By 1910 Newton Creek was transforming into a select residential satellite just beyond the boundary of Plymouth, boasting rows of villas, holiday cottages and holiday houseboats. The impetus for this change was initiated by one man in particular and can be dated from 15 January 1898, when the Great Western Railway's branch line from Plymouth to

The LADY BEATRICE *of 1904 pictured approaching Torpoint pontoon.* ALAN KITTRIDGE COLLECTION.

The Torpoint landing stage with the *LADY BEATRICE* at the pontoon. A carrier's cart, on the ferry beach, awaits the arrival of goods and packages from the steamer and floating bridge, for distribution around Torpoint ALAN KITTRIDGE COLLECTION.

Yealmpton was opened by the Countess of Morley. The branch ran along the eastern shore of Cofflete Creek turning east to run alongside the river itself into Yealmpton. Near the confluence of creek and river at Steer Point a station was provided to serve local passenger traffic and goods. This was to be the nearest railway station to the villages of Newton Creek which were nearly three miles further down-river.

James Ford, a Plymouth architect and property developer, was the man largely responsible for promoting the residential potential of Newton Creek. In 1898 his company, the River Yealm Building Estate, completed the Yealm Hotel on a point of land on the northern shore of Newton Creek, overlooking the Pool. A year later he inaugurated a steamboat passenger service between his hotel and the railway at Steer Point and later built a landing pier on the shore below the hotel. The steamboat was a river day-launch or ex-Admiralty pinnace of about forty feet in length, with a well-deck forward, a small after-

The *YAM YAM* leaving Steer Point, with another small, unidentified steamer heading downstream on the right. CITY OF PLYMOUTH LOCAL & NAVAL STUDIES LIBRARY.

Newton Creek with: the Lifeboat Station (1878-1927) on the far left; the Yealm Hotel; the first of many villas – in the middle distance; Kiln Quay; and the church of St Peter in Noss Mayo on the right in the background. Moored off the Yealm Hotel is the YAM YAM *– the first Steer Point steamer.*
ALAN KITTRIDGE COLLECTION.

saloon, a counter stern and a slim upright funnel amidships. She was fitted with canvas dodgers around her deck-rail and provided with awnings fore and aft. From her oversized jack-staff astern she flew her triangular name pennant – *Yam Yam* (Yealm is pronounced 'Yam').

The *Yam Yam* was operated on a waterman's licence – permitted to carry only twelve passengers. She was provided primarily to serve guests of the Yealm Hotel and prospective buyers for the plots of land that James Ford was laying out on the slopes of the creek above Newton Ferrers – any locals carried were by nature of a courtesy or favour only. There was a limited public service offered by a Mr Hartnell who operated a paraffin engined launch, but with the creek's population growing from the introduction of large households and their staff, and with the expanding horizons offered to the local population by the nearby railway, the opportunity arose for the provision of a full time public river steamer service calling at various landings in the creek and river and linking with the trains at Steer Point.

George Hodge of Noss Mayo was the captain of Lord Revelstoke's steam yacht, which was kept in the boat house at Kiln Quay. When the Yealmpton branch railway opened Lord Revelstoke sold his steamer and George Hodge was redundant. Seeing the need for a ferry to Steer Point, George Hodge started a rowing boat service but soon acquired from the STT&DSCo.Ltd the ex-John Parson Millbrook steamer *Lady of the Lake*, which was either renamed or nicknamed *Puffing Billy* – on account of the puffs of steam exhausted by her non-condensing engines. There were nine trains a day each way on weekdays and the *Lady of the Lake/Puffing Billy* met each arrival – keeping her busy for most of the day. Plymouth bound trains created the biggest demand for up-river passage. The steamer left Pope's Quay about an hour before the train was due and called at Kiln Quay in Newton Ferrers, Wide

George Hodge's attractive KITLEY BELLE *was built by the Hocking brothers of Stonehouse in 1905. She is moored at Popes Quay in Noss Mayo with Newton Ferrers and the church of Holy Cross in the background.*
ALAN KITTRIDGE COLLECTION.

Slip near Passage Road, the Yealm Hotel pier from about 1905 (when James Ford stopped running the *Yam Yam)* and, if hailed, would call at Warren Point on the opposite shore of the Pool and at Thorn Quay, about half way up on the Wembury side of the river. When the tide was out the run started from the mouth of the creek at Wide Slip and called at the Yealm Hotel pier. Near high tide at Steer Point the steamer could land at the slipway just inside Cofflete Creek. On other tides a small beach just around the corner on the river served as a landing but on low spring tides the steamer's dinghy had to ferry passengers ashore and crewmen had to carry some of the passengers across the remaining mud to the beach.

Excursion steamers from the Three Towns usually proceeded past Newton Creek, turning in midstream below Steer Point, and returning either to land passengers at Kiln Quay, where a tea garden was established, or anchor in the Pool, from where passengers were taken ashore by small boats 'landing for two hours to visit the romantic villages of Newton and Noss'. Some excursions offered the alternative round trip of proceeding to Steer Point by Hodge's steamer and returning to the Three Towns by train. This extra excursion business prompted George Hodge to order a second steamer in 1905 which Hodge family memory recalls as being built by the Hocking brothers of Cremyll Street in Stonehouse. She was a wooden, screw steamer, similar in appearance to the steamers of the O&TSCo.Ltd. Attractively proportioned and painted white, with a red funnel, she measured 54 feet long x 12 feet wide and was fitted with seating on her deckhouse roof. Licenced to carry 78 passengers she was named the *Kitley Belle* – locally the river was also known as the Kitley river, as Kitley Quay was the highest navigable quay.

Following the arrival of the *Kitley Belle* the *Lady of the Lake/Puffing Billy* was refitted and re-entered service as the *Kitley Girl,* to be used as an extra steamer in the summer months, attending visiting steamers and running excursions. Such was the popularity of the Yealm at this time that Hodge still lacked capacity – most of the visiting Three Towns steamers carried in excess of 200

The Kitley Belle turning in Newton Creek c1910, with Newton Ferrers on the right, Kiln Quay in the middle distance and the River Yealm beyond.
ALAN KITTRIDGE COLLECTION.

The Kitley Girl on the Pool of the River Yealm c1908.
ALAN KITTRIDGE COLLECTION.

A fully laden Kitley Belle *backing away from Steer Point. It is thanks to Mary Lewis (daughter of Elliot Hodge) and Alec J. Short (grandson of George Hodge), that this picture came to light.* Courtesy Mary Lewis

passengers. This shortfall was remedied by purchasing two ex-ships' lifeboats and when circumstances demanded these boats were filled with passengers and towed behind the *Kitley Belle* or *Kitley Girl*. If this procedure didn't actually break safety regulations, it certainly broke the spirit of the law and Hodge probably survived undetected owing to the river's remote location and escape from accidents.

The Yealm steamers were crewed exclusively by members of the Hodge family. George Hodge skippered the *Kitley Belle* with his son, George jnr, as deckhand (later to be the relief skipper and eventually skipper of the *Kitley Belle*) and another son, Ernest, as engineer. A third son, Elliot, was a boatbuilder, with his workshop adjacent to Popes Quay. In addition to building small boats and repairing local crabbing boats, Elliot also maintained and repaired his father's steamers and served as a relief crewman at times. Lionel Baker, George Hodge's nephew, served as a relief engineer on either steamer.

The steamer service survived two threats to its existence. The first was the promotion of the South Hams Light Railway in 1906, to run from Yealmpton to Newton Ferrers. The scheme got as far as preparing a site for a station between Kiln Quay and the Yealm Hotel before it was abandoned. The second threat occurred three years later with plans for a major docks development in Wembury Bay. The Wembury (Plymouth) Commercial Dock and Railway Co Ltd proposed to construct an ocean liner terminal and, while the planned docks were to be on the opposite side of the river, in Wembury Bay, the building of a railway station nearby would certainly have superseded the tortuous alternative offered by Hodge's steamers and the Yealmpton Branch. In the event the Bill was rejected by Parliament, Hodge's steamers survived, and the communities of the River Yealm continued in relative isolation, an isolation that would only be effectively ended with the introduction of motor omnibuses after the Great War.

CHAPTER SIX

EVIDENCE OF SOME RIVALRY

Millbrook and Saltash steamers 1894–1914

THE MILLBROOK FERRY

Strictly speaking the Millbrook Ferry was not a ferry at all, but two non-statutory steamboat lines calling variously at seven different stations on both sides of the Hamoaze. However, steamboat crews and passengers alike have always referred to the service as the Millbrook Ferry and it seems pedantic therefore to call it anything else.

The O&TSCo.Ltd had only been operating their experimental Mutton Cove–Cremyll steamer service for six months in September 1894 when John Parson approached the company to buy both the service and their steamer, the *Despatch*, on his own account. A price of £650 was agreed with H. E. Elford and the sale was completed on 13 November. In purchasing the complete business Parson took over the existing landing rights or agreements at Mutton Cove and Cremyll Beach and extended the route into Millbrook Lake. Within a month he placed an order with Plenty & Son Ltd of Newbury for a compound condensing engine and a boiler, destined for a new boat which was being built for him at Watermans Yard at Cremyll. These events occurred while Parson was still one of the largest shareholders in the STT&DSCo.Ltd. Furthermore he placed the *Despatch* in direct competition with the STT&DSCo.Ltd's brand new, purpose built, Millbrook Ferry paddle steamer, the *Lady Ernestine*.

The ex-Cattewater passenger steamer DESPATCH *at Anderton on Millbrook Lake c1900. Purchased by John Parson in 1894, she was the first boat in what would become his second fleet of Millbrook steamboats.*
CITY OF PLYMOUTH LOCAL & NAVAL STUDIES LIBRARY.

The Lady Ernestine

The *Lady Ernestine* (59.27tg, 71 x 16 x 5ft.), named after the Earl of Mount Edgcumbe's sister, was built of steel by Willoughby Bros Ltd in 1894. She was one of the smallest paddle steamers on the Tamar, designed specifically to

In this postcard view c1905, the LADY ERNESTINE *can be seen on the right, making her way up Millbrook Lake. Behind the paddle steamer is Southdown – usually the low tide limit for screw steamers. The industrial buildings of various companies were largely consolidated as the South Down Metal, Chemical and Brick Company, when this picture was taken. St Johns Lake and Torpoint are top left, with Devonport opposite (top right).*
ALAN KITTRIDGE COLLECTION.

The LADY ERNESTINE *at Higher Pier, Millbrook c1905, from a postcard dramatically titled 'Last boat home from Millbrook'.* ALAN KITTRIDGE COLLECTION.

maintain the Millbrook Ferry services for the STT&DSCo.Ltd. Her 20hp, two cylinder, compound, oscillating engines were also built by Willoughby's. She had a long forward well deck, a short counter stern and was the only steamer in the STT&DSCo.Ltd fleet to have her funnel positioned forward of the paddle boxes. She sat well down at the stern when under way and had a such a shallow draught that it sometimes rendered her difficult to handle on the exposed crossing of the Hamoaze – boatmen eulogised that she could float on the morning dew. James Goss recalled her draught constantly causing problems, 'She was far too shallow draught...'

The Saltash, Three Towns & Steamship Co Ltd inherited landing rights on Cremyll Beach from John Parson's earlier Millbrook steamer fleet. The LADY ERNESTINE *is pictured there c1900, with Mount Wise in the background.* CITY OF PLYMOUTH MUSEUMS & ART GALLERY.

This light draught was designed to enable the steamer to navigate Millbrook Lake at most states of the tide. She also specialised in trips to St Germans Quay and Lopwell Quay, where her draught proved particularly useful.

No sooner had the Saltash company placed their new steamer on the Millbrook Ferry than Parson started running the *Despatch* in opposition. The stage was thus set for an acrimonious battle on the lake, which in turn sparked an era of aggressive competition between John Parson's emergent fleet of Millbrook steamers and the STT&DSCo.Ltd. For fifteen years the two companies would fight a steamer war, a rivalry that became legend in Millbrook and Saltash, a competition that was financially damaging to both, and was only resolved following the demise of one of the protagonists. But what caused so dramatic a split between Parson and the STT&DSCo.Ltd ? Local accounts maintained that following the death of William Gilbert, Parson was in dispute with the board of the Saltash company – possibly over the operation of the Millbrook Ferry – and that he stormed out of a meeting vowing to run them off the river. Shareholding changes in the STT&DSCo.Ltd three years later in 1897 show that E. P. Gilbert – then living in Eastbourne – had inherited William Gilbert's shares and had also acquired three quarters of Parson's. While Parson's split from the STT&DSCo.Ltd is thus documented, evidence regarding the reason for the dispute has yet to be discovered.

The Cornubia

The compound, condensing engine and boiler ordered by Parson in December 1894 was delivered during the following March and installed in his new steamer, the *Cornubia*, which was nearing completion at Watermans Yard. The *Cornubia* was a wooden screw steamer, remembered as being cramped for space but a fast boat. She had a well deck forward, a single pole mast, and was distinctive in having a tall upright funnel and portholes along her cabin sides. The helm was on the top deck (cabin roof) squeezed between the mast and funnel requiring the helmsman to stand beside the wheel. The new steamer was designed for use on the Millbrook Ferry and could carry 150 passengers. She appears to have spent her entire civilian life on the service, offering only a few evening trips to Lopwell Quay early in her career.

The Devonia

In 1895 Parson ordered a second set of machinery from Plenty & Son Ltd. The compound, condensing engine was destined for another new steamer, the *Devonia*, built by Watermans and launched in 1896. Unlike the *Despatch* and the *Cornubia*, the *Devonia* was designed principally as an excursion steamer, although she was also used on the Millbrook Ferry. She had very short bow and stern rope handling decks, all of her outside passenger

A Frederick James Johns photograph of the DEVONIA *passing Insworke on Millbrook Lake in 1898.* COURTESY JOHN DODDRIDGE.

The sender of this postcard noted, 'Arrived Devonport at five minutes to six, arriving Millbrook 7.10...' The stamp was cancelled in Devonport 7.45pm 15 April 1911. The photograph shows the CORNUBIA *(nearest) at Higher Pier, and the* LADY ERNESTINE *at the STT&DSCo.Ltd's own landing at the end of Molesworth Terrace in Millbrook (later known as Worth's Pier). The Saltash company's pier was the better equipped – with oil lamps at either end and a ticket and parcels office at the entrance.* ALAN KITTRIDGE COLLECTION.

The DEVONIA *at Millbrook in 1898.* COURTESY JOHN DODDRIDGE

space being on top of her long saloon. She was larger than the *Cornubia* and had a raised helm deck in front of her amidships funnel. Her saloon was built to the sheer of the hull and her saloon windows slanted in line with the rake of her funnel and two pole masts. The *Devonia* was an attractive looking steamer but suffered badly from vibration – an anonymous observer stated 'I have never known another boat vibrate so badly'. James Goss recalled her passengers visibly shaking and the hull trembling in the water as she idled at the landing places. This unfortunate characteristic, coupled with her faintly oriental appearance, earned the *Devonia* the nickname 'the Junk'.

Initially the *Devonia* specialised in shallow water trips, probably to offer competition to the *Lady Ernestine*. She visited Maristow and Lopwell on the Tavy, and Apple Tree Cot in Forder Lake on the River Lynher – landing for two hours. These early excursions were run by T. Sayers Marine Excursions but by 1900 the Millbrook steamers' excursions were being managed by messrs J. Slee and R. Gliddon.

The *Despatch* was relegated to a cargo and parcel service between Devonport and Millbrook, which was run in connection with carriers on both sides of the Hamoaze. Competition between the *Cornubia* and the *Lady Ernestine* meanwhile became so intense that a number of court cases resulted. Deliberate groundings were effected by the faster steamer closing up to the slower boat, dragging it along in its wake and altering course suddenly to follow the narrow, winding channel, leaving the slower steamer struggling to regain control before she hit the mud. Sometimes the protagonist gave the victim a parting nudge towards the shore. Captain Ryall of the *Lady Ernestine* usually emerged as the villain but in mitigation on one occasion the magistrate noted 'evidence of some rivalry' and 'spirited competition'. Between January 1895 and February 1899 sixteen claims, amounting to £291. 15s. 6d. had been awarded to John Parson. Some endearing stories have survived the years, apocryphal in nature perhaps, but indicative of the impression the rivalry created.

Mutton Cove c1900 with Parson's steamers BRITANNIA *(outside),* DEVONIA *and* CORNUBIA *(inside).* CITY OF PLYMOUTH MUSEUMS & ART GALLERY.

Mutton Cove landing stage c1900. The steamer is believed to be the IOLANTHE, *built by the Waterman brothers in 1887 for John Parson and taken over by the Saltash Three Towns & District Steamboat Co Ltd in 1892. The* LADY ERNESTINE *can be seen behind.*
ALAN KITTRIDGE COLLECTION.

Jack Kingston, writing in the *Torpoint Parish Magazine,* recalled that passengers aboard the stranded steamer wouldn't dream of transferring to the victorious rival, but waited until the tide had receded enough to cross the mud to the shore, and walked home. More doubtful is the story of a 'mixed' Millbrook/Saltash marriage, where the betrothed travelled separately on their respective home town steamers.

The Britannia

In August 1900 the *Lady Ernestine* finally met her match in the shape of a new steel paddle steamer, the *Britannia*, built by Philip & Son of Dartmouth for John Parson. Resembling the *Lady Ernestine* the new steamer measured 63tg 75.3 x 16.1 x 5.5ft. Philip also built her 30hp two cylinder, compound diagonal engines (cylinders set in an incline plane). Similar to the *Lady Ernestine* the *Britannia's* stern sat very low in the water. This characteristic, coupled with the distinctive flapping sound of her paddle floats as they hit the water (she had six floats per paddle-wheel as opposed to the customary eight), contributed to the comparison of her progress through the water being like a duck squattering along. In addition to working the Millbrook Ferry the *Britannia* was also used for excursions. The *Britannia* differed from the *Lady Ernestine* in being flush decked, with all of her open air passenger space on top of the saloons.

During her first season the 'Millbrook Steamboat Company's New Saloon Steamer Britannia' ran excursions to Weir Head (landing at Morwellham), the Breakwater and Cawsand, departing from Pottery Quay, North Corner, the Promenade Pier and Phoenix Wharf. Some evening runs were made to St Germans Quay.

Iolanthe

On 9 July 1900 Orlando Davis, Secretary of the STT&DSCo.Ltd, minuted debenture shareholders of the Company for permission to sell one of their steamboats:

> My directors are desirous of selling the steam launch Iolanthe which has become very old and useless for their work and the cost of repairing is more than she would be worth after repair.

Surprisingly the *Iolanthe* returned to the ownership of John Parson and partnered the *Cornubia* on the Millbrook Ferry. Considering the rivalry between the two companies it seems an unlikely transaction, unless it was in settlement of the legal penalties which resulted from collisions on Millbrook Lake.

The opposing LADY ERNESTINE *and* IOLANTHE *at Lower Pier, Millbrook, after the latter steamer was sold back to John Parsons in 1900. Parsons' tide mill can be seen in the background. Note the wagonnette in the foreground.*
COURTESY JACK KINGSTON

The AERIAL *on the slip at Commercial Wharf, Saltash, probably undergoing her annual maintenance. The paddler is supported upon timber baulks from the Saltash company's own timber stock, kept at the adjacent Sand Quay. Behind her a topsail schooner is discharging coal, note the horses and carts on the left. In the background, moored in the river, is one of the Admiralty's 'gunpowder' ships, which were kept upstream of Saltash – as their present day counterparts still are.* DOUGLAS VOSPER COLLECTION.

RIVER EXCURSIONS

The Aerial is scrapped

In 1900 the 35 year old *Aerial* was showing signs of her age. She spent the year as relief steamer on the 'Dockyardies' service from Saltash and during the summer worked the Cawsand run – exchanging her characteristic saloon windows for portholes to satisfy Board of Trade requirements for operating outside the Breakwater. On one of her trips in 1901 the *Saltash Gazette* reported that she broke down in Cawsand Bay and suffered the ignomy of a tow from a Gun Wharf tug back to West Hoe Pier. With her boilers worn out and plates wearing thin she filled in the remainder of the season running the shuttle between the Promenade Pier and Cremyll Quay. Surviving the winter laid up at Saltash, the *Aerial* was broken up in 1902. In a final display of affection for the old steamer, many of her fittings were bought as souvenirs, including the ship's bell, nameplates and helm, none of which have come to light during many years researching this subject.

The Prince Edward

In 1904 John Parson and the STT&DSCo.Ltd each added a new paddle steamer to their fleets. Willoughby's built the *Prince Edward* for the Saltash company. She was a steel paddler measuring 62 tg, 84.2 x 15.1 x 4.7 feet, with two cylinder, compound engines built by Willoughby's. Although smaller, she

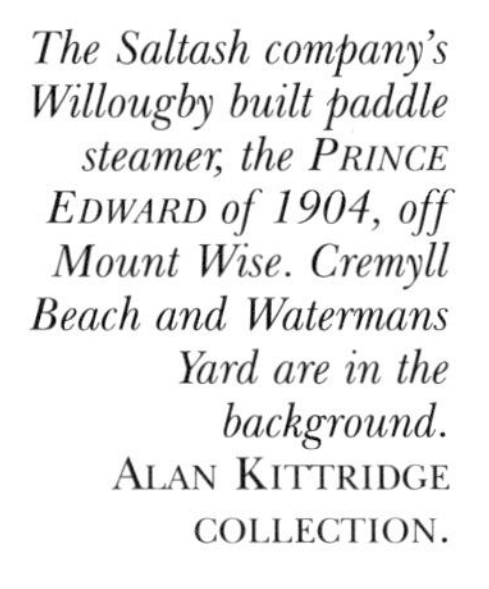

The Saltash company's Willougby built paddle steamer, the PRINCE EDWARD *of 1904, off Mount Wise. Cremyll Beach and Watermans Yard are in the background.* ALAN KITTRIDGE COLLECTION.

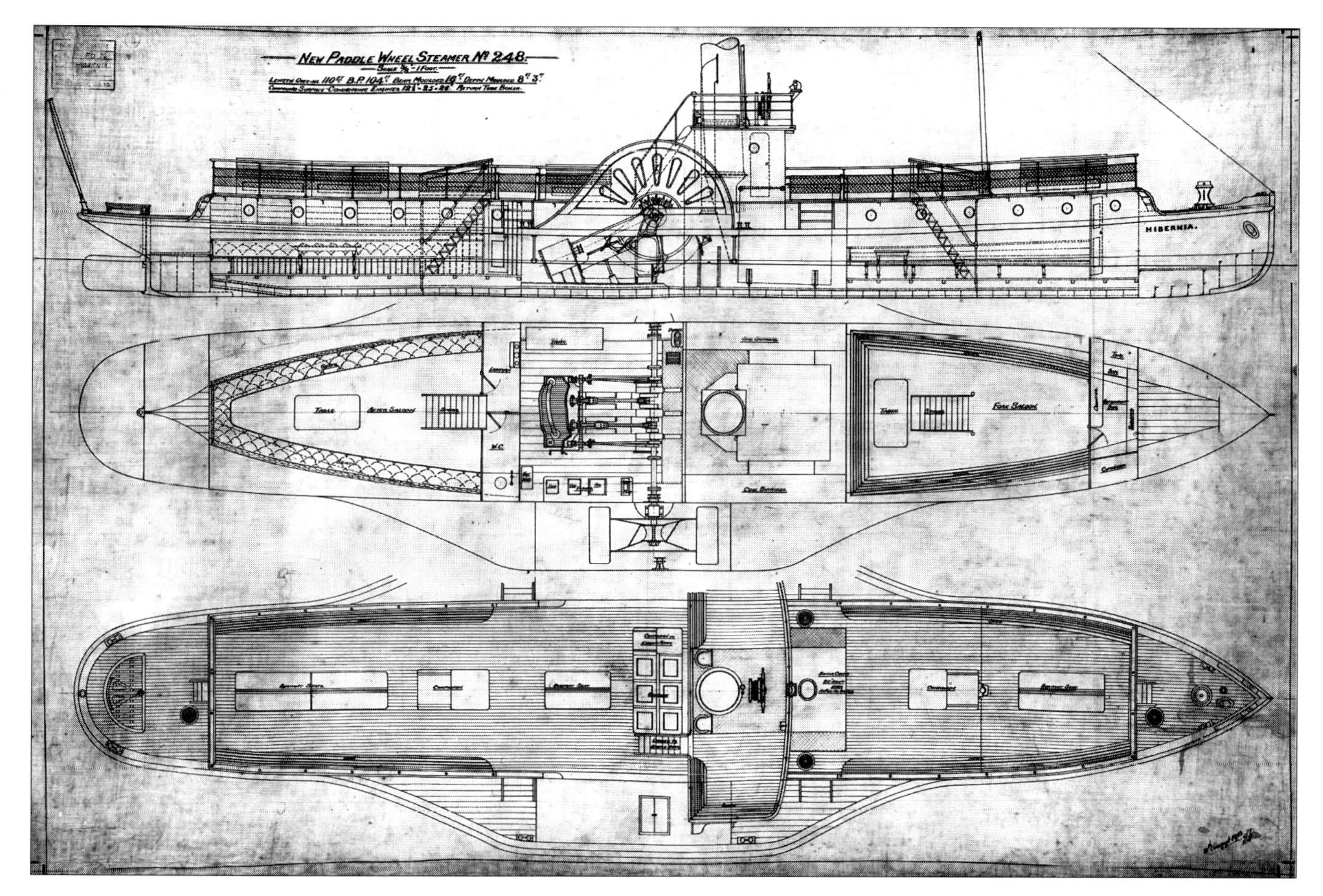

General arrangement diagram of the HIBERNIA. Note the diagonal engines. NATIONAL MARITIME MUSEUM

resembled both the *Empress* and the *Alexandra* and had a similar 11 knot speed. Initially the *Prince Edward* was mostly used on the Cawsand Bay run – from Saltash and the Hamoaze landings – but she also ran on Four Rivers trips and Tamar excursions. Some Mount Batten landings were made during her first season.

Edward Gill, an ex-Saltash company crewman, recalled the *Prince Edward* as being very difficult to steer, owing to the combination of a shallow draught and short length. Jack Abbot, an ex-Millbrook company crewman, was more forthright when he described the paddler as 'a pig to steer in any conditions'. As a Calstock boy, known to steamer crews, Jack recalled that the *Prince Edward* was the only paddler that he couldn't steer when offered the opportunity. Her last skipper, Albert Watts, rarely wore a jacket due to the effort required to navigate her. Another crewman aboard the *Prince Edward* in her later years was Edward Hughes of Saltash who, writing to Graham Grimshaw, the author of *British Pleasure Steamers 1920-1939*, asked:

> ...if it was possible to receive from you a copy of your manuscript when you have compiled your full edition, to keep as a memento, as my heart and soul were in the work appertaining to these vessels.

The Hibernia

John Parson meanwhile, in 1903, placed an order with Philip & Son of Dartmouth for a steel paddle steamer measuring 99 tg, 104.6 x 16.2 x 8.25 feet. Her compound diagonal, surface condensing engines were also built by Philip's, and her boiler by Barclay, Curle & Co Ltd. She was launched in February 1904 and completed in the following month. With a capacity of 366 passengers and a 10.5 knot speed, the *Hibernia* was a major new addition to Parson's fleet. She

The HIBERNIA pictured soon after delivery in 1904 – seemingly on her maiden trip. ALAN KITTRIDGE COLLECTION.

The BRITANNIA (right) and the HIBERNIA on Millbrook Lake. Although crowded, passengers were rarely admitted to The Hibernia's bridge deck seats. CITY OF PLYMOUTH LOCAL & NAVAL STUDIES LIBRARY.

boasted steam steering gear and was the first river steamer in the district to be fitted with electric lighting. Similar to the *Princess Royal* the *Hibernia* had a bridge deck fitted with seats – although passengers, apparently, were rarely admitted. Similar to the *Britannia*, her boiler and funnel were forward of the paddle wheels. The *Hibernia* became the Millbrook company's principal charter steamer and was also used on public Tamar excursions alongside the *Britannia* and *Devonia*. She ran regularly to the River Yealm.

One of the *Hibernia's* skippers was William H. Crawford who had previously commanded the *Cornubia* as the youngest passenger boat skipper on the river. His son William T. Crawford became the Managing Director of the Millbrook fleet after the Great War and members of the Crawford family would remain

The crew of the HIBERNIA with John Parson on the far left of the bridge deck in a peaked cap. Next is the Mate. At the helm is William Grylls, who worked aboard Tamar barges from Calstock until employment by Parson necessitated a move down river to Southdown. During the Second World War William's son Arthur worked on the Cremyll Ferry for the Millbrook Steamboat & Trading Co Ltd, and later skippered the EASTERN BELLE and PLYMOUTH BELLE until retiring in 1983. Captain William H. Crawford leans confidently on the deckrail next to the helm. Captain Crawford was Parson's right hand man and had commanded nearly all of the company's steamers at some stage. His son, William T. Crawford, became Manager of the Millbrook Steamboat & Trading Co Ltd, the family name being represented on the board until 1980. The gentleman on the right, in the Panama hat, might be J. Slee, Parson's excursion agent. Below, the Engineer and Stoker stand either side of the seated group that includes saloon staff and deck crew. COURTESY ARTHUR GRYLLS.

One of a series of Fred. J. Paul postcards which he issued at fortnightly intervals to mark progress on the PD&SWJR viaduct at Calstock. This photograph was taken in 1906 (postally used 20 July 1906) and shows the HIBERNIA *approaching the restricted channel. Behind the viaduct is James Goss' shipyard with the trading ketch* GARLANDSTONE *on the stocks – built on speculation she was launched in 1909 and is currently the subject of a long term preservation project at Morwellham Quay Museum on the River Tamar.* ALAN KITTRIDGE COLLECTION.

at the forefront of the company until 1980. Ernest Pengelley took over the *Hibernia* when William H. Crawford moved on to command the *Brunel*. Captain Pengelley was later the piermaster at Mutton Cove. After Calstock viaduct was built, bargeman William Grylls moved to Millbrook as helmsman of the *Hibernia*. His son Arthur was still with the Millbrook company in the 1980s as skipper of the motor vessel *Plymouth Belle*.

The arrival of these two new steamers coincided with the building of the railway viaduct across the river at Calstock between 1904 and 1908. It is difficult now to imagine Calstock without its graceful twelve arch viaduct forming a gateway to the upper reaches of the River Tamar. The PD&SWJR built the viaduct to link their isolated line from Kelly Bray (Callington) to Calstock (formerly the 3ft 6ins gauge East Cornwall Mineral Railway) to the P&DSWJR mainline at Bere Alston. This branch line was the only part of the PD&SWJR to be worked by the company's own rolling stock – all the way into Devonport.

Similar to the construction of the Royal Albert Bridge half a century earlier, the viaduct worksite attracted the curiosity of excursionists from the Three Towns. The railway was opened in 1908 and was a contributing factor towards a steady decline in the use of the river as a commercial highway – it soon won most of the mineral traffic. The line became increasingly busy in summer with 'school treats' and other group outings to Calstock, where games and a picnics were laid on in fields above the village – Vennings Pleasure Gardens on Hingston Down even had a railway halt provided nearby (Sevenstones, between Latchley and Luckett). The line also offered cheap market day tickets on Thursdays and Saturdays. However, the railway didn't immediately supplant river traffic, barges still called at quays along the river. Ketches and schooners still traded to Calstock and other quays. And steamers continued to visit Calstock, Morwellham and Weir Head

The Brunel

In 1909 the largest and fastest paddler ever to ply regularly on the Tamar was purchased by John Parson for just £500. This bargain presented itself following the collapse of London County Council's (LCC) Hammersmith to Greenwich water bus service in 1907, which put thirty similar vessels on the market. Parson selected the appropriately named *Brunel*, a steel paddler measuring 126tg, 129.9 x 18.5 x 6.7

Calstock children, including photographer Fred. J. Paul's daughters on the right, size up the BRUNEL *in 1909 – still in her LCC livery.* COURTESY MARJORIE DEACON.

feet. She had been built by the Thames Iron Works in 1905, with two cylinder, compound diagonal engines by Scotts of Greenock. With a 12.5 knot speed and a capacity of 533 passengers the *Brunel* offered considerable competition to the STT&DSCo.Ltd. Parson's advertisements optimistically suggested 'Every resident should take a trip on the Brunel'. Purchased on 20 July 1909, no time was lost in bringing the *Brunel* around the coast to the Tamar where she made her superstition defying maiden voyage to Calstock on Friday 13 August, still carrying her LCC livery and lettering. She kept the London livery for the rest of the season and was still being referred to as 'The LCC Steamboat Brunel' in 1913. She only ran to Weir Head on the highest tides as she could only just turn there.

The Tamar passenger steamer fleet thus reached its peak and in 1910 the Millbrook and Saltash companies comprised:

STT&DSCo.Ltd

Eleanor	Tamar excursions, Hamoaze and Cawsand services
Albert	Cawsand, coastal excursions and Hamoaze service
Prince	Hamoaze service
Princess Royal	Tamar, Yealm and coastal excursions
Empress	Market service, Tamar excursions
Alexandra	Tamar and Yealm excursions
Lady Ernestine	Millbrook Ferry
Prince Edward	Tamar excursions, Cawsand

(The *Lady of the Lake* was sold to George Hodge on the River Yealm after 1898)

John Parson's Millbrook Steamboat Company:

Cornubia	Millbrook Ferry
Devonia	Tamar excursions
Britannia	Millbrook Ferry and Tamar excursions
Hibernia	Tamar and Yealm excursions
Brunel	Tamar excursions

(The *Iolanthe* was withdrawn before 1910 and her hull used in some capacity by the Millbrook company at their base at Parson's tide mill buildings on Millbrook Lake)

Having described Parson's Millbrook steamers and both the *Lady Ernestine* and *Prince Edward* in some detail, there follow some memories and notes about the older units of the Saltash fleet during this period.

Another Fred. J. Paul postcard, phototyped for mass production, shows the BRUNEL, *with her white saloon sides, above Calstock.* ALAN KITTRIDGE COLLECTION.

The BRUNEL *at Morwellham Quay (facing upstream) c1910. Note the lime kilns behind the steamer.* MORWELLHAM QUAY MUSEUM.

The Eleanor

The *Eleanor* was lengthened in 1886 by 4.7 feet to 109.5 feet length overall. By 1906 she was forty years old but would soldier on for many years beyond that. Following the failure of the *Aerial* and until the *Prince Edward* entered service in 1904, the *Eleanor* was the principal Cawsand Bay steamer. She was also used on the Grand Circular excursion when the *Empress* was otherwise engaged on market day service or charters. Originally her speed was 10 knots but by 1910 it was remembered as 'considerably less'. An oddity of the *Eleanor* was a small well deck in the bows for rope handling, while other paddlers in the fleet (excepting the *Lady Ernestine*) were flush decked.

The Princess Royal

The *Princess Royal* was probably the best remembered Tamar paddler, due to her distinctive appearance and belief that she was the biggest in the fleet. Not only did she look bigger than the *Alexandra,* but she was also the flagship of the fleet, commanded by the Saltash company's senior skippers – foremost c1900 being Captain Whitburn of Calstock, who had previously commanded the *Aerial* for messrs Rickard and Spear. Captain Whitburn eventually emigrated to New Zealand. Captain Moyse was another of *Princess Royal's* skippers and as the senior Captain was in charge of the company's other certificated skippers including Captains Craven, Gill, Foot and Sutton. The crew of most Saltash company boats comprised: skipper, mate, deckhand, boy, engineer, stoker and steward. She was re-boilered in 1909.

Edward Gill recalled that on one occasion the *Princess Royal*, full with a charter party from Saltash Wesleyan Chapel, was going to Weir Head but stayed too long at Morwellham while the excursionists danced on the quay. They eventually left late, arriving at Weir Head after the tide had turned and while the *Princess Royal* was turning at the lock gates of the Tamar Manure Navigation she went aground. Prompt action got all the gangways out, boats lowered and crowds of people landed. All who could, manned the ropes to pull the vessel around but with no success. Eventually the lock keeper arrived and as everyone made a last effort he opened the lock paddles. The resulting rush of water floated the steamer off the bottom and into the channel.

The Empress

In the Tamar Valley the name *Empress* is synonymous with the market boat service – a service the *Empress* maintained for half a century. Jack Abbot recalled:

> When the Empress was loaded up on Market days, baskets and boxes of vegetables and fruit were piled high, all along the promenade deck and people had to pick their way between.

The PRINCESS ROYAL, *depicted in a Saltash, Three Towns & District Steamboat Co Ltd, official postcard.* CITY OF PLYMOUTH LOCAL & NAVAL STUDIES LIBRARY.

The EMPRESS, *on an excursion, passes beneath Calstock viaduct in 1907. One of the* EMPRESS' *distinctive features was a metal ring on her funnel below the black top, being too far down for the regulation black to reach. Note the the old D&CTSPCo.Ltd's quay office immediately upstream of the viaduct and Bowdens Steam Packet Hotel behind. The metal structure under construction on the viaduct was a wagon hoist, to lower railway wagons to the quayside line – supplanting the old ECMR incline. The hoist was dismantled in 1934. On the right is an unidentified ketch rigged barge, similar to the* SHAMROCK, *now preserved at Cotehele Quay.*
CITY OF PLYMOUTH LOCAL & NAVAL STUDIES LIBRARY.

Livestock was penned in with boxes.

Empress also made a cargo run, including bringing beer up-river for the Calstock pubs, on Wednesdays and Fridays. Rowe was the carrier at Calstock. Salmon fishermen bagged up their catch and Empress took them to Bigwoods Cold Storage in Plymouth for local shops such as Churchills the Fishmongers and hotels.

The *Empress* left Calstock Quay at 6am on Tuesdays, Thursdays and Saturdays. After calling at Cotehele, Halton Quay, Hole's Hole, Cargreen and Saltash she arrived at North Corner at 9am. Carriers such as Pickfords and Hayes queued to carry the produce up Cornwall Street to Devonport Market. The return trip departed at 4pm. Writing of the market steamers in the *Western Morning News* in 1951, George Umpelby said :

> It is a pity the artists of those days, who have bequeathed us so many impressions of the river, its scenery, and shipping, do not seem to have left us any of the richly-characteristic scenes those little boats must have presented. But it would have needed the discerning eye of a Degas, the sympathetic brush of a Monet to have translated to canvas the stout, jolly figures and the homely features of the passengers, with their colourful merchandise of flowers, fruit, butter, eggs, poultry, and other Tamarside produce.

Similar in appearance to both the *Alexandra* and *Prince Edward*, one of the *Empress'* distinguishing features was her funnel which had a metal funnel ring below the black top, the ring being too far down for the regulation depth of black. One of her regular skippers in the 1890s was Captain Trennance who had previously commanded her one-time arch rival, the *Aerial*. Captain Trennance later moved to coastal excursion steamers on the south coast where he commanded the sea going paddle steamer, *Plymouth Belle*. Mary Hocking is remembered as another regular member of the *Empress'* crew, she was the caterer aboard the steamer on market days. A hard worked steamer, the *Empress* was reboilered in 1889 and 1908.

Although primarily the market steamer, the *Empress* filled in with charters and other work. In 1905 the Independent Order of Good Templars chartered her for a day, visiting Cawsand in the morning and Weir Head in the afternoon. In the same year St Judes Church in Plymouth chartered her for their annual excursion to Weir Head. The *Empress* was the handiest of the big steamers at Weir Head, and according to James Goss she was the only one that could turn on her engines, i.e. without the assistance of poles or ropes. It is also said that a young crewman fell and drowned while the steamer was turning there.

William (Bill) Worth, one of the *Empress'* later skippers, sometimes let young Jack Abbot (who's uncle was the engineer) take the helm. Jack recalled one such occasion when some female passengers looked up and, seeing only Jack, with typical Three Towns understatement exclaimed 'ere look at the boy, I 'ope ee knows what ee's doing'.

The ALEXANDRA *pictured turning off Calstock, with the Passage House Inn behind her funnel smoke. On the right is James Goss' shipyard and the Calstock Ferry boat.* CITY OF PLYMOUTH MUSEUMS & ART GALLERY.

The Alexandra

Edward Gill said that the *Alexandra* was fastest in the fleet and the favoured steamer of Saltash company crews. Gill had been a deck hand aboard the *Eleanor* and *Empress*, and stoker on the *Princess Royal* and *Alexandra*. After the Great War he would progress to be the helmsman on the *Prince Edward*, eventually becoming her skipper.

Our intrepid test driver, the young Jack Abbot, found *Alexandra* beautiful to steer. She had a three inch keel which gave a bite in the water and helped prevent drift in the wind. This keel later proved advantageous when she gained a certificate after the Great War to call at coastal destinations between the limits of Mevagissey and Salcombe.

Regularly seen on the Tamar and Yealm the *Alexandra* made at least one fateful trip on the Tavy, as remembered by Edward Gill:

> On one trip the 'Alex' was engaged by a Tamerton Foliot party from Warleigh Quay. On Tavy trips the after mast was dropped and the forward mast lowered. On the 'Alex' the funnel just cleared the railway bridge. On this occasion the Mate, Captain Squance, was knocked overboard, washed into the paddle wheels and killed. He had been reduced to mate when held responsible for a collision with one of the Dockyard boats.

In 1891 *Alexandra's* skipper was Captain Lamerton, who had once commanded the *Queen* for the D&CTSPCo.Ltd. A later skipper was Captain Foot, of Calstock. She was re-boilered in 1902.

Her most distinctive feature was a seemingly continual wisp of white steam escaping her waste steam pipe on her funnel – there are few photographs where it does not appear. Calstock folk said it was: 'Alex's pennant flying'.

The ALEXANDRA *negotiates the viaduct works in 1906, with her 'pennant flying' – the almost perpetual wisp of steam from the waste pipe on her funnel.* COURTESY MARJORIE DEACON.

Passengers embarking aboard the DEVONIA *(outside) and the* PRINCESS ROYAL, *on the Sea Front c1910*
ALAN KITTRIDGE COLLECTION.

In the 1890s the industrial and mining boom in the Tamar Valley was drawing to a close. A visitor to Morwellham in 1896, found the inland port deserted, trucks lay derelict on the dockside and ruined winding gear littered the hill beyond. Lime burning at New Quay ended in 1904, when Messrs Perry and Spear centralised the Tamar Valley's lime burning at the Halton Quay kilns. Similar to neighbouring Morwellham, the community at New Quay began to drift away to new employment. Agriculture, meanwhile, expanded as the Great Western and London & South Western railways opened up huge new markets for the produce of the fertile valley, particularly for early fruit crops of strawberries and cherries. The Tamar Valley market gardens also enjoyed increased prosperity from the continued growth of the Three Towns which provided a healthy trade for the market steamer *Empress*.

The population of Devonport grew from nearly 55,000 in 1891 to over 83,000 just ten years later. There was a corresponding increase in the membership of Friendly Societies, Methodist congregations, and other working class clubs and societies. Since the August Bank Holiday Act of 1871 a tradition of club and society outings had been established over the Bank Holiday weekend. Additionally, as working hours were reduced with the adoption of a maximum working week, Mondays, Wednesdays or Saturdays became half working days for many. The established steamboat owners reaped the benefit as the large artisan workforce of the Three Towns looked for somewhere to go on their time off.

Escape to the seaside and countryside by steamer was readily available and mostly inexpensive. In 1900 one penny could get you across the Plym to visit Jennycliff and Radford Grounds Tea Gardens; or over to Cremyll and Mount Edgcumbe. Similarly the Millbrook Ferry cost only a few 'coppers' and was met by fleets of wagonettes for the beaches of Tregonhawke, Withnoe and Freathy in Whitsand Bay. Steamers also ran seasonally to the beaches at Kingsand and Cawsand. The River Yealm was a regular destination. Excursions to St Germans on the Lynher, and to Lopwell or Maristow on the Tavy were still run, but difficulty in navigating the former and the L&SWR bridge (of 1889) at the mouth of the latter, reduced excursion opportunities on these rivers. Any vessel visiting the Tavy after 1889 needed a striking mast, i.e. a mast set in a tabernacle which could be lowered to clear the bridge. The perennial favourite, however, remained a trip up the River Tamar to Calstock and, when the tide served, to Morwellham and Weir Head.

A TAMAR EXCURSION IN 1909

Safely ensconced aboard a comfortable steamer at the Sea Front piers, the day tripper could settle back to enjoy an afternoon steaming up-river aboard the perfect grandstand to view the beautiful scenery of 'Devon's Rhine'. Time ashore at Calstock or Morwellham added to the experience of going away for the day, out of the bustle and grey urban landscape of the Three Towns and into the beautiful surrounding countryside. The STT&DSCo.Ltd was well placed to benefit from an excursion boom which lasted until the Great War – or would have been had John Parson not instigated a damaging price war. By 1909 rivalry between the Millbrook and Saltash fleets had brought the price of a day on the Tamar down to just one shilling – the cheapest it had ever been.

The after saloon aboard most steamers was designated as the Ladies Saloon, providing non-alcoholic refreshment and on the larger paddlers the comfort of upholstered seating and a carpeted floor. Hot water was dispensed from nickel plated urns, steam heated by a pipe from the ship's boiler. The forward Mens Saloon invariably offered beer and spirits from a small counter. *Hibernia's* bar was fitted with shelves, a cupboard, a drinking water tank and a small sink. The *Britannia* had slatted seats in both her forward and after saloons, positioned around the cabin sides. The *Empress* was also fitted with slatted seats throughout – more serviceable for the year round market service. The bar and men's toilet aboard the *Empress* were beneath the forward cabin companionway, while the buffet and ladies' toilet were similarly positioned in the after saloon. The *Alexandra* and *Princess Royal* had panelled bulkheads, rows of tables and upholstered seats in their saloons.

The crowded smoke-filled atmosphere of the forward saloons, contrasted sharply to the

From right to left: the EMPRESS, *the* ELEANOR *(her funnel visible behind), the* PRINCESS ROYAL *and the* ALEXANDRA *at West Hoe Pier, with the* HIBERNIA *at the Promenade Pier, c1905.*
ALAN KITTRIDGE COLLECTION.

bright daylight and fresh air on deck. Buoyant seats, saloon companionways and the engine room skylight occupied the central run of the steamers' decks. The area around the funnel and paddle sponsons amidships offered a popular meeting place and the boiler casing, which usually projected about 20 inches above deck level, was a favoured location as the evening drew on. Slatted seats lined the deckrail of all the steamers, while the *Princess Royal* and the *Hibernia* had additional seating on their bridge decks.

Both *Empress* and *Alexandra* were fitted with conning bridges, a narrow raised walkway, forward of the funnel, which spanned the paddle boxes and housed the helm, engine telegraphs and binnacle. Where no such raised deck was provided, both the skipper and helmsman were sometimes boxed into a 'monkey bridge', as featured aboard the *Eleanor* and *Britannia*.

A canvas awning sometimes protected the fore deck of Reynolds' *Marguerite* and the after decks of the *Hibernia* and *Brunel*, casting a cool yellow or light green shade over the passengers. The *Eleanor* and the *Princess Royal* could rig an after awning but no evidence has come to light indicating that other steamers of the STT&DSCo.Ltd were so equipped.

At the height of the season the steamers were well patronised, especially over the August Bank Holiday weekend when they worked to capacity. The *Eleanor* had a Class 5 (smooth water) certificate for 341 passengers, but while on the Cawsand run her Class 4 (partially smooth water) passenger numbers were limited to 188. The *Hibernia* had a similar Class 5 capacity of 366. The *Empress*, *Princess Royal* and *Alexandra* carried 444, 462 and 468 passengers respectively on their Class 5 certificates. The *Brunel's* 533 passenger capacity was the largest of any Tamar paddle steamer.

Potential passengers on the Sea Front were touted by agents from the Promenade Pier (for Parson's, and O&TSCo.Ltd steamers) or from West Hoe Pier (for STT&DSCo.Ltd steamers). In the days before public address systems the inquisitive excursionist could glean points of interest from a number of guide books including: *The Illustrated Western Weekly News Holiday Booklet for the Rivers Plym, Tamar, Lynher and Tavy* by Chas. R. Rowe; and *McBryde's River and Sea Trips* by H. Scrine Hill. McBryde's book noted 'Each steamer carries a stewardess and assistants, and tea and light refreshments are served on board, and fruit in season'.

Steamers from the Sea Front piers called at North Corner after about fifteen minutes to pick up passengers from Devonport. The North

The PRINCESS ROYAL, *departing from the Promenade Pier c1910*
COURTESY MARTIN LANGLEY.

North Corner, looking down on the pontoon landing. The wall on the extreme left is the 'north corner' of South Yard – the extent of the original dockyard. The steamer at the pontoon is the DEVONIA *of the Millbrook Steamboat Company. In attendance are carriers' wagons of Pickfords and Hayes. The Dutch-style brick building on the right is the Piermaster's house and storeroom, while the wall behind encloses Morice Yard.*
ALAN KITTRIDGE COLLECTION.

Corner pontoon had waiting shelters at each end of the pontoon. The Devonport call gave passengers the chance to view the dockyard and warships at close quarters. The trip up the Hamoaze was always a popular part of the excursion and in 1909 'Jacky' Fisher's Royal Navy was nearing its apogee, especially in numbers of Dreadnoughts, some of which were being built in Devonport Dockyard. In addition to being one of the largest naval dockyards in Europe, Devonport was also a Naval Base, a manning depot for ships of the Royal Navy, and anchorage for many partially manned ships of the Reserve Fleet. Immediately inside the mouth of the Tamar, the grandeur and gaiety of Plymouth's famous Hoe and the spectacular scenery of Plymouth Sound were abruptly replaced by a dominating naval presence, both ashore and afloat, all the way to Saltash. Pleasure steamers passed close to Sir John Rennie's imposing Royal William Victualling Yard; the historic South Yard; Sir John Vanbrugh's Gun Wharf (Morice Yard); Keyham Steam Yard – with its landmark Quadrangle steam factory; the immense new North Yard Extension; and the Royal Naval Barracks at Keyham. Warships of the Royal Navy lined the docksides and were moored in trots in the Hamoaze. Reminders of Nelson's navy were represented by ex-ships of the line – the 'wooden walls of England'. Converted to training ships they were dotted around the Hamoaze from Cremyll to Saltash.

Saltash was the last pick-up point and was reached in about fifteen minutes after North Corner. At the head of the Saltash Town Quay pontoon the SSTT&DSCo.Ltd had fitted a deck with seats and various coin machines. Tickets for the steamers were sold from a window of the booking office which adjoined the Passage House Inn. Brunel's Royal Albert Bridge naturally excited attention and passengers had plenty of time to view the bridge towering above them because the Saltash pontoon lay alongside it. Parson's steamers called at a small pontoon

Crowds embarking aboard the PRINCESS ROYAL *at Saltash Town Quay pontoon c1910*
ALAN KITTRIDGE COLLECTION.

immediately upstream of the bridge at Ashe Torre (or Ash Tor) Wharf.

Once up-stream of the Royal Albert Bridge the vista altered dramatically to a wide expanse of water surrounded by low, fertile agricultural land. The River Tavy, with the eight arch girder railway bridge at its mouth, was passed on the right and the one time river port of Cargreen, a stopping place for steamers of the O&TSCo.Ltd, was passed close on the Cornish bank. The channel switched to the opposite Bere Peninsula side passing Egypt Bay – a maze of channels through reed beds to Liphill Quay. Next, on the Bere shore came Weir Quay and the market steamer depot at Hole's Hole. In 1893 the STT&DSCo.Ltd reached an agreement with the Mount Edgcumbe Estate to lease the quay, store and other premises at Hole's Hole for £4 per annum The lease stipulated that the tenant was to allow steamers and other boats to land at payment of one shilling a day. The Tamar Hotel at Hole's Hole closed in 1903, indicating a shift in the quay's usage. A building behind the road was used for basket making and at one time served as a tea pavilion for steamer passengers who also picnicked in nearby cherry orchards. Early season trippers could enjoy the colourful spectacle of cherry blossom covering the hillsides and the 'carpet of gold' daffodils and Bere Ferrers' own distinctive Double White narcissi.

At Weir Quay and Hole's Hole were the first

The ALEXANDRA and the Hamoaze steamer PRINCE at the Saltash company's Town Pier and pontoon landing. Upstream of the Royal Albert Bridge is the Industrial Training Ship MOUNT EDGCUMBE. The Willoughby built Saltash floating bridge of 1892 is visible behind the pontoon bridge.
ALAN KITTRIDGE COLLECTION.

A rare picture of a passenger steamer at Cargreen, in 1926. She is an Oreston & Turnchapel Steamboat Co Ltd boat, probably the SWIFT. *The 'Bovril Club' was a group of army petty officers who chartered her for the afternoon.* ALAN KITTRIDGE COLLECTION.

of the valley's lime kilns – mostly disused by 1909 – which would be seen at every major quay up to Morwellham. Lime, sand, seaweed, and the euphemistically named 'dock dung' were all used to manure the market gardens and farms. There was no limestone in the Tamar Valley but the Three Towns had it in abundance, so the once ubiquitous Tamar sailing barge developed, transporting produce and goods on the river, always assured of a return cargo of manure.

After the great meander of South Hooe the steamer passed Pentille Quay – an occasional landing place by prior arrangement with the Coryton family of Pentille Castle. The scenery on the Cornish side was more hilly now, passing the strangely named Mount Ararat and Strawberry Hill – which was adjacent to the market steamer quay at Halton. Halton Quay was the market garden distribution centre for St Dominick, St Mellion and the surrounding district and in 1909 its bank of four kilns remained as the only ones in the valley still burning limestone. Beyond the long, wide reach off Halton the beautiful setting of Cotehele Quay was glimpsed across the reed beds. Cotehele was a market steamer landing but excursion steamers could land by special arrangement only.

Once past Cotehele Estate, a sharp turn to the right around Danescombe Bend brought excursionists into the Calstock reach, where a landing was invariably made. It was not unusual

The HIBERNIA *steaming up the River Tamar off Halton Quay.* CITY OF PLYMOUTH MUSEUMS & ART GALLERY.

The EMPRESS, *with the* ALEXANDRA *astern, heads up river, towards Morwellham and Weir Head, in this Fred. J. Paul postcard, taken from the Bere Alston peninsula in 1907.* ALAN KITTRIDGE COLLECTION.

for six or more steamers to be moored at Calstock some evenings – on charter trips and public excursions. Jack Abbot and his young friends could identify a steamer from her paddle beat echoing around the valley, as she steamed around Danescombe Bend. Indeed, I have heard Jack's impressions – although I had to take his word for their authenticity.

A number of writers reminiscing in later years described the scenes at Calstock, George Johnson (jnr):

> At Calstock during the summer boats were met by a host of white aproned dames selling strawberries at twopence a punnet, about a pint of fruit. The punnets were made at Calstock, by hand, at the princely remuneration of one shilling and ninepence a gross.
>
> A character who boarded the boats at Calstock was one William Jane. He exhibited a sort of revolving peep show and an excerpt from his pamphlet reads:
>
> *I am here to give you an interesting exhibition of mineral specimens, with an apparatus, consisting of a great variety, from various parts of the world, collected and arranged by myself, who has been for 52 years a practical miner. This apparatus contains some of the most beautiful and brilliant specimens of the following kinds of minerals: Quicksilver, Diamonds of Tin, Carbonate of Copper, Silver, Lead, Crystalized Antimony, Maleable Copper and a variety of others very interesting. These are not imaginary shadows or pictures without substance, they are realities in their raw state as taken from the bowels of the earth and are remarkable for their great value and worth. The scenes to be exhibited are worthy of the attention of all classes of society. Come and see for yourselves this wonderful Mineralogical Specimen Box.*
>
> Poor old William Jane. He became the butt of the various crews and on one occasion his box of tricks was hoisted to the top of the mast. When, on his return to the boat, he at long last discovered the trick played upon him his remarks had a vividness all of their own.

Alfred Pengelly writing in the 1950s:

> Providing that the sun shone and that the tide was suitable, trippers from Plymouth would call in at Calstock every day on their way to Weir Head. This 'calling-in' was a great help to the folk of Calstock, for there were no cafés or restaurants in our village in 1899.
>
> The housewives would stand on the quay, clad in spotless white aprons and smart frocks awaiting the steamer's arrival, then calling out with varying, nevertheless, equally eager shouts, 'Place for tea! Place for tea!' They would each take a bevy of trippers home for tea and

The HIBERNIA *passing the community of New Quay c1910. The two girls are Fred. J. Paul's daughters. Marjorie – confidently holding the boat steady with the oar – recalled their apprehension as the* HIBERNIA *approached, making a sizeable wash, but her father persuaded them to hold their pose until the last second.* ALAN KITTRIDGE COLLECTION.

The BRUNEL *at Morwellham Quay with a charter party and brass band.*
COURTESY ARTHUR GRYLLS

strawberries and cream. On occasional Saturday evenings hundreds of pleasure-seekers would throng the little Fore Street, of Calstock, spending their diminutive pocket-money mainly on fruit.

Copper mining was finished by 1900 and since the 1880s the principal mining activity in the Tamar Valley was for arsenic which was mined from the walls of failing copper lodes. Towards the end of the nineteenth century Devon Great Consols was producing half the world's arsenic for pesticides and industrial uses. The refined white powder was packed in blue paper lined casks and shipped out from Tamar quays. Devon Great Consols stopped working in 1901 but there was a short revival of arsenic refining in the 1920s.

Granite would be quarried at Pearson's Quarry in Gunnislake until 1914, but the brick boom had ended, although some brick and tile making continued until the 1930s. Near Calstock, across the river at Gawton, bricks had been fired in a circular Hoffmann brick kiln and in 1909 the steamers passed close to this imposing structure and a nearby arsenic calciner – its tall chimney stack positioned high up on the hillside.

The steamer continued, passing the dwindling community of New Quay – which would revive briefly in 1914 to burn its last limestone and subsequently fall derelict; past Morwellham – devoid in 1909 of deep sea shipping but still an active village; past the towering Morwell Rocks – a popular picnic site in the days of the paddlers, particularly when Morwellham was still open as a dock; around the very tight Impham Turn and our Edwardian excursionists were on their last lap. The river was narrow now and the water had been brown for some distance. To borrow a derisory but appropriate phrase from deep sea mariners, the

The HIBERNIA *at Morwellham Quay with a charter party.*
ALAN KITTRIDGE COLLECTION.

The E*LEANOR* *turning at into the lock gates inlet at Weir Head with the* H*IBERNIA* *waiting to do likewise.* F. M. STEVENS COLLECTION CITY OF PLYMOUTH MUSEUMS & ART GALLERY.

Heading down river, after visiting Weir Head, the PRINCE EDWARD *approaches Morwell Rocks in the 1920s.* COURTESY DAWN TAPPER.

steamers were 'ditch crawling' the final yards to the limit of navigation. The five feet deep channel between Morwellham and the canal at Gunnislake was still supposed to be maintained, but lack of dredging caused deterioration of the navigable channel for the large paddlers. It is said that the steamers dragged chains astern to help scour the river bed, although it seems more likely they were dragging anchors or weights to help check their heading amidst the vigorous flood of a spring tide – which can fill the river above Calstock with startling speed. Fleet rivalries were put to one side when opposing paddlers passed each other on the final stretches to the weir. One witness observed:

> Pre 1914 and up to say 1925, the paddle boats could go right up to Weir Head on a flowing tide and it was then possible for two boats to pass one another on the final stretch of the river near the lock and the next bend in the river. The river has silted up so much that this would not be possible today, but I remember one occasion when I was on the Brunel and, having turned at the Head we passed the Alexandra quite easily a few hundred yards downstream. The Alexandra would have measured some 35 feet across the sponsons, and the Brunel a shade more.

Long 'quant' poles were used to help pivot the paddle steamers around in the shallow water at Weir Head (and on the mud banks in Millbrook Lake). These huge poles were approximately four inches wide and over twenty feet long with a forked end to dig into the mud. Care needed to be exercised to avoid leaving the pole firmly embedded in the mud while the deck of the steamer moved away.

Twenty four miles inland, lost amongst the trees and undergrowth with the river reflecting the hue of the greenery around, the head of navigation stood out as a shot of white water, rushing over the step of Weir Head. What an extraordinary sight for the unsuspecting visitor amongst this sylvan scenery of water meadows and river banks – to be suddenly confronted with one or two 125 feet long paddle steamers, each loaded with around 400 excited excursionists. And, once their well practiced procedure for turning had been completed to an accompaniment of engine room bell signals and skippers' commands, back down river they went, the human and mechanical noises gradually fading into the distance, while river and observer alike regained their composure and proceeded quietly on their way.

COASTAL EXCURSIONS

In addition to river trips, the immediate coastline of Devon and Cornwall and the Eddystone Lighthouse also offered excursion opportunities aboard a number of coastal steamers which ran from the Three Towns. It was during the 1870s that a tradition of coastal excursions from Millbay Docks was established by the ocean liner tenders based there. The GWR tenders never suffered any prolonged competition for their coastal excursion business – they outclassed most of the occasional interlopers and outlasted all of them. But, for over a quarter of a century, 'Saltash' steamers offered an alternative coastal programme and in 1895 some directors of the STT&DSCo.Ltd were involved in the only serious bid to eclipse the tenders, with the purpose built coastal paddle steamer *Plymouth Belle*.

The GWR's summer excursion programme was initially managed by A. E. Rowe, and profits helped subsidise the tenders' running costs. They ran to the River Yealm 'landing for two hours at the romantic villages of Newton and Noss'. Excursions were also operated further afield to Salcombe, Looe, Fowey and to Mevagissey – which was to become one of the most popular coastal destinations before the Great War. Since the earliest days the tenders offered frequent excursions to view the Eddystone Rocks and lighthouse – establishing a tradition for evening cruises that survived until the 1960s.

The Tamar paddler *Alexandra* gained a certificate for trips outside the Breakwater to the River Yealm and – 'circumstances permitting' – to visit the Eddystone. Following her alterations in 1891, the *Princess Royal* gained a certificate to visit ports along the Devon and Cornwall coast between Salcombe and Mevagissey. She also ventured as far as Torquay and Falmouth on occasions such as Naval Reviews or regattas, but no passengers were carried *en-route*, public excursions or charters were undertaken on arrival. Edward Gill, while serving as a stoker aboard the *Princess Royal*, recalled one foggy evening in 1910 returning from a Naval Review at Torquay. No passengers were aboard but as the fog became thicker a crabbing boat was encountered off Bolt Head and a deal was struck for pilotage into the safety of Salcombe harbour in return for towing the crab boat. Edward Gill landed to telephone his wife about the delay but found a postcard of the *Princess Royal* on sale at the post office and sent that

The GWR tender SIR RICHARD GRENVILLE *at Mevagissey, c1909. Ahead lies the* ALEXANDRA *of the St Mawes Steam Tug & Passenger Co Ltd, she was later purchased by W. J. Reynolds of Torpoint, but used solely as a tug.* ALAN KITTRIDGE COLLECTION.

The ALEXANDRA *at the mouth of the River Yealm, with the Great Mewstone and Wembury Bay beyond.* ALAN KITTRIDGE COLLECTION.

The ALBERT and the PRINCESS ROYAL at the Promenade Pier c1910. Both steamers undertook coastal excursions. ROYAL INSTITUTION OF CORNWALL

The unpopular BANGOR CASTLE pictured before her time at Plymouth. ALAN KITTRIDGE COLLECTION.

instead. The steamer continued on her way in the morning. An unusual public excursion was run by the *Princess Royal* annually to Bigbury Bay, Burgh Island and up the River Avon to Bantham, landing for 1½ hours. These excursions caused some excitement locally and many years later Mrs Daisy Cole of Bantham recalled 'the yearly arrival of the steamer from Plymouth that came in on a Sunday and anchored at Bantham Quay where her passengers disembarked'.

The Saltash steamer *Albert* was also used for coastal excursions, visiting the River Yealm and Mevagissey.

Seemingly the most unpopular coastal paddler to ply from Plymouth was the 246tg *Bangor Castle*. She was originally launched as the *Palmerston* in 1866 and found her way to Plymouth twenty eight years later. She was owned by the Plymouth Excursion Co Ltd and Captain Samuel Vincent took command. The *Bangor Castle* was both old fashioned and austere, especially when compared to the local favourite *Princess Royal* – her main competitor for the sea front coastal excursion trade. That the Three Towns public preferred the latter steamer is illustrated by an incident that occurred on 9 June 1895. The *Bangor Castle* arrived at Salcombe, not unusually less than full. However the *Princess Royal* added insult to injury by following them into harbour so overloaded that her paddle sponsons were 'in the water'. A police sergeant waited at the harbour to count the *Princess Royal's* passengers off, later explaining that 'it was in consequence of a communication made by the officers of the *Bangor Castle* that he decided to interfere'. The engineers of the *Bangor Castle* readily

The PRINCESS ROYAL *landing passengers at Town Quay, Fowey, on Regatta Day c1910. This unflattering view of the Saltash steamer highlights her rather shapeless lines – a simple 'U' section hull, devoid of any flare in the bows and with little sheer to her decks.*
ALAN KITTRIDGE COLLECTION.

volunteered to help the sergeant's count, when it was discovered that the *Princess Royal* carried fifty passengers too many. At the subsequent Kingsbridge Petty Sessions the *Princess Royal's* captain was fined lightly (£5. 10s), the magistrate observing that 'there was evidence of a little jealousy between the crews'.

Captain Vincent didn't go out of his way to increase the *Bangor Castle's* popularity. Later in 1895 the paddler arrived at Fowey twenty minutes behind schedule, so the captain decided to reduce the landing time by half an hour. Unfortunately not all the trippers were informed and after a last minute scramble at departure time, ten passengers were left stranded on the quayside. The anxious parents of two girls included in the unhappy group pleaded with Captain Vincent to return to pick up their daughters but he refused. The stranded party were eventually rescued by a tug skipper who was returning to Plymouth. Captain Vincent plodded on regardless for a few more years but in 1899, in need of essential reboilering and repairs, the *Bangor Castle* was sent to Turnchapel where she was broken up.

It was not unusual in the 1890s to find the GWR liner tenders from Millbay Docks – *Sir Francis Drake*, *Smeaton* and *Sir Richard Grenville* – joined by the *Princess Royal* and *Bangor Castle* offering excursions variously to Salcombe, Bigbury Bay, Looe, Polperro, Fowey, Charlestown, Mevagissey, Dodman Point and, of course, to the Eddystone. However these coastal trips suffered their share of bad weather. In 1895, while returning a party of excursionists to

The ALBERT *at the inside landing steps of the South Pier of the Outer Harbour at Mevagissey c1910 with the St Mawes Steam Tug & Passenger Co Ltd's* PRINCESS MAY *astern, at the outside steps.* ROY STRIBLEY COLLECTION.

The PLYMOUTH BELLE *leaving Penzance. Judging from her 'dressed' appearance (i.e. all the flags) this might be her maiden departure from the port on Saturday 13 July 1895 en-route to Falmouth, Plymouth, Torquay and the Channel Islands.* GRAHAME FARR COLLECTION COURTESY NIGEL COOMBES.

Mevagissey after a visit to Plymouth Races, the *Princess Royal* encountered heavy seas and was forced to seek shelter in Fowey Harbour, where both the passengers and crew endured the entire night aboard. In the same storm even Captain Vincent put *Bangor Castle* into shelter at Looe, joined temporarily by the *Sir Richard Grenville*. However, the tender's primary function was attending liners at Plymouth and although many of her passengers were seasick the *'Grenville* put to sea again and battled home regardless.

THE PLYMOUTH BELLE

On 2 July 1895 a large party of Plymothians cruised in perfect weather on the Firth of the Forth. The event marked the delivery trial of the magnificent new ocean going paddler *Plymouth Belle* (654tg, 220.5 x 26.3 x 9.1 feet). Her owners were the Plymouth Belle Steamship Co Ltd, an operating company set up by its Managing Director, William Dusting. Local newspapers initially credited her ownership to the STT&DSCo.Ltd, for which Dusting was the General Manager. Indeed, further close links are indicated by the running of STT&DSCo.Ltd steamers to link with the *Plymouth Belle* at the Promenade Pier.

The *Plymouth Belle*, built by J. Scott & Co of Kinghorn, was an exceptionally beautiful steamer incorporating some of the very latest design features. Her promenade deck ran almost the entire length of the ship, the main deck being entirely plated in. Lifeboats were supplied for each of her maximum 1,350 passengers. She drew 9 feet of water and was fitted with a bow rudder. Her 232hp, two cylinder, compound, diagonal engines were also built by Scotts.

An invited compliment of passengers for her maiden voyage on 9 July 1895 cruised around the Eddystone Rocks. Her first fare paying cruise, the following day, visited Dartmouth to land passengers for one hour. The remainder of the week was filled with trips to Fowey, Mevagissey, Falmouth, Start Point, Torquay and 'Moonlit' Eddystone excursions. At least one trip was run from Torquay to Plymouth and Falmouth and across to the Isles of Scilly, returning from Penzance the following day. On Saturday 13 July she inaugurated her regular weekend feature. Departing from Penzance and calling at Falmouth, Plymouth and Torquay she crossed the Channel to visit Guernsey and Jersey, arriving back in the westcountry the following Monday. This basic pattern of sailings continued throughout the year, until her last trip of the season when an extended weekend excursion was offered from Plymouth to Penzance and the Isles of Scilly.

The *Western Daily Mercury* had carried an air of enthusiasm throughout the season, even shortening her name to a more endearing 'Belle' and placing a reporter aboard for one weekend trip to Jersey and St. Malo. It therefore came as a surprise the following season when *Plymouth Belle* was chartered to R. R. Collard of Newhaven, commanded by Captain Trennance, ex-skipper of the *Aerial* and *Empress* (Captain Trennance remained on the South Coast, later commanding the excursion steamer *Brighton Queen* of 1897. After serving in the Royal Navy during the Great War Captain Trennance returned to the Tamar Valley to establish a market garden). The *Plymouth Belle* completed two seasons of South Coast excursions before eventual sale to the Hamburg America Line for use as a tender at Cuxhaven, appropriately renamed *Willkommen*.

The American Line and the London & South Western Railway inaugurated improved liner passenger facilities at Ocean Quay, Stonehouse on 9 August 1904, when the L&SWR's 704tg steel twin screw steamer *Victoria* ferried passengers and mail from the American Line's *St Louis*, which anchored in Cawsand Bay. (The railway company had previously chartered the *Princess Royal* as a tender to Union Line ships from South Africa). The L&SWR's 'magnificent screw steamship' *Victoria*, was also available for trips to land at Dartmouth and Torquay or Fowey and Falmouth. Needless to say most evening and short trips visited the Eddystone. Many in the Three Towns were unfamiliar with the newly developed area on the Devonport side of Stonehouse Pool, so advertisements instructed 'passengers arriving by Plymouth, Stonehouse & Devonport Tramways Company tramcars alight at Richmond Walk'. The *Victoria* was replaced in 1907 by a purpose built 577tg steel screw steamer named *Atalanta*. The new tender continued to offer a regular excursion programme from Ocean Quay until 1910 when the L&SWR closed the ocean passenger facility as part of a wider operating agreement with the GWR.

The popularity of coastal excursions at this time can be gauged from advertisements which appeared in July 1910. The GWR offered the *Antelope* and *Lynx* (both temporarily transferred from Weymouth); *Sir Francis Drake* and *Sir Walter Raleigh* (new 478tg steel screw tenders of 1908); *Sir Richard Grenville; Smeaton;* and the paddle steamer *Helper* (ex *Sir Francis Drake* – the GWR's original tender); on trips to Looe, Fowey,

The WILLKOMMEN*, ex-* PLYMOUTH BELLE*, on the River Elbe c1900.* COURTESY E. C. B. THORNTON.

Falmouth and Eddystone. The L&SWR operated the *Atalanta* to Dartmouth and Torquay while the *Princess Royal* visited Salcombe and Eddystone.

In 1911 The GWR tender fleet at Millbay comprised of four screw steamers: the *Smeaton*, *Sir Richard Grenville, Sir Francis Drake* and the *Sir Walter Raleigh*. The only alternative to their virtual monopoly of local coastal excursions was still being provided by the *Albert* and the ever popular *Princess Royal*.

The GWR's SIR FRANCIS DRAKE *or* SIR WALTER RALEIGH *of 1908 off the Jubilee Steps, Salcombe. The idea behind the enormous funnel was to clear the superstructure of liners they were attending. The 'DRAKE's and 'RALEIGH's funnels were later shortened.* COURTESY L. FAIRWEATHER

Following the amalgamation of the Saltash, Three Towns & District Steamboat Co Ltd and the Plymouth Promenade Pier & Pavilion Co Ltd as the Plymouth Piers, Pavilion & Saltash Three Towns Steamboat Co Ltd in 1910, the Saltash steamers finally gained permanent access to the Promenade Pier. With the exception of the PRINCE EDWARD *the company's fleet of paddlers arrive and depart. From left to right:* ALEXANDRA, LADY ERNESTINE *(a rare visitor to Plymouth Sound),* EMPRESS *making her way to the River Yealm, the* PRINCESS ROYAL *and the* ELEANOR. *Excursionists bought their steamer tickets from the round kiosk, which also gained them admission to the pier.*
COURTESY DAWN TAPPER

PYRRHIC VICTORY

While Edwardian steamer passengers of the Three Towns district benefited from cheap prices and a profusion of steamers, the competition between the Saltash and Millbrook companies was damaging both. The Millbrook Steamboat Company was wholly owned by John Parson and documented evidence regarding his financial position at this time is not in the public domain. However, local memory suggests that Parson never recovered financially from his one-man war against the Saltash company. Meanwhile, at Saltash, the arrival of Parson's *Brunel* towards the end of 1909 seems to have prompted W. H. Gilbert of Maida Vale, London, to sell out his family's remaining interests in the STT&DSCo.Ltd before the next season commenced. Most of these shares were purchased by William C. Leader Lieut RN – a STT&DSCo.Ltd director since 1906. On 9 February 1910 the Board of Directors proposed liquidation of the STT&DSCo.Ltd. An Agreement was reached with the board of the Plymouth Promenade Pier & Pavilion Co Ltd (which was also struggling financially) to amalgamate their interests and the *Albert, Alexandra, Eleanor, Empress, Lady Ernestine, Prince, Prince Edward, Princess Royal* and the tug *Victoria*, were each sold to the PPP&PCo.Ltd on 27 April 1910. The base for the fleet remained at Saltash and the public at large discerned little change but the pier company now controlled the STT&DSCo.Ltd fleet and its landing places. On the Sea Front the Saltash steamers immediately

The ALEXANDRA *at the Promenade Pier.*
ALAN KITTRIDGE COLLECTION.

The Millbrook Steamboat Company's annual opportunity to tender for landing rights at the Promenade Pier was withdrawn by the new the Plymouth Piers, Pavilion & Saltash Three Towns Steamboat Co Ltd in 1910 and the Millbrook steamers were banished to the Princess Royal Pontoon in Millbay Docks. This turn of events forced John Parson to negotiate an operating agreement with the new Plymouth Piers, Pavilion & Saltash Three Towns Steamboat Co Ltd. The HIBERNIA *(left) and the* BRUNEL *are pictured at the Princess Royal Pontoon in 1910. The GWR's tender* SMEATON *is moored at Millbay Pier on the left.*
COURTESY JACK KINGSTON.

supplanted the Millbrook Steamboat Company at the Promenade Pier, indeed they monopolised the Sea Front, as the pier company now owned both the Promenade and West Hoe piers. John Parson quickly reached agreement with the GWR at Millbay Docks for landing rights at their Princess Royal pontoon. Later in the year sanction was given by the Registrar of Companies to change the PPP&PCo.Ltd's name to the Plymouth Piers Pavilion & Saltash Three Towns Steamboat Co Ltd (PPP&STTSCo.Ltd) with W. C. Leader as its new Managing Director. (Although PPP&STTSCo.Ltd was the pier company's new name, the steamers had been sold earlier in the year while it was still the PPP&PCo.Ltd and no correction ever seems to have been made to subsequent Mercantile Navy Lists or the Lloyds Register). Parson could at last have claimed the accomplishment of his threat to drive the STT&DSCo.Ltd off the river but it was a Pyrrhic victory, he found himself at such a disadvantage, hidden away in Millbay Docks, that a truce with the new PPP&STTSCo.Ltd was sought.

On 8 April 1911 the PPP&STTSCo.Ltd and John Parson signed a seven year agreement. The pier company agreed to stop running steamers in Millbrook Lake, or to charter any steamers for the same purpose. In return Parson agreed to stop running steamers to the Yealm, or any destination east of the Mewstone and also agreed to stop running public trips to Cawsand Bay (between Picklecombe Point and Penlee Point).

Minimum public excursion fares were to be:

	Single	Return
Plymouth or Devonport to Weir Head	1s 0d	1s 6d
Plymouth or Devonport to Calstock	10d	1s 3d
Saltash to Weir Head	10d	1s 3d
Saltash to Calstock	8d	1s 0d
Plymouth to Mount Edgcumbe	3d	4d
Plymouth to Saltash	4d	6d
Devonport to Saltash	2d	4d
Four Rivers, Three Rivers, Circular	1s 0d	
Evening trips to St Germans, Pentille	9d	

The companies also agreed some minimum charter fares: On Sundays, Wednesdays and Saturdays no less than 6d per head/per day; 5¼d per half day; and 3d for an evening trip. The minimum fares for the remaining days (Tuesday, Thursday and Friday) were 5¼d, 4½d and 2½d respectively. They agreed to notify each other of their public excursion timetables and prevent duplication by alternating their programme. The seven year agreement would never run its course, being interrupted by the Great War. Before that the 'Saltash' fleet enjoyed four successful years, once more restored to its position as the foremost river steamer fleet in the district. During this period the only change to the two fleets was the sale of the tug *Victoria* by the PPP&STTSCo.Ltd in 1914, to new owners in Hull. The Millbrook company struggled on, but two world wars would pass before the Millbrook Steamboat & Trading Co Ltd (the direct descendent of Parson's fleet) could lay claim to being the pre-eminent passenger boat fleet in the district

CHAPTER SEVEN

THE PASSING OF THE PADDLE STEAMERS

Excursion fleets 1914–1939

AMALGAMATION OF THE THREE Towns had been debated at various times for decades. In May 1914 consensus was finally reached and the County Borough of Plymouth absorbed the County Borough of Devonport and the Urban District of Stonehouse. Over half a century would elapse, however, before the old 'Three Towns' name faded away.

Industry in the Tamar Valley declined further during 1914. New Quay burned its last lime and the community was subsequently abandoned. In Calstock Pearson's granite quarry closed. The once thronging river and industrious Tamar Valley was retreating into isolation, soon to be virtually forsaken by visitors from the 'Three Towns'. During the first year of the Great War river excursions continued as before but as increasing numbers were encouraged to enlist in the armed forces both the steamer crews and excursion parties steadily declined.

Saltash steamers laid up off the Gas Works in the 1920s. From left to right: the LADY ERNESTINE – dismasted and disused for five years or more, this is one of the last photographs she appeared in; the ALEXANDRA – seemingly in a poor condition; and the relatively presentable PRINCE EDWARD. This was a regular winter lay up berth for Saltash steamers. ALAN KITTRIDGE COLLECTION.

REQUISITIONED

War was declared on Germany and her allies on 4 August 1914 and the PPP&STTSCo.Ltd's *Albert* was immediately hired as a tug by the Admiralty. The *Princess Royal* was the next to be pressed into naval service on 23 June 1915, when she was chartered for harbour duty at Rosyth naval base. In spring 1916 a large number of British river paddlers, tugs etc were purchased by the War Office for service with the Inland Water Transport Service of the Royal Engineers of the Mesopotamia Expeditionary Force. The reinforcements were to help secure lines of communication and prepare for an attack on Baghdad in 1917. Together with nine or ten other ex-LCC paddlers the *Brunel* was purchased in 1916. The muster and departure point was Fowey, where steamers were either towed in batches or made their own way to Basra. Some of these steamers were specially adapted as ambulances, but the *Brunel* was listed as a tug, PT24, and fitted with a fixed awning and a wheelhouse. The *Cornubia* was hired in the same year for use as a fleet tender at Devonport Dockyard. The *Hibernia* was also chartered as a fleet tender in 1916 but was sent to the other end of the British Isles, to Scapa Flow in the Orkney Islands – the wartime anchorage of the Grand Fleet. In 1917 the *Alexandra* was chartered as a fleet tender and followed the *Princess Royal* to Rosyth.

By 1916 the MSCo fleet was reduced to just two steamers, the *Devonia* and the *Britannia*, which calls to question reports that the *Devonia* was scrapped at the end of the same year. Whatever the timing or circumstances of her demise, the *Devonia* never re-appeared on passenger or any other service after the war. The *Britannia*, now fitted with a wheelhouse, continued on the Millbrook Ferry throughout the war. The ferry timetable for 1916 lists some changes to landings on the Devonport side, introduced to serve dockyard workers, with calls made at: Mutton Cove for South Yard and the shipbuilding slipways; North Corner for South Yard and Morice Yard Ordnance Depot; and Pottery Quay for Keyham Steam Yard and the North Yard Extension.

The Limekilns at Halton Quay burned the last limestone in the Tamar Valley in 1916 (for increased wartime agriculture) but the *Empress* continued to call and maintained the market service from Calstock throughout the war.

RETURNED IN A DAMAGED CONDITION

Following the Armistice of November 1918 steamer services of the Plymouth district slowly returned to normal. Steamers were returned to civilian ownership, usually with an agreed cash lump sum – for repair, replacement or as compensation. The *Alexandra* arrived back from Rosyth in 1919 in such poor condition that sky could be seen through holes in her funnel. She

The PRINCESS ROYAL *at Town Pier pontoon, Saltash in the early 1920s.*
ALAN KITTRIDGE COLLECTION.

was taken to Rogers & Co. (Shipbuilders) Ltd's Cremyll Yard and replated, refitted and overhauled. Both the *Alexandra* and *Princess Royal* had originally boasted elaborate Victorian decor, including panelled bulkheads and plush velvet seating, but their post war refits proved more utilitarian with unpanelled bulkheads and slatted seating. However, the *Alexandra* gained a certificate to visit ports between the limits of the Eddystone Lighthouse, Salcombe and Mevagissey, having previously been limited to the Eddystone, Yealm and Looe. Unfortunately she broke down with paddle wheel trouble on her first trip since the war, *en-route* to the River Yealm on Whitsun Bank Holiday in 1920. At the same time, thousands of miles away on the River Tigris, the *Brunel* was sold to the Mesopotamian Corporation, never to return to Great Britain.

After the war Plymouth College student, Bernard Williams, saw the *Cornubia* lying out of service on the mud at Southdown. In February 1921 the MSCo offered her for sale to O&TSCo.Ltd who purchased her for £325 later in the year. They took out her boiler in March 1922 as a replacement for the *Rapid's* and the *Cornubia* subsequently disappeared from records. A 'small paddle steamer' spotted by an anonymous observer laid up off Saltash in 1922, would appear to have been the redundant Millbrook Ferry paddler *Lady Ernestine*, which was withdrawn early in the war (or before) and never returned to service.

The *Hibernia* returned to excursion service in 1921 and, judging from one post war photograph, some replacement or alteration to her paddle boxes and sponsons were made during her refit. In October 1922, during the Irish civil war, the *Hibernia* was chartered by the Cork, Blackrock & Passage Railway to ply between Cobh and quays at Cork, until the railway between Monkstown Pier and Cork reopened after the civil war. She returned to Plymouth in April 1923.

The year 1923 saw the demise of the 54 year old paddle steamer *Eleanor* – the one time 'dry' boat, the favourite of Temperance organisations. The *Eleanor* was the last paddler with direct links to the earliest days of the river steamers, having been in William Gilbert's Saltash & Devonport Steamboat Company fleet in the 1860s, contemporary with the likes of the *Gipsy* and the *Fairy*.

She made her way to the breakers yard in the company of the Saltash to Devonport steamer *Prince*. The Hamoaze steamer service she once provided had been largely superseded by improved tram services between Saltash Passage and Devonport. For two more seasons the remaining 'Saltash' steamers *Prince Edward, Empress, Princess Royal* and *Alexandra* plied their

The ALEXANDRA *at Looe in the 1920s passing the GWR's* SIR FRANCIS DRAKE *or* SIR WALTER RALEIGH. *Unlike the GWR steamers, which had to anchor off the Banjo Pier, the* ALEXANDRA'S *shallow draught enabled her to go alongside the pier, saving her passengers time and a penny each way to the local boatmen.*
ALAN KITTRIDGE COLLECTION.

usual routes. Few in the Tamar Valley could remember or even imagine a summer without their presence on the river. But the end was near, four years after the *Eleanor* was scrapped the entire 'Saltash' fleet vanished from the rivers and lakes of the 'Three Towns'. One event in particular sealed the fate of the remaining PPP&STTSCo.Ltd paddle steamers – the coal dispute of 1926. But a major contributing factor leading up to the fateful event was the proliferation of motor buses after the Great War.

CHAR-A-BANCS

The Great War generated improvements in road transport and advanced the development of internal combustion engines. By the end of the war many ex-servicemen had driving and mechanical experience. Plymouth Corporation bought its first motor-bus fleet – twenty Straker Squires – in 1921 and A. C. Turner's Tours of Plymouth acquired their first 'char-a-banc' around the same time – a 28 seat Karrier with solid tyres, folding hood and oil lamps. Other char-a-banc fleets were established immediately after the war, including the Plymouth Co-operative Society (15 char-a-bancs purchased in 1919) and Embankment Motors. Princess Square in the town centre of Plymouth became the haunt of the owner-operators and their evocatively named char-a-bancs: *Lorna Doone,*

In this 1926 postcard view the PRINCE EDWARD *(left),* EMPRESS *– having lost her market trade, and the* ALEXANDRA*, are alongside the Promenade Pier. Offshore (just to the left of the pier) is the Plymouth Piers, Pavilion & Saltash Three Towns Steamboat Co Ltd's only motor vessel, the* LADY ELIZABETH*. Heading towards the River Tamar is the Millbrook Steamboat Company's* BRITANNIA *with a Tamar barge in tow.* ALAN KITTRIDGE COLLECTION.

Golden Ray, Violet Tours, Princess Tours, Glider and *Come With Me*. Competition for passengers was intense and drivers would sometimes place friends and relatives in the buses to make them look more popular. In east Cornwall three bus operators, namely Skinner's, E. S. Haddy and the Millbrook Steamboat Company, competed for passengers on the Rame Peninsula.

The PPP&STTSCo.Ltd, meanwhile, viewed this enthusiasm for road transport and its competition for day trippers with trepidation. Plymouth Promenade Pier was already viewed as old fashioned and run-down – even seedy, while the paddle steamers, so familiar to Plymothians, were well past their Victorian prime. Many trippers had seen the district's rivers time and time again, so the prospect of a day out in a char-a-banc offered new and exciting alternatives. An additional benefit of the char-a-bancs was their availability for hire by small parties to go wherever, whenever they wanted.

Typical of new competition for day trippers after the war was Eddystone Motors of W. Coath & Son, who ran excursions and maintained stage services to Plymstock.
ALAN KITTRIDGE COLLECTION.

Another post war trend was for a day out swimming and sunbathing at one of the district's many surrounding beaches. Nearby was Bovisand and Wembury in the South Hams, and in east Cornwall the ever popular Cawsand Bay and the spectacular sweep of Whitsand Bay which included the big sandy beaches at Tregonhawke, Freathy and Tregantle. Wagonettes and buses on the Rame Peninsula met ferries at Cremyll and Millbrook to take passengers to Whitsand Bay. At Cawsand the *Prince Edward* still called but remained anchored offshore while boats ferried passengers to the beach. In the 1920s diesel engined passenger launches, running from the Barbican, Sea Front, Stonehouse Pool, the Devonport landings and Saltash, started taking day trippers right onto the beaches at Bovisand, Cawsand and Kingsand. Diesel engined passenger launches, crewed by just two men, also started appearing on the local rivers. The message could not have been lost on the directors of the pier company – their expensively crewed, ageing, coal fired, paddle steamers were looking sadly out of date and their worth as assets of the company had declined to scrap value.

The ALEXANDRA coming alongside a ship in Plymouth Sound in the 1920s, presumably to land passengers for a visit. An O&TSCo.Ltd steamer also approaches in the background.
KEN SAUNDERS COLLECTION.

A post-war postcard of Cawsand Bay – which was postally used in 1923. The PRINCE EDWARD is anchored offshore. Local fishermen earned extra money ferrying passengers ashore from visiting steamers. Within five years of this photograph the PRINCE EDWARD was scrapped and her place on the Cawsand Bay run was taken over by a multitude of diesel engined motor launches. ALAN KITTRIDGE COLLECTION.

The ALEXANDRA turning at Weir Head in 1927 – two of her crewmen are using quant poles to help bring her around. Meanwhile two launches – possibly the TAMAR QUEEN and the PRINCESS – are manoeuvring with ease at the lock gates of the Tamar Manure Navigation. By the 1920s the channel of the Tamar Manure Navigation, which extended from Morwellham to Gunnislake, was no longer being dredged, making it even more difficult for the surviving paddle steamers to reach Weir Head. The weir is the line of white, in the river above the steamer's fore deck. ALAN KITTRIDGE COLLECTION.

The PRINCE EDWARD *in September 1927, her last month in service. The captain is believed to be Albert Watts, who rarely wore a jacket due to the effort needed to steer the paddler.*
B. Y. WILLIAMS.

COAL DISPUTE

A national financial crisis led to the withdrawal of a subsidy the Government had granted the coal industry in 1921. So in April 1926 the mine owners locked the miners out until they agreed a cut in wages and harder working conditions. In May the General Council of the Trades Union Congress called a National Strike in support of the miners. The strike only lasted for ten days but the miners remained locked out until November, by which time huge quantities of more expensive foreign coal was being imported. The regular ferry services at Saltash, Torpoint and Cremyll were permitted to continue using coal throughout the dispute. Likewise regular steamer services including the *Britannia* on the Millbrook Ferry; O&TSCo.Ltd steamers on the Plym; the *Kitley Belle* on the Yealm; and the *Empress* on her market day service; could burn coal. But all other steamers remained laid up until foreign coal became readily – but expensively – available in July.

Halton Quay was purchased by the Plymouth Co-operative Society in 1918 from where the Society's own river barges served their produce warehouse in Sutton Harbour. By the mid-1920s Kelly Bray – the Southern Railway station (ex PD&SWJR) near Callington – had become the district's principal agricultural supply depot. In 1926, with the agricultural trade at Halton Quay in decline, the PPP&STTSCo.Ltd failed to renew their landing rights. Reduced market day trade and loss of the Halton Quay call made continued year round operation of an expensive coal-fired market steamer uneconomic and the *Empress* was withdrawn. Her skipper, Bill Worth, left to establish his own market boat service so 'Billy' Skelton commanded the *Empress* for the remainder of the season.

Both the *Alexandra* and the *Prince Edward* remained laid up until 1 July 1926 when they recommenced excursion services. The *Empress* too was put on excursion service running to both Cawsand and the Yealm, advertised as 'The Calstock Steamer Empress'.

THE PADDLERS ARE SCRAPPED

At the end of September 1926 the *Empress* was laid up for the first time in her life, as she no longer ran the market service which had been year-round. She remained at her Saltash moorings off the Gas Works throughout the following year. The *Princess Royal* – which had been laid up since the end of the 1925 season – never returned to service but lay at her moorings throughout 1926 and 1927. The *Prince Edward* returned for a full season in 1927, running to Cawsand, Calstock and Weir Head. The *Alexandra* too returned for 1927, running to the Yealm, Calstock and Weir Head. The Millbrook company returned the *Hibernia* to

A rare post war view of the HIBERNIA, pictured landing passengers by boat at Millbrook. She would appear to have been fitted with new, or different, paddle boxes. ALAN KITTRIDGE COLLECTION.

service in 1927 – the first time since September 1925. All three paddle steamers were laid up, as usual, at the end of September, but for the last time. During the winter of 1927-8 the *Princess Royal, Alexandra, Prince Edward* and the screw steamer *Albert* were sold for scrap. The three paddlers were spotted lying at a scrapyard in Cattedown that winter by Bernard Williams (then working for the GWR in Devonport). The *Hibernia* was also sold for scrap and was broken up, probably in Stonehouse, during 1928. The *Empress*, the sole remaining paddle steamer of the Saltash fleet, remained at her moorings off Saltash in 1928 – 'for use if traffic justified' – but she never entered service again. However, she was saved from the scrap yard and sold as a houseboat to be moored on the River Yealm. Her registry was not closed until 27 August 1931. Edgar Foster of Newton Ferrers was a part time caretaker of a number of summer houseboats on the Yealm and recalled that the owners of the *Empress* were two retired schoolmasters, brothers with the surname of Gilbert. On the Millbrook Ferry the *Britannia* continued to ply the choppy waters of the Hamoaze as the sole surviving Three Towns district paddle steamer.

The EMPRESS laid up off Saltash in September 1927. She had been there since the end of September 1926, never to enter service again. B. Y. WILLIAMS.

Given the financial problems of both the PPP&STTSCo.Ltd and the MSCo, the age of their steamers, the sudden rise in the price of coal, and competition from char-a-bancs, the demise of the paddle steamers was inevitable. The final nail in their coffin, however, must have been the proliferation of comparatively cheap to run motor launches after the war. River excursions were still an attractive alternative to char-a-banc trips and the lives of both the *Hibernia* and the *Prince Edward* might well have been prolonged, but by 1927 there were already at least ten licenced motor boats competing for passengers on the very same river excursions.

THE TAMAR TRANSPORT COMPANY

When the *Empress'* market service closed in 1926 her skipper, Bill Worth, left the PPP&STTSCo.Ltd and started a market service in partnership with the agricultural merchant Gideon Spear, trading as the Tamar Transport Company (TTCo). Spear owned landing rights at most of the Tamar quays, a legacy from the lime burning days of Messrs Perry & Spear. He had also been a part owner of the paddle steamer *Aerial* and was a shareholder in the STT&DSCo.Ltd. Initially the TTCo operated a Kelvin engined launch named *Aerial*, after the paddle steamer, and another named the *Prince*. They soon acquired two larger, ex-naval motor launches – the *Tamar Queen* and the *Calstock*.

The *Tamar Queen* was a long open motor boat with a closed forepeak. She had a diagonal built wooden hull and a very shallow draught. The crew were Bill Worth and Norman Southey (ex-fireman on the *Empress*). Originally both the *Tamar Queen* and *Calstock* were used mainly as market-cargo boats with the *Tamar Queen* being cleaned out for excursions during the summer – with her jib crane unshipped and buoyant seats fitted. As the market trade declined further the *Tamar Queen* was used full time on excursions and carried 80 passengers. During 1926 and 1927 she was running Four Rivers trips and to Calstock and Weir Head from Phoenix Wharf, North Corner and Pottery Quay. When they ran from Plymouth on consecutive days Bill and Norman slept in the forepeak.

The *Calstock* was soon renamed *Princess*. Similar to the *Tamar Queen* she was a long open motor boat with a closed forepeak and a mast and jib crane forward. Her crew were Charles 'Charlie' Southey, skipper (Charlie had been engineer on the *Empress* and was Norman's father) and Jack Abbott, crewman (whose uncle had also served in the engine room of the *Empress*). The *Princess* was to be the last dedicated market boat. During the late 1920s, when Gawton Quay was briefly re-opened, the *Princess* took casks of arsenic, from Gawton and Greenhill arsenic works, down to the Victoria Wharves in Cattedown for Coast Lines ships to take out. The *Princess* also carried livestock on market days – calves were up-ended and had their legs tied, while the trick with sheep,

Amongst the early motor boats in the district was the Tamar Transport Company's TAMAR QUEEN, *seen here at Morwellham(?) in the late 1920s, with the Young Womens' Club of Gunnislake leaving on a day's charter to Mount Edgcumbe House. Skipper William (Bill) Worth is in the bow, with a quant pole. Nearest the camera is crewman Norman Southey ex-fireman of the* EMPRESS. *The 'box' the young women are sitting on in the stern of the boat is the engine 'room'.* COURTESY R. T. PAIGE.

according to Jack Abbot, was getting the first one aboard. She was mainly used as a cargo boat but was also run in the summer from Pottery Quay to Cawsand with a licence for 70 passengers.

In 1927 the TTCo bought a substantial new vessel, a steel hulled motor boat, the *Tamar Belle* (26tg, 54.1 x 12.2 x 4.8ft) built by H. Gale & Co of Cowes and fitted with a 50hp Atlantic diesel engine. Her flush deck gained her a certificate for Yealm excursions. In 1928 agreement was reached with the O&TSCo.Ltd and the Millbrook Steamboat & Trading Co Ltd (MS&TCo.Ltd, see below) for each company to run their principal excursion boat from the Promenade Pier so, in that year, the *Tamar Belle* departed from the Promenade Pier, North Corner and Pottery Quay. At the end of the following season the TTCo accepted a good offer for the *Tamar Belle* and sold her to the King's Bargemaster in London.

In 1930 the Steer Point 'steamer' *Kitley Belle* was bought by the TTCo from the Hodge family, but she was in a poor condition having been laid up for some time. She was repaired by Rogers & Co (Shipbuilders) Ltd, fitted with an Atlantic diesel engine and renamed *Tamar Belle*.

By 1932 Messrs Spear and Worth wanted to dissolve their partnership and in February unsuccessfully offered to sell the *Tamar Belle*(2), *Tamar Queen* and *Princess* together with their landing rights etc, to the O&TSCo.Ltd for £1000. The partnership subsequently managed to sell the *Tamar Queen* to Exmouth where she was used on the Starcross Ferry until 1954.

The Tamar Transport Company's steel hulled TAMAR BELLE *of 1927 was only in the Plymouth district for three years, being sold to the King's Bargemaster on the Thames at the end of 1929. She is pictured arriving at Putney with her delivery crew: Bill Worth – on the forward deck, leaning over seats; Les Worth – Bill's nephew, later to become a director of the Millbrook Steamboat & Trading Co Ltd; and on the left, Jack Abbot – who stayed in London for a while to overhaul the engine and 'drive' the* TAMAR BELLE *on Thames excursions.* ALAN KITTRIDGE COLLECTION.

Dwarfed by the towering Morwell Rocks is the Tamar Transport Company's second TAMAR BELLE *(ex-*KITLEY BELLE*). She was purchased in 1930 and fitted with an Atlantic diesel engine. She was the last boat to offer a market/produce service from Tamar Quays. Bill Worth kept her after the Tamar Transport Company ceased trading in 1932, until she was sold to the Millbrook Steamboat & Trading Co Ltd in 1942.*
ALAN KITTRIDGE COLLECTION.

On 10 March 1932 the steel paddle steamer *Kenwith Castle* was purchased for £300 by Bill Worth, on his own account. She had been built in 1914 by Willoughby's of Millbay and measured 53.5tg, 80.2 x 13.5 x 4.8 feet. Since 1927 the *Kenwith Castle* and the year round steamer service on the Kingsbridge Estuary that she maintained, had been owned by the GWR but after 1929 she was only used on summer excursions from Salcombe. Jack Abbot recalled taking the *Princess* out towards Bolt Head, to meet Bill Worth who was bringing the *Kenwith Castle* to Plymouth. Jack had previously travelled aboard the paddler when he and the skipper of a trading ketch he was crewing, boarded the steamer at Salcombe with a view to trace the channel to Kingsbridge, thus saving the cost of a pilot – the ketch subsequently went aground. At Plymouth the *Kenwith Castle* ran from Phoenix Wharf to Calstock but proved a huge disappointment when it was found that she was unsuitable for long Tamar trips. She had compound, diagonal engines but was a poor steamer, constantly losing pressure. So bad was the problem that the hapless crew were sometimes forced to stop to raise a sufficient head of steam again. A part of the problem seems to have been the provision of only one fire hole as opposed to customary two in Plymouth district paddlers. Bill Worth was therefore relieved to sell her during the winter of 1932-3 to the MS&TCo.Ltd She was overhauled by Willoughby's, and registered in Plymouth with her new name, *Whitsand Castle*, in April 1933.

Following the demise of the TTCo and the *Kenwith Castle*, Bill Worth established a road transport business at Calstock, but kept the *Tamar Belle*(2) for excursions. During the mid 'thirties she was running from Phoenix Wharf, North Corner, Pottery Quay and Saltash to Calstock calling at Cargreen. She also made some rare calls to Pentille with permission to land to view the grounds. In 1939 the *Tamar Belle*(2) was operating from the Mayflower Steps. She was purchased by the MS&TCo.Ltd during the Second World War and used as a reserve to the ferry steamers, *Armadillo* and *Shuttlecock* – when the Millbrook company took over running the Cremyll Ferry in 1943.

BOVISAND BOATS

The O&TSCo.Ltd was amongst the first of the local passenger boat operators to own a motor launch when, in June 1919, they purchased a 32ft long boat from Devonport Dockyard for £140. They planned to develop a new summer service running to the beach at Bovisand, just around the eastern headland of Plymouth Sound. In October 1921 the company was provisionally granted permission by the C-in-C Devonport Dockyard to land passengers from motor boats at Bovisand Pier. During the following winter the O&TSCo.Ltd installed an Atlantic engine in their launch and prepared her for service in the following spring, she was named *Tiger*. A second 32ft cutter was purchased from the Dockyard in March 1922, she was altered for passenger service, fitted with a diesel engine and named *Hustler*. A five year lease was agreed with the Sutton Harbour Improvement Company in May 1922 for the launches to run from New Quay Jetty in Sutton Harbour. When that lease expired they moved to the Corporation owned Mayflower Steps. Unfortunately, permission to land at Bovisand Pier was soon withdrawn because watermen had taken it as an open invitation and crowded the landing with their own boats. Instead the *Tiger* and the *Hustler* ran onto the beach at Bovisand (similar to Cawsand), but owing to the exposed nature of the bay – facing south west – the launches experienced difficulty getting off the beach and turning in the swell. In October 1922 agreement was reached with the Duchy of Cornwall surveyor to build a landing place on the eastern shore of Bovisand Beach extending from the rocks. The plans were accepted by the Board of Trade and the Admiralty and a 31 year lease was signed in 1923. In 1926 gates and turnstiles were erected at Bovisand so that passengers paid ashore. The local police officer, Richard Badge, recalled cycling from Turnchapel to count the passengers off as the launches were 'regularly overcrowded'. Two years later the landing rights at Bovisand were transferred to the Bovisand Sands & Pier Company (financially connected to directors of the O&TSCo.Ltd), which planned various developments in the area. In 1931 Captain Wilcocks agreed to work the *Hustler* to Bovisand on a three share basis (one share for the owners, one for the crew and one for maintenance and running of the boat). The *Tiger* meanwhile seems to have continued operating with a paid crew – Billy Phillips and his son – and the service continued to be run at half hourly intervals charging 6d each way. The *Hustler* was last mentioned in the O&TSCo.Ltd minutes in 1937 when she was being used as the company's work boat.

CAWSAND BEACH BOATS

Cawsand had been a popular landing place since the earliest years of excursions. Steamers anchored offshore and for a small extra charge passengers were rowed ashore by local boatmen. Latterly, since the 1911 Agreement with the MSCo, the PPP&STTSCo.Ltd more or less had the trade to themselves. But after the Great War the situation altered dramatically, as fleets of motor launches – not party to any such Agreement – started running from various Plymouth district landings to Cawsand Bay, driving their boats right onto the beaches at the twin villages of Cawsand and Kingsand. Although Cawsand Bay was only a short distance beyond the Breakwater, it seemed a world away from Plymouth (as it still does to some degree) – a picturesque Cornish fishing village on Plymouth's doorstep. After the war increasing numbers went to swim in the crystal clear water of the bay and to sunbathe and picnic on the beaches.

Surprisingly the PPP&STTSCo.Ltd were early innovators in the new generation of beach boats with the only motor boat they ever owned. In 1924 the company took delivery of a 50ft motor launch with a covered passenger cabin, built by Mashfords of Saltash. She was named the *Lady Elizabeth*, to commemorate the recent marriage of Lady Elizabeth Bowes-Lyon to the Duke of York. The boat had been designed to visit the increasingly silting channel to Weir Head on ordinary high tides or even neap tides (the lowest high tides), while the paddle steamers were restricted to visiting the head of navigation on spring tides only. The *Lady Elizabeth* was powered by two 20hp Atlantic diesel engines driving twin screws. During the coal dispute of 1926 she was used on 'emergency trips', whilst her coal fired fleet sisters remained laid-up. Advertisements for 1927 show her running regularly to Cawsand from Saltash for one shilling return. Following the demise of the PPP&STTSCo.Ltd as passenger boat operators in 1927 a 'free-for-all' competition developed for the Cawsand trade. The *Lady Elizabeth* was sold to Parson's MS&TCo.Ltd in 1929. Jack Abbot considered her one of the best he had ever handled – until she was converted to single screw in 1949.

Charles Cload, a Ships Chandler on the Barbican in Sutton Harbour, sold supplies to the Mevagissey herring fleet. Included in their number was the Mitchell of Mevagissey built 'tosher' *Westward*, which so impressed Cload that he ordered a 32ft passenger launch from Percy Mitchell. She was duly built, launched in the summer of 1926 and named *Violet* (later renamed *Gweneth*). The *Violet* was towed to Sutton Harbour where Cload fitted the machinery. In the same year a second boat was ordered and built, named the *Speedwell*. The *Violet* and the *Speedwell* ran from the Mayflower Steps to Cawsand Bay, landing on the beaches. In 1934 Cload returned to Mitchell's Portmellon Yard for the first of his locally remembered 'Content' launches, starting with the 50ft *Sweet Content* and followed by the 45ft *Heart's Content* in 1935, the 50ft *Good Intent* in 1937 and the 50ft *Content*, which was on the stocks when the

Charles Cload's first passenger launch, the VIOLET/GWENETH. Cload was the local agent for Kelvin engines and fitted all his launches with Kelvin F4, four cylinder, petrol-paraffin engines (petrol for ignition and paraffin for running). These engines survived at least until the 1960s and Charles Cload's grandson, C. R. Cload, recalled taking paraffin to the launches from the family chandlery on the Barbican.
COURTESY C. R. CLOAD.

Cload's SWEET CONTENT, pictured off Mutton Cove on what would appear to be her maiden trip in 1934, with Charles Cload standing amidships dressed in a dark overcoat and light coloured Homburg hat. COURTESY C. R. CLOAD.

Aboard Cload's passenger launch, the HEART'S CONTENT, pictured at Kingsand in the 1930s. All of Cload's launches were worked on a third share basis – one for the crew, one for the owner and one for the boat (i.e. to recover initial cost and pay for maintenance and running costs etc). Most of the district's 'beach boats' were were worked on the same basis, but the system was open to abuse and regularly caused friction between the crews and owners. COURTESY C. R. CLOAD.

Second World War broke out in 1939 and was completed in the following year. Each of these big open launches were fitted with their Kelvin F4 engines by Cload. The 'Content' launches were a familiar sight at Cawsand right up to the 1960s

Another customer of Percy Mitchell was Jack Worth of Millbrook, Bill Worth's brother. In 1927 Jack Worth ordered a 35ft Kelvin engined launch, the *White Heather*, from Mitchell. She was followed by the 40ft *Silver Star* in 1929 and the 34ft *Pride of the West* in 1930. Each of these launches were used on river excursions or to Cawsand running from Millbrook and the Devonport landing stages – particularly Pottery Quay. Percy Mitchell, his wife and son delivered the 50ft *Guiding Star* in 1933. Fred Lee of Cawsand recalled that the *Guiding Star* was the first boat to carry 100 passengers onto the beach at Cawsand. A fifth launch, the 45ft *Endeavour*, was completed by Mitchell in 1935 and fitted with a Kelvin Ricardo diesel engine. Finally, in 1946, the *Guiding Star* was replaced by a smaller namesake, a 24ft cabin launch, fitted with a Parsons diesel engine. Other boats associated with Jack Worth and his son Les Worth included the *Southern Star, Reliance* and the *Majestic*. Worth's launches also ran to Calstock, St. Germans and even up the River Lynher to view Notter Bridge.

Two unidentified motor boats at Cawsand in the 1930s. These are possibly watermens' boats, licenced by the City of Plymouth to carry up to twelve passengers. Boats like these ran from the Sea Front, Stonehouse Bridge, North Corner and Saltash.
ALAN KITTRIDGE COLLECTION.

There were also Luscombe's boats, the *Rose of Cawsand I* and the *Rose of Cawsand II*. These two launches ran from the slipway adjacent to Stonehouse Bridge to Cawsand and were well remembered by the local children of run-down Stonehouse, because they took them virtually from their back doors to the glorious beaches of Cawsand Bay. The clinker built *Cawsand Belle* also ran from Stonehouse Bridge. Another launch was the *Quick Step*, of which Fred Lee recalls her skipper who didn't like people standing on the seats. There were also the *Morning Star*, *Kiaora* and numerous twelve seater watermen's boats which ran from the old waterman stations at Pebble Beach (between West Hoe Pier and the Promenade Pier), Mutton Cove and North Corner. Two of those from North Corner were the Kelvin engined *Argyle I* and *Argyle II*, owned by the Behennas, a waterman family of Cornwall Beach.

THE MILLBROOK STEAMBOAT & TRADING CO LTD.

After the Great War John Parson's Millbrook Steamboat Company was practically restricted to fulfiling the service indicated in its title, namely maintaining the Millbrook Ferry. The *Hibernia* appeared on excursions in fits and starts until she was finally withdrawn in 1927, while the *Britannia* remained as the only other major unit in the 'fleet'. However, she was assisted on the Millbrook Ferry by two shallow draft motor launches which met the paddler at Southdown at low tide to take passengers up to Anderton or Millbrook. The wooden motor launches were named *Princess Mary* and *Queen*. Each measured about 30ft long and were fitted with an awning. The *New Queen* replaced the *Queen* between 1933 and 1935. The motor boats were also used in the summer months running all the way from North Corner to Millbrook 'for Whitsands'. Another addition to the company in 1919 was a solid tyred Napier char-a-banc allegedly named *Big Ben*, which maintained a service around the Millbrook district linking with the ferry.

The *Hibernia* was withdrawn and scrapped in 1927 and replaced by a modest, more economic, steel motor vessel, the *Manna*. Built in 1922 by Albert Hang of Berlin as the *Marie*, the motor vessel measured 38tg, 61 x 13.4 x 3.6 feet. She was fitted with a 48hp Kamper diesel engine (replaced with an 50hp Atlantic diesel in 1928). It is thought that the *Marie* was claimed by Belgium during the war reparation settlements which followed the Armistice of 1918 and that her new owners had appropriately renamed her *Manna*. In 1926 however her Belgian owners dispensed with their 'miraculous gift' and the *Manna* found her way to Great Yarmouth from where she was inspected and purchased by John Parson. At Plymouth the *Manna* ran Four Rivers excursions from the Promenade Pier and afternoon trips to Calstock – where she would become a familiar sight for the next half a century.

This just about sums up the Millbrook company's activities in the decade after the war, a far cry from the 'red funnel' steamer fleet which had once challenged the Saltash fleet's monopoly. Local memory recalls that John Parson never recovered from the bruising competition and had lost the private means to rebuild the business again. The Millbrook Steamboat Company was, and always had been, John Parson alone, the steamers were wholly owned by him and he was personally liable for the company's finances. It is not surprising

One of the Millbrook Steamboat Company's motor boats, PRINCESS MARY or NEW QUEEN, on Millbrook Lake in the 1930s
ALAN KITTRIDGE COLLECTION

Pictured off Southdown in the 1930s are the Millbrook Steamboat & Trading Co Ltd's two motor vessels: nearest the camera, the LADY ELIZABETH *(ex-Plymouth Piers, Pavilion & Saltash Three Towns Steamboat Co Ltd); and the* MANNA *(renamed* DEVON BELLE *in 1936).* COURTESY ARTHUR GRYLLS.

therefore that on 28 March 1929 the Millbrook Steamboat & Trading Co. Ltd (MS&TCo.Ltd) was incorporated with a nominal capital of £6,000 in £1 shares...

> ...To acquire and take over as a going concern the business of a Steamship and Bus owner and the conveyance of passengers and goods thereby and a dealer in coal, corn and feeding stuffs and also engineers which are now carried on by John Parson of Insworke under the style of the 'Millbrook Steamboat Company'

Parson's personal finances were thus safeguarded at last, but he evidently intended keeping a tight rein on the distribution of shares as the subscribers numbered just two – himself and Francis (Frank) Parson. William T. (Bill) Crawford, son of Capt William H. Crawford of the *Cornubia, Hibernia* and *Brunel*, was appointed as Manager.

The first acquisition of the MS&TCo.Ltd, in 1929 or 1930, was the *Lady Elizabeth*, the last passenger boat of the PPP&STTSCo.Ltd. She was variously used by her new owners and established the short, but popular, Dockyard and Warships trips from the Promenade Pier.

John Parson, owner of the Millbrook Steamboat Company. COURTESY JACK KINGSTON.

John Parson's perseverance in maintaining the Millbrook ferry began to pay dividends. Beaches in the Bovisand, Wembury, Cawsand and Whitsand bays became increasingly popular with bathers and trippers from the Plymouth district after the war, and just as the O&TSCo.Ltd sought to benefit from a monopoly at Bovisand, so too the MS&TCo.Ltd. found themselves well placed as part of the route to Whitsand Bay. In addition, scores of small weekend beach cabins began appearing on the land above the beaches. Between the world wars much of the cliffs between Freathy and Tregonhawke became dotted with these brightly coloured, picket fenced, holiday chalets, each one a unique creation of their proud owners. The chalets generated extra weekend and even week long holiday traffic, complete with the necessary baggage for their stay. Unfortunately for the MS&TCo.Ltd, in Millbrook Frederick Skinner had established a garage and taxi service and was acquiring a fleet of buses to run stage services on the Rame Peninsula. Skinners 'Yellow Coaches' – the 'Yellow Peril' to MS&TCo.Ltd drivers – met each Cremyll ferryboat and on weekends competed for the Whitsand traffic by advertising services to Polhawn and Whitsands.

In his book, *Cornwall's Forgotten Corner*, Tony Carne explains that Richard Willcox, proprietor of the Tea Hut at Withnoe Beach in Whitsand Bay, owned Withnoe Farm across which lay the only direct access from the Withnoe road to Whitsand Bay. Willcox only permitted Skinner's buses to use the road, effectively shutting out conveyances from the Millbrook landings from direct access to Withnoe and Freathy beaches (the military road along the cliff top was not yet a public thoroughfare). This was like showing a red rag to a bull and in 1930 John Parson bought Tregonhawke Farm to construct his own road up to Tregonhawke Cliff, thus establishing the MS&TCo.Ltd's own monopoly of Tregonhawke Beach. The MS&TCo.Ltd then purchased three or four Crossley buses, each named *Whitsand Belle* (suffixed 1-3 [or 4]) and in 1932 bought the *Kenwith Castle* from Bill Worth, her dissatisfied owner, trusting they would have more success with the paddler on the shorter Millbrook ferry route. In the winter of 1932-3 she was overhauled by Willoughby's and registered in Plymouth with her new name, *Whitsand Castle*. The inclusive steamer and bus fare from North Corner to Whitsands was 1s 6d and on weekends the *Whitsand Castle* was met by *Whitsand Belle* buses on every crossing. Jack Kingston of Torpoint recalled that such was the clamour for a return passage in the evening that feigned faintness was regularly employed to jump the queue and on at least one occasion, a well acted total loss of consciousness, willingly carried aboard by accompanying friends. Bernard Williams remembered the Millbrook ferry and bus timetables, printed on coloured paper and bound into small twelve page booklets. They were available in Millbrook and Devonport from newsagents, shops etc. Bernard used them in his capacity as a GWR goods clerk in Devonport where he dispatched goods and packages by carrier to North Corner to be put aboard the first available steamer going all the way to Millbrook (as opposed to changing boats at Southdown).

After only two seasons – 1933 and 1934 – the *Whitsand Castle* was sold in May 1935 to run

Following on from their success with the 'Whitsand Belle' buses the Millbrook Steamboat & Trading Co Ltd enlarged their bus fleet with a number of additional vehicles to connect villages and beaches on the Rame Peninsula with their Millbrook Ferry.
A Chevrolet pictured at Cawsand in the mid-1930s could belong either to the MS&TCo.Ltd or E. S. Haddy & Sons of Kingsand, who ran similar looking buses to Cremyll and Millbrook.
ALAN KITTRIDGE COLLECTION.

A MS&TCo.Ltd Chevrolet, registration number CV4541, in the 1930s.
COURTESY SKINNER'S GARAGE.

cruises from Bangor on Belfast Lough. This venture only lasted one month and her registry was closed in January 1936, reported variously as 'scrapped' or 'constructive loss'. Her sale by the MS&TCo.Ltd indicates some dissatisfaction with her performance but also heralded a brand new replacement in the following year.

On Saturday 30 November 1935 Fellows & Co of Great Yarmouth launched from their Southtown yard a 56.24tg steel motor vessel built to the order of the MS&TCo.Ltd. At the launching ceremony Miss Molly Thorne, youngest daughter of Mr E. J. Thorne, manager of Fellows & Co, christened the new vessel the *Western Belle*. She was 69.9ft long x 15.3ft wide x 5.4ft deep and was fitted with a raised passenger deck over a long, porthole lined saloon. Her capacity was for 283 passengers who were also seated on a long, flush fore deck and a small after deck. She was powered by two six-cylinder

The Millbrook Steamboat & Trading Co Ltd's Whitsand Castle (ex-Kenwith Castle of the Kingsbridge Estuary), moored off Southdown in 1933.
ALAN KITTRIDGE COLLECTION.

The WESTERN BELLE *approaching Phoenix Wharf to pick up passengers for an evening Tamar excursion.*
B. Y. WILLIAMS.

Atlantic diesel engines driving her twin screws. When the *Western Belle* entered service in 1936 the *Manna* was renamed the *Devon Belle*, establishing the 'Belle' nomenclature which lasted for fifty years. The *Western Belle* immediately established herself as the company's new flagship and for many years the firm favourite on Tamar and Yealm excursions. Meanwhile the faithful old paddle steamer *Britannia*, or simply 'Brit' as she was known to regulars on the Millbrook ferry, continued in service. Her distinctive paddle wheel 'flapping' echoed around the hills of the lake, a familiar and reassuring sound for nearly forty years. Following the arrival of the *Western Belle* there were fears regarding the *Britannia's* immediate future. Bernard Williams, who took some photographs in the last year of the 'Saltash' fleet, photographed the *Britannia* during Whitsun 1935, believing it to be her final year. But she survived the year and was used to relieve the *Western Belle* and *Devon Belle* on the Millbrook ferry during the following summer excursion season. Therefore, during the years leading up to the Second World War the MS&TCo.Ltd fleet comprised:

Western Belle	Tamar / Yealm excursions and Millbrook Ferry
Devon Belle	Excursions, Millbrook Ferry
Britannia	Millbrook Ferry / laid up 1937
Lady Elizabeth	Cawsand and Dockyard & Warships excursions
Princess Mary	Millbrook Ferry
New Queen	Millbrook Ferry

The wheelhouse of the WESTERN BELLE *on 25 June 1937 with Jack Abbot (left) and Derek Crawford – later a Director of the Millbrook Steamboat & Trading Co Ltd.*
ALAN KITTRIDGE COLLECTION.

In addition the MS&TCo.Ltd was also expanding its fleet of buses and before the Second World War had established various stage services in the Rame Peninsula.

The *Britannia* could not go on forever but it took a declaration of war against Germany in May 1939 to finally prompt W. T. Crawford to dispose of the steamer. There is some uncertainty regarding the actual date of her demise. Most suggest that she was withdrawn and laid up at the end of 1936 and scrapped during the early years of the war – Bernard

Similar to foreseeing the demise of the remaining Saltash paddle steamers in 1927, Bernard Williams, working in Paddington Station since 1930, suspected the end was nigh for the BRITANNIA *following the arrival of the motor vessel* WESTERN BELLE. *On a Whitsun visit in 1935 he took a series of photographs of the* BRITANNIA *off Southdown in what would prove to be her penultimate season in service. This picture shows the paddler going astern from Southdown.* B. Y. WILLIAMS.

The BRITANNIA in the scrapyard of Vick Bros (Metals) Ltd, Stonehouse. A note on the reverse of the photograph suggests this was 1937 but the Millbrook company has recorded a date of 1940 for her sale to Vicks Bros (Metals) Ltd. ALAN KITTRIDGE COLLECTION.

Williams recalled seeing the paddler before 1939, 'laid-up' in Stonehouse Pool. A fleet list, drawn up by the MS&TCo.Ltd in 1962 notes 'During war years coal was expensive and in 1940 this vessel [*Britannia*] was sold for scrap to Vick Bros (Metals) Ltd. Stonehouse'. There appears to be a consensus, therefore, that she was laid up from the end of 1936 and scrapped between 1939 and 1940. There is a hint of sentimentality on the part of Bill Crawford in saving her from the breaker's torch for as long as he did. He and two others from the company were photographed standing sadly on her deck when she finally 'finished with engines' at Vick Bros scrap yard beside Stonehouse Bridge, bringing to an end 110 years of passenger paddle steamers on the River Tamar.

The Oreston & Turnchapel Steamboat Co Ltd's MAY QUEEN at Phoenix Wharf c1930. Rarely used on the Cattewater service in peacetime, the MAY QUEEN seems to have been reserved for excursions and charter work. She is easily distinguished from her fleet sisters by her white-lifebelt lined deckrails. ALAN KITTRIDGE COLLECTION.

ORESTON & TURNCHAPEL CO LTD EXCURSIONS

After the Great War the O&TSCo.Ltd recommenced excursions with the *May Queen* and the *Swift*, running from Phoenix Wharf, the Promenade Pier and the Devonport landings to St Germans and Calstock and maintaining shorter Grand Circular trips around the Sound and the Hamoaze.

The O&TSCo.Ltd usually maintained between 40 and 50 tons of coal at the company's coal store at Turnchapel and when the stock fell to 20 tons more was ordered. Welsh coal was obtained from Craig Merthyr colliery and before the war was delivered by coal schooners, chartered through Cory's of Cardiff. By 1917 coal was sent by rail *via* the Turnchapel Branch of the L&SWR. In 1926 the company's stock fell to 10 tons, with no immediate supply guaranteed. On account of the coal dispute the company was prohibited from using Welsh coal for pleasure parties, so two steamers remained laid up in Hooe Lake. A stock of expensive Belgian coal was purchased in July 1926 and the *May Queen* was put back into excursion service.

Until the local paddle steamers were finally withdrawn in 1927 the O&TSCo.Ltd's excursion business remained secondary to maintaining 'the line' on the Cattewater. But in May 1928 the district's three remaining excursion operators – the O&TSCo.Ltd, the TTCo, and the MSCo – each received a letter from the Plymouth Publicity Committee, who were concerned regarding the sudden lack of major excursion boats in the Plymouth district. As a result Messrs

In 1928 Royal Letters Patent designated Plymouth a City and the Oreston & Turnchapel Steamboat Co Ltd's new motor vessel, which was ordered from M. W. Blackmore & Sons of Appledore in the same year, was named the CITY OF PLYMOUTH *to commemorate the occasion. The* CITY OF PLYMOUTH *and her crew pose off the Promenade Pier, with Capt Tucker in his specially purchased uniform, holding the rigging, beside the funnel.*
The speedboat in the background ran trips from the Promenade Pier and in 1929 was driven by Bob Rooney, in contrast to his previous berth aboard Westcott's (of Sutton Pool) barquentine, the FRANCES & JANE.
ALAN KITTRIDGE COLLECTION.

Elford (O&TSCo.Ltd), Spear (TTCo) and Parson (MSCo) met with the Manager of the Promenade Pier to arrange a working agreement and fix minimum prices to run one boat each from the pier – namely the *Swift*, *Tamar Belle* (of 1927) and *Manna*.

At the end of the 1928 season the O&TSCo.Ltd's ferry steamer *Dart* was described as 'practically condemnable', so the *Swift* joined the *Rapid* and *Lively* on the Cattewater steamer service. To permanently replace the *Swift* on summer excursions the company decided upon a major new boat – a motor vessel of about 69ft long x 14ft wide with a flush deck suitable for Yealm excursions. M. W. Blackmore & Sons of Appledore won the contract, quoting a price of £2,170. During the same year Plymouth was designated a City by Royal Letters Patent, so the O&TSCo.Ltd fittingly settled on the name *City of Plymouth* for their new excursion boat. On 9 May 1929 the *City of Plymouth* (46tg, 66 x 15.1 x 6.8 feet) was launched at Appledore by Mrs W. H. Elford, also present were Mr and Mrs Sydney Elford, Miss W. Elford and Mr and Mrs Clarence Elford. Her twin screws were powered by two Thornycroft diesel engines giving a speed of around 10 knots. After fitting out and trials the *City of Plymouth* left Appledore at 4am on 18 June and arrived at Turnchapel at 11pm on the same day. Her first public voyage on 29 June was to the River Yealm, and she was proudly advertised as the 'New Passenger Yacht'. She had been designed specifically to visit the Yealm, consolidating the company's passenger services in this westernmost corner of the South Hams of Devon. Unfortunately the *City of Plymouth* rolled badly in the open sea outside the Breakwater and the beleaguered Captain Tucker is recalled on occasions declaring that as there was a 'nasty lop' outside the Breakwater, they would be doing the 'Four Rivers' instead. In a complete departure from their ferry livery the new vessel was painted light grey with white saloon sides and a buff funnel. As built she had her funnel positioned well forward, immediately behind a small wheelhouse. However, the exhaust fumes were causing annoyance to passengers seated near the stern and in the following year the funnel was moved further back amidship. At the same time the boat was repainted with a white hull and the two changes improved the *City of Plymouth's* appearance. In 1936 the O&TSCo.Ltd and the Western National Omnibus Company introduced bus return tickets for steamer passengers landing at Newton Ferrers – trippers could enjoy a walk along the spectacular cliff paths nearby and catch a bus home later in the day.

The O&TSCo.Ltd further improved their excursion business in 1932 when they negotiated sole landing rights with the PPP&STTSCo.Ltd at the Promenade Pier and Steamer Quay at Calstock. The MS&TCo.Ltd and TTCo could still run one boat each from the pier but now had to pay a toll to the O&TSCo.Ltd. It was at this time that Messrs Worth and Spear unsuccessfully offered to sell the business of the TTCo to the O&TSCo.Ltd

The LADY BEATRICE *at Calstock in 1932 soon after being purchased by the O&TSCo.Ltd – before being repainted in 1932-3. She is moored at Steamer Quay.* ALAN KITTRIDGE COLLECTION.

for £1000. Instead, in July of the same year, the O&TSCo.Ltd made an offer for the Torpoint steamer, *Lady Beatrice* – her Hamoaze passenger service having been closed following doubling of the Torpoint floating bridge. Their offer of £500 was accepted and she started a new career, running from the Promenade Pier to Calstock. The only alteration made to the *Lady Beatrice* was in 1938, when a gentlemans' toilet was provided – the steamer only having had a ladies' toilet until then. For the remainder of the decade the O&TSCo.Ltd annually renewed their landing rights at the Promenade Pier and until the *Western Belle* appeared four years later, the company became the principal passenger boat operator in the Plymouth district. In 1932 the fleet comprised:

Lively	Cattewater steamer service
Rapid	Cattewater steamer service
Swift	Cattewater steamer service
May Queen	Charters and reserve
City of Plymouth	Yealm excursions
Lady Beatrice	Tamar excursions
Tiger	Bovisand
Hustler	Bovisand

The LADY BEATRICE *is pictured approaching the Promenade Pier. In the background, work is underway on the sea front's two tier road and observation deck, which swept around in a curve from the Pier to Madiera Road.* ALAN KITTRIDGE COLLECTION.

EXCURSIONS DURING THE LATE 1930S

Following the arrival of the *Western Belle* the O&TSCo.Ltd and the MS&TCo.Ltd chose to co-operate rather than compete. They issued joint leaflets advertising and describing their Four Rivers Trip, their Calstock and Weir Head excursions and trips to the Yealm. They also ordered a loudspeaker from Moons of Plymouth to promote their excursions at the pier – a marketing device that resulted in a reprimand from the police, following complaints about the noise.

Not being a company to squander money the O&TSCo.Ltd had never provided uniforms for their crews – any nautical pose struck by the district's boatmen after the Great War was usually either coincidental or thanks to remnants of service uniforms. But in a rush of blood, brought about by the imminent arrival of the *City of Plymouth,* the company splashed out on a full uniform for Captain Tucker and, probably to placate petty jealousies, caps were bought for the piermaster at Turnchapel and captains of the other boats in the fleet. By the late 1930s the MS&TCo.Ltd were also providing uniforms for the crews of the *Western Belle* and *Devon Belle*. Jack Abbot remembered W. T. Crawford sending him to Sweets in Union Street – 'OUTFITTERS FOR THE BIG, SMALL, STOUT AND TALL' – for his new uniform: black trousers, black jacket and two white shirts. The shirts had detachable collars and Jack carried a spare clean collar if they were working an evening trip.

On the Millbrook ferry and during the peak summer season on the excursion boats, Millbrook company crews worked a sixteen hour day – on a day-on / day-off basis – each boat having two crews. MS&TCo.Ltd personnel during the 1930s included Jack Samuels and Dick Daymond – *Britannia's* last skipper and

The CITY OF PLYMOUTH *(outside) and the* WESTERN BELLE *embark passengers at the Promenade Pier in 1937. The Plymouth Piers, Pavilion & Saltash Steamboat Co Ltd still owned the pier but it was losing money and falling into disrepair. In the following year the pier company was placed in receivership.*
AEROFILMS LTD.

engineer. Tom Crawford – W. T. Crawford's son – successively skippered the *Devon Belle* and *Western Belle*, while brothers Reg and Harry Crawford were also crewmen as some stage. Yet another generation of Crawfords – Douglas, Donald and Derek – would also crew MS&TCo.Ltd boats, with Derek becoming a director of the company in the 1970s. Engineers included Harry Webber and Jack Abbot.

For the O&TSCo.Ltd Harry Tucker and Billy Phillips were captain and engineer of the *City of Plymouth*. Harry Tucker doubled as the company's carpenter. Billy Phillips and his son Billy also ran the *Tiger* to Bovisand for a number of years while Fern Phillips was engineer on the *Swift*. Jakie Phillips was in charge of the company's machine shop. Capt H. Johns was latterly Piermaster at Turnchapel. The names Brown, Burridge, Ellis, Gregory, Hine, Holland, Lane, Oxland, Taylor and Tugwell – some familiar names from the villages of Turnchapel and Oreston – were also found amongst crewmen of the Cattewater steamers. The turnstiles were in the charge of Gwen Phillips, Edie Townshend, Bessie Dungey and Ivy Tucker.

By the 1930s the maritime tradition of Calstock was already consigned to history, the Tamar Transport Company had been the final passenger boat operator to draw its crews from the village. After the war the majority of Tamar passenger boat crewmen came from Millbrook, although some, like Jack Abbot, Arthur Grylls' family, and the Millbrook Worths, had migrated down from Calstock.

In the Tamar Valley the old industries and mines were overgrown and memory of the area's industrial and maritime past was fading away. Excursions to Calstock numbered just one or two boats a day. Shorter afternoon and evening trips had become the norm and the duration of the Calstock call dwindled to less than an hour. Weir Head remained as a special trip, but run only on spring tides as the river was increasingly silted and overgrown above Morwellham. Jack Abbot also remembered some trips to Lopwell and Bere Ferrers in the *Western Belle*, but crews disliked going on the Tavy because the railway bridge at the mouth was hard to navigate at high tide – and they needed the tide to get to Lopwell. Navigation to St Germans was also becoming difficult – skippers would follow the channel from memory, crossing to Wearde on the Saltash side, then across to Jupiter Point, back across to Ince and back again to the Sheviock side. Poles set in the river by local mariners marked the remaining channel to St Germans Quay. Some river boat skippers and bargemen viewed the rivers at low tide and marked or memorised changes in the channel themselves. Little wonder that trips on the Lynher and Tavy have long since been consigned to memory, besides, insurance and certification restrictions prevent such adventures today.

Thus, on the eve of the Second World War, the river excursion fleet in the Plymouth district had been transformed. From seven paddle steamers and two screw steamers in the early 1920s, the regular excursion fleet now

Millbay Docks in 1929 with the Sir Walter Raleigh *at Millbay Pier (on the right), the* Sir John Hawkins *of 1929 at Princess Royal Pontoon (in the centre) and the* Sir Richard Grenville *of 1891. The* 'Grenville *was replaced by her 901tg namesake in 1931 – the GWR's last tender at Millbay, which would continue to provide coastal excursions until the 1960s.* Douglass Hoppins collection.

The GWR's excursion booking office window in the octagonal Custom's Office adjacent to Millbay Pier gates. Alan Kittridge.

comprised of only three motor vessels: *Devon Belle*, *Western Belle* and *City of Plymouth*, and one steamer: *Lady Beatrice*. In addition there were around twelve motor launches – including the MS&TCo.Ltd's *Lady Elizabeth* – running Dockyard and Warships trips on the Hamoaze or to the beaches at Bovisand and Cawsand, and the *Tamar Belle* (ex *Kitley Belle*) which was operating from Phoenix Wharf. Sadly, during this inter-war period, Plymothians had largely turned their back on the local rivers, indeed, had it not been for the growth in popularity of the nearby beaches there would have been even fewer passenger boats available. Railways, coaches and bus routes were carrying ever increasing numbers of day trippers to beaches and resorts further afield, such as Paignton and Torquay, or inland to Dartmoor. Private motor cars enabled families to go out exploring Devon and Cornwall by themselves. A boat trip on the river might still be enjoyed, but it was no longer an annual tradition.

On 19 July 1938 debenture shareholders of the PPP&STTSCo.Ltd appointed a receiver, C. E. B. MacFarlane Smith, to administer the property of the company. Such had been the decline in the structure of the Promenade Pier that at the start of the 1939 season the O&TSCo.Ltd and MS&TCo.Ltd considered the landing steps were in too dangerous a condition to use. Work was put in hand by the impoverished pier company but in the interim excursions had to start from Phoenix Wharf.

The threatening international situation in 1939 was matched by a build up of naval shipping in Devonport Dockyard and the passenger boat operators profited from an opportune change to their regular excursions by increasing the number of Dockyard and Warship trips. Unfortunately the naval presence only grew in proportion to the threat of hostilities which culminated with the declaration of war with Germany on 3 September. Unlike 1914, all excursions ceased forthwith and any boats not employed on regular passenger and ferry services were withdrawn from public service – many of them were placed on Dormant Charter with government departments, i.e. reserved for use when required by establishments like Devonport Dockyard.

The Sir John Hawkins *pictured on an excursion off Looe in the 1930s.* Alan Kittridge collection.

Coastal excursions

Following the demise of the PPP&STTDSCo.Ltd fleet in the mid 1920s the remaining history of Plymouth's coastal excursions lay almost entirely with the GWR at Millbay. In 1929 the old excursion favourite *Smeaton* was sold to make way for one of the largest passenger tenders to operate in the United Kingdom, the *Sir John Hawkins*. She was a 172 feet long steel twin screw vessel of 930 tons, built by Earles Shipbuilding of Hull. The *Sir John Hawkins* was joined two years later by a 901 ton sister ship, *Sir Richard Grenville*, also from Earles. She replaced her Victorian namesake, which was renamed *Penlee* and sold to the Dover Harbour Board in 1931. The tender fleet now comprised of the four vessels that are probably best remembered, due in part no doubt to their stirring westcountry nomenclature: the *Sir Walter Raleigh*, *Sir Francis Drake*, *Sir John Hawkins* and the *Sir Richard Grenville*. In terminally declining numbers, units of this fleet would continue to provide coastal excursions – mostly to Salcombe, Looe, and Fowey to land; and to view Dodman Point and the Eddystone Lighthouse – until the *Sir Richard Grenville's* farewell sailings in 1962. Subsequently the MS&TCo.Ltd offered coastal trips – to Looe, once or twice a year, subject to favourable weather conditions.

CHAPTER EIGHT

LINES OF COMMUNICATION

Ferries 1914–1939

The KITLEY BELLE *at the slipway landing, just inside Cofflete Creek at Steer Point c1925.* COURTESY A. L. CLAMP.

YEALM STEAMER SERVICES

The *Kitley Belle* was kept active on the Steer Point ferry throughout the Great War because an Officer Training Centre was established in nearby Membland Hall with an intake of up to 300 men – some with their families lodging nearby. Mrs N. J. Croft, granddaughter of George Hodge snr, recalled the steamer service as being very busy at this time and with Hodge's sons away in the armed forces, grandchildren and female members of the family were recruited to maintain the service.

George Hodge retired after the war and the steamer service to Steer Point was continued by his sons, with George jnr as the senior partner. Passenger traffic on the Yealmpton branch was at its peak in the 1920s – the GWR offered a through rail and steamer ticket to Newton Creek for 1s 6d, and the paddle steamers from Plymouth were calling again. The *Kitley Belle* and the *Kitley Girl* enjoyed a busy period maintaining the ferry and offering excursions on the river.

A threat to the steamer service appeared in 1919 when the GWR started running a bus service from Yealmpton to Noss Mayo. Further competition appeared in 1925 when Devon Motor Transport (acquired by the Western National in 1927) opened a route from Plymouth to Yealmpton and Newton Ferrers (to compete both with the GWR's bus service and their trains on the Yealmpton branch). The coal dispute of 1926 therefore happened at a particularly bad time for the Hodges. A catastrophe befell the *Kitley Belle* when, unable to afford imported coal, the Hodges replaced her boiler and steam engine with a paraffin engine. They also removed her funnel and demolished the forward section of her cabin, the attractive Hocking built steamer of 1905 was barely recognisable once Elliot Hodge had finished converting her.

The *Kitley Girl,* laid up since 1926, was replaced by a motor boat purchased from St Mawes. Named the *Pioneer*, the newcomer looked like a converted yacht and was fitted with a 'hot-bulb' Gardner diesel engine (to start the engine, glass bulbs were heated with a blow torch to pre-heat the cylinders, it was quickly replaced with a Kelvin engine). She was fitted with a small cabin, probably built by Elliot Hodge. The *Pioneer* was soon favoured over the paraffin engined *Kitley Belle*, which subsequently swung idly at her moorings for her remaining time on the Yealm. Some time after July 1929, a year before the Yealmpton branch line was closed to passenger traffic, the Hodges withdrew their Steer Point ferry service. The deciding factor was the withdrawal of the combined rail and steamer tickets following amalgamation of National and GWR buses as the Western National – which then ran most of the bus services in the district including those to Newton Ferrers and Noss Mayo. The Hodges operated their own short lived twelve seater bus service between Newton Ferrers and Yealmpton for a

The KITLEY BELLE *after her conversion to a paraffin engined motor vessel. Her funnel and the engine room part of her cabin have been removed. However, the conversion was not successful and she spent most of her remaining time on the Yealm out of service.* COURTESY A. L. CLAMP.

The KITLEY BELLE *conversion appears to have been unsuccessful and she was soon replaced on the Steer Point service by this singular motor vessel, the* PIONEER, *which proved popular with the crew once her 'hot-bulb' Gardner diesel engine was replaced with a Kelvin diesel. She is pictured at the beach landing at Steer Point – which was just outside and upstream of Cofflete Creek.* ALAN KITTRIDGE COLLECTION.

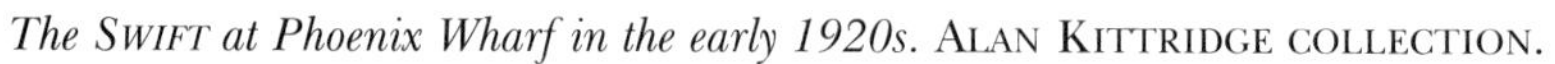

The SWIFT *at Phoenix Wharf in the early 1920s.* ALAN KITTRIDGE COLLECTION.

Pictured by Bernard Williams in 1935, the LIVELY *approaches Phoenix Wharf.*
B. Y. WILLIAMS.

year until Ernest Hodge took a job with the Western National in 1930.

The *Kitley Girl* was never used again. In the late 'twenties she broke from her moorings and went aground at Bridgend in Newton Creek – Bernard Williams recorded seeing her ashore there on 26 April 1930. She was broken up in-situ soon after. The *Kitley Belle* was sold in 1930 to the Tamar Transport Company. George Hodge used the *Pioneer* during the early 1930s operating her with a waterman's licence for twelve passengers. He then moved to Saltash to run a market garden, leaving the *Pioneer* out of use on the foreshore near Popes Quay in Noss Mayo, where she lay slowly deteriorating throughout the Second World War.

CATTEWATER STEAMER SERVICE

In February 1917 the Government took possession of a field and cottages at Mount Batten to establish a flying boat station, RNAS Cattewater. The air station then refused the O&TSCo.Ltd permission to land passengers there, except those engaged in works at the base. The O&TSCo.Ltd in turn refused to replace their pontoon landing, which had been removed for repair. Later in the year the O&TSCo.Ltd issued special passes for soldiers stationed at forts and gun emplacements in the district. Ten turnstiles were purchased 'to help ease the workload' of ticket collectors and the daily treasurer – some were installed on Turnchapel Pier and at Gutter in Oreston. The *Lively* was hired as a liberty boat by Devonport Dockyard in 1917 and returned damaged, so the O&TSCo.Ltd, exercising a clause in their charter agreement, sent her back to the Dockyard for repair. A more lucrative charter was agreed with the Commanding Officer of Mount Batten air station in April 1917. Regretting their hasty action in banning the O&TSCo.Ltd from the Mount Batten landing, it dawned upon RNAS Cattewater that their personnel needed a ferry service to Plymouth. They agreed to charter the *Rapid* for £72 per month and to provide their own Royal Navy crew, coal and stores. It was further agreed that the steamer would be returned in the same condition as at the commencement of the charter. In June a letter was received from the Ministry of Transport requesting a new, substantially reduced contract of only £3.5s per week – which was a lot nearer the going rate. The O&TSCo.Ltd refused, demanding their original terms agreed with the C.O. of RNAS Cattewater – revenge was sweet, but trifling compared to what followed after the war. The *Rapid* was released from her profitable charter on 14 August 1919 and, subject to the contract, was sent to the Dockyard for a full overhaul. The charter realised £1,152 and the boat was returned as good as new. The American Naval Base at Victoria Wharves, Coxside were also looking for a ferry steamer in September 1918 but the O&TSCo.Ltd had none to spare because the *Rapid* was then still on charter and the *Dart* was being repaired. The other three steamers, *Lively, Swift* and *May Queen* were all needed to maintain their regular ferry services.

After the war the air station at Mount Batten was retained by the RAF and in 1920 the O&TSCo.Ltd was awarded £615 compensation by the War Losses Commission for the loss of its Mount Batten traffic. But the company appealed and in 1926 Arbitration awarded the O&TSCo.Ltd £2,575 for loss of business between 1918 and 1921, and a further £2,625 for the period 1921 to 1926. Additional compensation for compulsory acquisition of company's property amounted to £3,766. If one includes the lucrative charter of the *Rapid* to the Mount Batten air station between 1917 and 1919 the O&TSCo.Ltd realised £10,118 from the Mount Batten landing over a ten year period – without running a single steamer.

In January 1921 agreement was reached with the Duchy of Cornwall, the Cattewater Harbour Commissioners and the Admiralty, to install a pontoon landing at Gutter in Oreston. Subsequently the Dummy Landing fell out of use. In the same year a house and store, and the quay and foreshore adjacent to Turnchapel Pier was purchased by the company. Tolls on the approach road to the Laira Bridge were abolished in 1924 – with little immediate ill effect to the Cattewater steamers. But four years later two bus companies began running services *via* the bridge to Plymstock: Palace Saloons *via* Hooe; and Eddystone Motors *via* Oreston. By 1932 the Western National had absorbed these independents and was operating comprehensive services in the district, including to Oreston and Mount Batten. But the Cattewater steamer service continued to thrive and the O&TSCo.Ltd bought the old school in Turnchapel to convert into a shop and office, and also planned to open a tea room. By the 1930s the core of the steamer service was the 'ferry' between Phoenix Wharf and Turnchapel Pier – especially on summer weekends and Bank Holidays, when thousands from Plymouth visited Jennycliff and tea gardens in Hooe. The only other regular call on most, but not all, crossings was Gutter pontoon. Mount Batten still appeared on the timetable, but mainly as a worktime service for personnel at the RAF station.

W. H. Elford died in April 1934 and was succeeded as chairman of the O&TSCo.Ltd by his brother, C. C. Elford. Sydney Elford was also elected to the Board.

Although the company experimented with diesel engines on their Bovisand and excursion boats, the Cattewater service remained a steamer stronghold:

SWIFT: The *Swift* had an overhaul and a new keel fitted by James Goss at Calstock in 1919 and in 1928 was fitted with new engines and boiler by Sissons of Gloucester. Well over fifty years old in

A nostalgic view of the Cattewater between the world wars. On the left an Oreston & Turnchapel Steamboat Co Ltd steamer heads for Turnchapel. Blackburn Iris flying boats based at RAF Mount Batten are moored in trots on the Cattewater. In the background, moored off Turnchapel, is one of the cable ships – the MACKAY BENNET *or the* JOHN W. MACKAY *– which were based there.* ALAN KITTRIDGE COLLECTION.

1930, the *Swift* had survived a disaster in 1902 having been burnt 'almost to the water's edge' and subsequently rebuilt. Herein might lay the secret of her longevity – by 1930 there could have been little of the original *Lily* left. Until the *City of Plymouth* and *Lady Beatrice* took over excursion duties around 1930 the *Swift* was the company's favoured boat for trips on the Hamoaze and to St Germans Quay, but she rarely left the Cattewater after 1932.

DART: After the war the *Dart* was repaired by Gerry Bros at Cattedown but the O&TSCo.Ltd was unhappy both with the work done and the time taken to complete the repairs – ten months. By 1926 considerable repairs were again needed but the O&TSCo.Ltd undertook the work 'in-house' this time, on the beach in Hooe Lake. They therefore discovered for themselves the poor condition of the steamer and declared her 'practically condemnable'. It was decided to order a new boat for excursions (the *City of Plymouth*) and release the *Swift* for full time service on the Cattewater. The *Dart* lingered on in reserve until scrapped in December 1930.

LIVELY: Thanks largely to her wartime repairs by Devonport Dockyard and post war renewal of her engines and boiler by Sissons of Gloucester, the *Lively* was in a far better condition than her ex-Greaney sister, the *Dart*. In 1934 she received a new saloon and top deck, new frames and planking – work which was undertaken by boatbuilder William Lucas of Oreston. Probably the most familiar boat on the Cattewater steamer service, the *Lively* rarely suffered breakdowns and, excepting her Dockyard charter in 1916, never left the Cattewater.

RAPID: The *Rapid* was another of the company's steamers to benefit from a dockyard repair, after her charter to RNAS Cattewater in 1919. In the following year a new set of engines were supplied by Sissons and the MSCo's *Cornubia* was purchased for the value of her machinery – her boiler being fitted to the *Rapid*. Thus the old Millbrook steamer's boiler survived until replaced by a new one in 1939. Major hull repairs were needed in 1926 and these were undertaken on the beach in Hooe Lake by O&TSCo.Ltd employees.

MAY QUEEN: The *May Queen* had originally been built to double as an excursion steamer and she maintained the Three Rivers and Four Rivers trips before the Great War. But after the war the *Swift* fulfiled this role until around 1930. However, the *May Queen* was never a regular on the Cattewater service. When Cornwall County Council took over the Torpoint Ferry in 1922 they continued the Hamoaze passenger steamer service with the *Lady Beatrice* alone. Subsequently, when she was out of service for overhaul or repairs, the *May Queen* was chartered to replace her. The only repair undertaken on the *May Queen* between the wars was a new boiler in 1924. It would appear that her good condition was a result of her light work load – she seems to have been held as a reserve excursion boat and for charters.

The SWIFT going astern from Turnchapel Pier in 1935. The crewman on the steps has to guide the helmsman, who has no view astern. Note the tiny canvas dodger to protect the helm from spray.
B. Y. WILLIAMS.

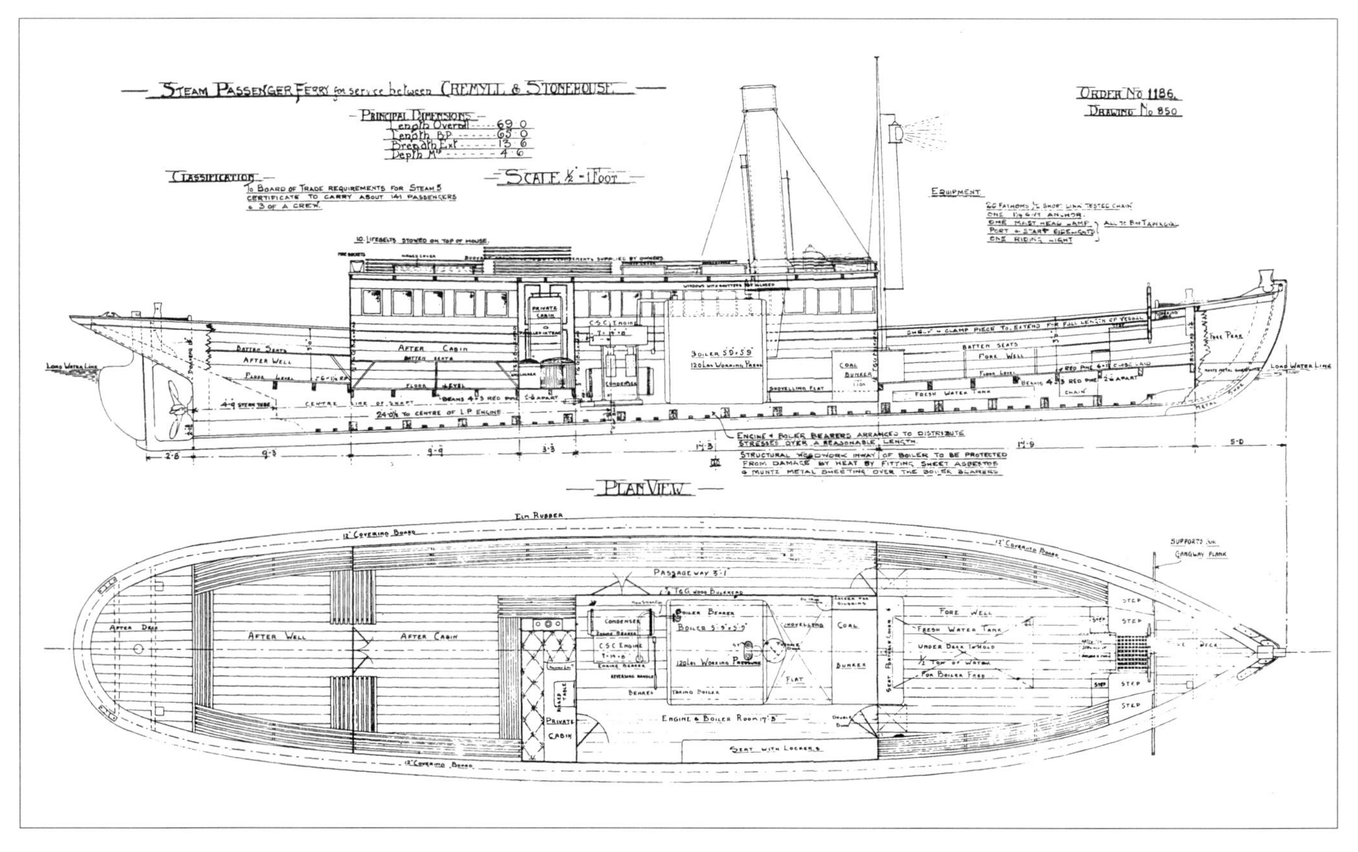

General arrangement diagram of the ARMADILLO *of 1926. A similar diagram of the* SHUTTLECOCK *(1925) shows a funnel cowl as fitted in the picture below. This diagram was discovered by Alan Gissing in the current Board of Trade file for the* NORTHERN BELLE *(EX-*ARMADILLO*). Note: the fresh water tank for the boiler feed, the boiler, the engine and condenser, and the Earl's tiny private cabin.* COURTESY ALAN GISSING.

THE CREMYLL FERRY

After the *Shuttlecock* was wrecked at Mount Wise in 1910 the Cremyll Ferry was maintained by the remaining two steamers, *Carrier* and *Armadillo*. Little in the history of the Cremyll Ferry seems straightforward and in 1923 the Mount Edgcumbe Estate began what was to prove a long drawn out and confusing programme of renewal of the steamers. In August 1923 the Mount Edgcumbe Estate ordered a compound, surface condensing engine and boiler from Plenty & Son Ltd. It was noted that the new machinery was intended for Rogers & Co. (Shipbuilders) Ltd's Cremyll yard, for yard number 599, 'Shuttlecock'. The boiler was subcontracted to Riley Brothers of Stockton-on-Tees and the completed machinery was delivered to Cremyll in December 1923. In the meantime Rogers drew up a specification for the new ferry boat. How accurately it describes the eventual steamer is open to doubt because the maker's plate on the *Shuttlecock* recorded the year 1925 as her building date (even though she appears to have acquired her yard number in mid-1923).

Rogers' specification gave the principal

The SHUTTLECOCK *(of 1925) at Cremyll Quay in the 1920s.* ALAN KITTRIDGE COLLECTION.

The Cremyll Ferry steamer ARMADILLO *(of 1926) at Admiral's Hard at low tide during the late 1920s. In the background is the L&SWR's Ocean Quay with the station buildings still evident from the time before 1910, when passengers from American Line and Union Castle liners were landed there.*
ALAN KITTRIDGE COLLECTION.

dimensions as 69 x 13.5 x 4.5 feet. She was to be designed to carry about 141 passengers (actual - 147) and 3 crew on a Class 5 certificate. Oak frames and pitch pine planking were specified and she was to have a well deck forward and a deckhouse for the engine room and passenger cabin. Also within the deckhouse a private cabin was specified, although there remains some debate whether this feature was eventually installed aboard the *Shuttlecock* or the new *Armadillo* of 1926 – or both. Provided for the use of the Earl of Mount Edgcumbe, his family, guests etc, the cabin was a small room located between the engine room and the main passenger cabin and was to be comfortably fitted:

> ...panelled out in teak, (with the) seating arrangement made round the cabin forming a settee with upholstered seats. The starboard side of the cabin to be fitted with Stone's under water type W.C. with flushing arrangements complete. Cabinet tip-up wash basin in mahogany to be fitted above the W.C. secured to the bulkhead...Two windows fixed on the port side of the cabin made to lower, of railway carriage type. Suitable curtains to be fitted on brass rods at each of the windows. One brass Gimball lamp to be supplied and fixed in place where convenient and one looking glass. One hinged table of hardwood to be fixed at the fore end of the cabin with the necessary swing legs to support same when up in place.

The Earl's paying customers meanwhile endured the solitary comfort of slatted seating.

The *Armadillo* continued alongside the new *Shuttlecock* throughout 1925. In January 1926 machinery was ordered from Plenty & Son Ltd for the new *Armadillo* which was being built at Cremyll Yard. The compound, surface condensing engine and boiler were delivered in June 1926 and, as the builder's plate on the *Armadillo* gave her year of construction as 1926, we can safely assume she was completed in the second half of that year – unprecedented accuracy in the history of the Cremyll Ferry. Similar to the *Carrier* the old *Armadillo* disappeared – presumably scrapped.

Alan Gissing remembered the two 'new' ferry boats before they were converted to diesel after the Second World War. As with many 'identical' ships and boats there was usually some feature which distinguished the vessels: the cabin sides of the *Shuttlecock* were almost vertical, whilst those on the *Armadillo* inclined inwards. Another anomaly was the *Shuttlecock's* passenger capacity – two fewer than the *Armadillo's* 145. Alan Gissing has no recollection of the private cabin(s) but he recalled that during the mid 1940s, just before the steamers were converted to diesel, Charlie Wilcox, the engineer, had a bench seat aft of the *Armadillo's* engine, in what could have formerly been the private cabin space

THE TORPOINT FERRY

Little had happened on the Torpoint Ferry since the Rendel designed floating bridges were replaced in the 1870s, other than the failed experiment in double ferry operation in 1905. By 1919 the whole operation was run down and out of date.

In his book *The Torpoint Ferry - a History and Review*, A. R. Warren, Manager of the Torpoint

The 1871 Willoughby built floating bridge of the Torpoint Ferry, pictured at Torpoint was old fashioned and worn out in the early 1920s, when this photograph was taken. On taking over operation of the ferry in 1922 Cornwall County Council immediately made plans to replace her. A new Philip & Son Ltd, bridge was completed in 1925 and in the following year the old Willoughby bridge was withdrawn and scrapped. ALAN KITTRIDGE COLLECTION.

Ferry, explained the circumstances of Cornwall County Council's acquisition of the Torpoint Ferry in 1922. The Ferries (Acquisition by Local Authorities) Act 1919 allowed Local Authorities, with the consent of the Minister of Transport, to purchase or transfer existing ferries to Local Authority ownership. The Torpoint Ferry was the main route into Cornwall from the Plymouth district. After the Great War a ferry committee looked after its operation but the floating bridge was in desperate need of new investment. The two bridges were over forty years old, designed for horse traffic, not motor vehicles. A proposal to double the tolls to help finance improvements met with strong opposition and Torpoint Urban Council asked Cornwall County Council to take the ferry over. On 21 July 1922 the County Council acquired the Torpoint Ferry rights, the floating bridges and the supplementary passenger service for £42,000.

The passenger steamer *Volta* was immediately condemned and broken up at Cremyll. The *Lady Beatrice* continued alone, being substituted during annual maintenance or breakdown by steamers chartered from the O&TSCo.Ltd. T. P. Endean, the Manager, was instructed to draw up proposals for a new floating bridge which was built by Philip & Son Ltd of Dartmouth at a cost of £14,650. The new bridge was completed in 1925. She measured 85 feet long x 53 feet wide x 8 feet deep and entered service in the following year. A fundamental change in design was the provision of a single traffic deck, located centrally with deck houses on either side – similar to the Saltash floating bridges. Another distinctive feature was the curvature of her decks, rising amidships to accommodate the horizontally positioned chain wheel. She was powered by a Philips two cylinder compound steam engine, with two boilers by Barclay, Curle & Co Ltd. There was capacity for 800 passengers and about 16 vehicles. However, one design flaw, perhaps better appreciated with the benefit of hindsight, was the perpetuation of coal fired boilers, which, compared to oil fired boilers, was both labour intensive and dirty. The Willoughby

The 1878, Willoughby built floating bridge, pictured here c1925 at Torpoint, served as the reserve ferry to the new Philip bridge for one year and was herself replaced by a second Philip built bridge in 1926-7. Note the supplementary passenger steamer landing on the left. ALAN KITTRIDGE COLLECTION.

The LADY BEATRICE *at the Torpoint pontoon landing c1920s.* ALAN KITTRIDGE COLLECTION.

built floating bridge of 1871 was withdrawn and scrapped. In 1926 a second bridge was built by Philips to the same design and after almost 50 years in service the 1878 Willoughby built bridge was withdrawn and, after laying out of service on the beach at Torpoint for a time, was scrapped. Unfortunately for the ferry users, to help pay for these improvements Cornwall County Council had to increase the tolls.

In the Parliamentary Session 1928-9 Cornwall County Council successfully promoted a Bill to extend and improve the ferry service. They were empowered to acquire land on both sides of the river for extension of the landing beaches and to lay a second set of chains for double floating bridge operation. The work

One of the new floating bridges at Torpoint. These Philip built bridges of the mid 1920s were the first Torpoint Ferry vessels to be specifically designed to take motor traffic. The distinctive hump back shape of her deck was to accommodate the horizontal chain wheel amidships, beneath the traffic deck. ALAN KITTRIDGE COLLECTION.

Pictured at Devonport is the third Philip built floating bridge. She was built in 1931 to ensure a reserve when double floating bridge operation was introduced in the following year. The Pottery Quay pontoon, on the right, was owned by Devonport Corporation and continued in use after the supplementary passenger service of the Torpoint Ferry was withdrawn in 1932. But the Torpoint passenger pier and pontoon was owned by Cornwall County Council and was subsequently demolished. ALAN KITTRIDGE COLLECTION.

The new shore turnstiles and office buildings (behind) at Torpoint, built in the early 1930s. ALAN KITTRIDGE COLLECTION.

started in June 1930 and was completed two years later. To ensure continuity of the service a third floating bridge was ordered from Philips in 1930 and delivered in May 1931. She was similar in design to the previous two but was distinctive in having more of her main deck passenger accommodation plated in. One of the bridges was kept in reserve and switched during maintenance or breakdowns. New buildings and shore layouts were designed by the County Architect of Cornwall and built with local limestone. Waiting rooms were erected on both sides of the Tamar and on the Torpoint side new offices were built and new turnstiles installed. Thus the ferry undertaking was transformed from its Victorian origins into a modern commuter system capable of handling thousands of passengers and about 64 vehicles hourly, in each direction. The new double floating bridge operation was inaugurated on 1 July 1932. These improvements, coupled with late night running, rendered the passenger steamer service redundant – the *Lady Beatrice* was sold in the same month to the O&TSCo.Ltd and the pontoon landing on the Torpoint side was dismantled.

THE SALTASH FERRY

Compared to Torpoint the Corporation run Saltash Ferry was in a far better condition after the Great War. Their two Willoughby built bridges were more efficient than those at Torpoint and much younger, having been built in 1892 and 1911 respectively. Nevertheless, in September 1927 a new bridge entered service. She was built by Philip & Son Ltd at a cost of £8,950. and measured 64 feet long x 36 feet wide x 6.7 feet deep. Her two cylinder, compound engine was built by Philips, and her boiler by Muir & Findlay. She carried three rows of about five vehicles each, and had mechanically operated prows. The 1892 bridge was withdrawn and scrapped by Vick Bros (Metals) Ltd of Stonehouse. During the early 1930s Saltash Corporation took advantage of a government job creation grant to order a replacement for the 1911 bridge. The replacement was ordered from J. I. Thornycroft & Co Ltd of Southampton from a plan by S. H. Hambling, Naval Architect and Marine Surveyor. The new bridge cost £10,750 and entered service in 1933. She measured 72 feet long and 42 feet wide with 28 feet long prows and could carry four rows of about six cars. The new vessel maintained a twenty minute service. The 1911 bridge, which since 1927 had been the reserve or winter ferry, was sold to the King Harry Ferry floating bridge on the River Fal. However, she proved too large and was subsequently sold for breaking in south Wales but sank *en-route* off Portreath in Cornwall. Saltash Corporation allocated their bridges with the operating numbers 1 and 2, thus the 1892 and 1911 steam bridges had been 1 and 2 respectively and the 1927 and 1933 bridges likewise were nos 1 and 2. In 1938 the Philip built No 1 bridge was widened by cutting it in half lengthwise and adding an extra 6 feet of carriageway.

The floating bridges were painted buff topsides, with a dark brown 'hull' and a black funnel. The ferry ran from 6am until 11.15pm.

Saltash floating bridge No.2 at Saltash Passage, with No.1 laid up on the gridiron. The latter, 1892 bridge, was replaced in September 1927 by a new Philip built floating bridge. Of interest in the background are the EMPRESS *and* PRINCE EDWARD *anchored behind the central pier of the Royal Albert Bridge and, in the distance on the right, two gunpowder ships on their traditional moorings – midstream and well away from anything.* ALAN KITTRIDGE COLLECTION.

From then until midnight the floating bridge could be hired for ten shillings plus the toll, and after midnight for £1. 2s. 6d plus the toll. Tolls were charged dependent on the length of vehicle and a 16 feet long wooden measure was kept aboard for this purpose. Pedestrians and cyclists resident in Saltash crossed free of charge, indeed, anyone with the confidence to look the ticket collector in the eye and knowingly say 'Saltash' travelled free. On both the Torpoint and Saltash Ferry a one minute warning bell was sounded prior to departure, which at Saltash could save a latecomer a twenty minute wait. At night the ferry was moored clear of the low water mark on the Saltash side with the fire damped down.

The Philip built Saltash floating bridge No.1 of 1927. Saltash's Town Pier, on the left, lost its pontoon landing when the paddle steamers were scrapped. The Royal Albert Bridge looks in sparkling condition following strengthening in the 1930s, when the long, horizontal bracing was added to the bridge spans. ALAN KITTRIDGE COLLECTION.

CHAPTER NINE
BRIDGES AND BELLES
A second golden age 1939–1985

THE SECOND WORLD WAR

The Admiralty assumed control of all British merchant shipping on 26 August 1939 and at 11am on 3 September war was declared against Germany. All river and coastal excursions were stopped but ferries on the Cattewater and Tamar would continue to ply throughout the ensuing war. Devonport Dockyard sent for the O&TSCo.Ltd's *May Queen* and *Lady Beatrice* on 22 September – a Dormant Charter of the two boats had been made earlier. The British Expeditionary Force was evacuated from Dunkirk in May 1940 but surprisingly, during the same month, permission was granted by the King's Harbourmaster for the O&TSCo.Ltd to restart public excursions from the Promenade Pier. The *City of Plymouth* was hurriedly returned to service and offered trips on the Cattewater, around the Sound and even beyond the protective Breakwater to Cawsand Bay. But in June 1940 France capitulated and within two weeks German bombers, flying from French airfields, attacked Plymouth, so the *City of Plymouth's* public trips were stopped on 1 July. In September 1940 a Dormant Charter was arranged with the military authorities to take three O&TSCo.Ltd steamboats in case of emergency (i.e. invasion). From October the air raids on Plymouth became heavier and continued all through the winter. The *City of Plymouth* was chartered by Devonport Dockyard on 7 November 1940, manned by O&TSCo.Ltd crews who were paid by the dockyard. The O&TSCo.Ltd decided to re-commission the open motor launch *Tiger*, as all of the company's other boats were either in the dockyard or under imminent threat of being taken over. On 28 November 1940 government oil storage tanks at Turnchapel were set alight by bombs and burned for five days. Further attacks in the Oreston, Turnchapel, Mount Batten district followed – the fire acting as a beacon to bombers. In the following month bombs fell on the slipway at Turnchapel and near the ferry steamer while on ferry service. The O&TSCo.Ltd bought 'tin helmets' from Plympton District Council and, thus protected, the doughty steamer crews of the O&TSCo.Ltd continued throughout the war. Following the death of his father Sydney, Henry Russel Elford was appointed as a director in 1939, he became Manager of the Company two years later. Both the *Swift* and the *City of Plymouth* were damaged by incendiary bombs on 13 January 1941. The *Swift* sank on the beach but was patched up and sent across the Cattewater to Hockings Yard for repairs.

The bombing raids culminated in two devastating periods of attack during March and April 1941, when the centres of Plymouth and Devonport were devastated. Plymouth suffered its biggest raids to date on 20 and 21 March 1941, during which the Luftwaffe obligingly hit and destroyed the decaying Promenade Pier – an event recalled with nostalgic regret after the war but a blessing at the time to the Receiver of the PPP&STTSCo.Ltd.

The Torpoint Ferry closed at night but a Naval crew stood by for emergencies and kept the boilers going. Both of the Torpoint floating bridges carried a barrage balloon as protection against dive bombing. The balloons were manned by RAF personnel who were housed in a cabin aboard. On 22 April 1941 the south floating bridge was hit by a bomb in the engine room, with no serious casualties, but she was put out of service until 22 May. The next day the reserve floating bridge, undergoing a refit, was damaged by bombs which straddled her and she was put out of service until 8 August – so for a month only one floating bridge was available. In the same year a bomb fell on the ferry beach, killing ferry employees Ernie Everingham and Bernard Gorman at the turnstiles and the RAF balloon crewman they were talking to. The floating bridges at Torpoint and Saltash were kept in steam throughout the 'Blitz' and ferried emergency services.

Two fatalities were suffered on the Cremyll Ferry when skipper Tucker and engineer Crowther were killed in an air raid – caught by bomb blast in the entrance to an air raid shelter. During the raids of April 1941 Mount Edgcumbe House was severely damaged by incendiary bombs. One of the Cremyll Ferry steamers sank at Cremyll during the war, a witness remembered seeing only the top of her funnel sticking out of water, general opinion suggests it was the *Armadillo*.

As a result of the Blitz attacks of March and April 1941 the commercial and government centres of Plymouth were virtually wiped out and large areas of the 'Three Towns' lay in ruins. The citizens of Plymouth were in the front line, left vulnerable by scarce and ineffectual air defences, and dependent upon the overwhelmed emergency arrangements of the local authorities. For many frightened Plymothians the only escape from the nightmare was to get out of the City and each evening tens of thousands of refugees 'trekked' into the surrounding countryside. Trekkers queued for steamers to Oreston and Turnchapel and sought shelter in open countryside at Jennycliff and Staddon Heights. They queued patiently at Admiral's Hard for the Cremyll Ferry. 'There were thousands of them', recalled Arthur Grylls, a Cremyll Ferry crewman during the war, 'they'd sleep in barns, under hedges, anywhere just to get out'. Once ashore on the Cornwall side trekkers made for Maker and Cawsand where local halls were opened for them. At Whitsands the summer chalets became a priceless haven for their weary owners. Jack Abbot was on the Millbrook ferry with the *Western Belle* during the war, he remembered the impossible queues winding up Cornwall Street from North Corner, all patiently awaiting salvation from the nightly purgatory. Many pleaded to be allowed aboard and there were not many boatmen who could refuse. The *Devon Belle* and the *Western Belle* were overloaded on most evening crossings during this period of the war, Jack could not say how many were aboard because he didn't count. He remembered on some trips the *Western Belle's* rubbing strake (the moulding that ran along her hull) was in the water. She was always a bad handler but this made her worse. These scenes were repeated on the Torpoint and Saltash ferries, and indeed, on all exits from the city.

The blackout meant there were no lights to help mariners after dark. Navigation was aided by dim blue lights at quaysides, otherwise skippers calculated their position by observing hills and other landmarks on the river which ironically, because of the blackout, were easier to see than before. But in bad weather and fog it was down to the skipper's intimate knowledge of his particular stretch of water.

In the second half of 1941 the Ministry of War Transport (MoWT) bought the O&TSCo.Ltd's *Lady Beatrice* for £950. Meanwhile the *Tiger*, which was being overhauled at Hocking's Yard, was damaged by a bomb and further repair work was stopped. In August 1942 the MoWT also bought the *City of Plymouth* for £2,250 and the *May Queen* for £1,050. The Ministry sought the O&TSCo.Ltd's permission to rename the *May Queen* – HMS *Foliot*. Perhaps one of the most optimistic requests the O&TSCo.Ltd made during the war was for the resumption of excursions from West Hoe Pier in 1942 – the request was refused. The MS&TCo.Ltd's *Lady Elizabeth* was sold to the MoWT in 1942, for use in Devonport Dockyard, and the Millbrook company purchased the *Tamar Belle* from Bill Worth to replace her.

In January 1943 the authorities released the O&TSCo.Ltd's three ferry steamers from

Plymouth Hoe and the Sea Front, pictured after the Second World War. Just beyond the 'Big Pool' at Tinside are the remains of the bomb damaged Promenade Pier. All traces of the pier vanished in 1952 when the structure was dismantled. Due to its poor state of repair West Hoe Pier was abandoned as a steamer landing and Phoenix Wharf in Sutton Pool has remained as the major passenger excursion pier ever since. The SIR FRANCIS DRAKE *lies at Millbay Pier, in the background, she was the first tender to resume coastal excursions on 2 July 1946.*
COURTESY SARAH ACKRILL HILL.

Dormant Charter, the threat of invasion having receded. In the following month Hockings Yard was instructed to recommence repairs on the *Tiger*. Further signs of a return to normality are indicated by repairs to the Gutter pontoon by Fox Haggart of Sutton Harbour, while at Turnchapel the landing steps were repaired by Hockings. HMS *Foliot* (ex-*May Queen*) collided with a trawler and sank in the Hamoaze in December 1943 and was written off as wreck. After the war Jack Abbot saw her, almost up to her funnel in the mud of Weston Mill Creek.

There was a major change on the Cremyll Ferry in 1943 when the Mount Edgcumbe Estate leased the ferry (including the *Armadillo* and the *Shuttlecock)* to the MS&TCo.Ltd.

The *Plan for Plymouth* was published in 1943 outlining proposals for the reconstruction of the City after the war. Important to this story was a high level road bridge at Saltash (a suspension bridge, as first projected in 1822).

The steamer service between Turnchapel and Oreston was suspended on order of the police from 27 to 30 March 1944 – for embarkation practice at Sycamore Slipway for D-Day landings in Normandy. On August Bank Holiday 1944 the weather was good and a huge number of passengers took advantage of the Cattewater steamers to visit Jennycliff – the company's minute books describe the takings as 'very good'. The country was still at war but the cold fear of the 1941 Blitz was becoming replaced by optimism for victory.

In February 1945 some navigation lights within the port were re-lit. On the Cattewater, in a fit of uncharacteristic concern for the well being of their crews, the O&TSCo.Ltd fitted the *Lively* with a wheelhouse in her bow – the first shelter that helmsmen on the Cattewater steamers ever had in over 75 years of continuous operation in all conditions. The war in Europe ended on 8 May 1945 and the O&TSCo.Ltd lost no time in applying to run trips to Saltash and Calstock. Permission was granted for most excursions to resume, excepting trips to Cawsand and Bovisand, because the defence boom was still in position off the Breakwater. The *Western Evening Herald* reported that on Wednesday 13 June 1945 pleasure cruises resumed when the *Swift* and the *Lively* carried about 150 passengers on a Tamar excursion. However, the *Western Morning News* claimed that the 'first trip since the war' was on 15 June 'from Phoenix Wharf, Plymouth to the Royal Albert Bridge', and the *Lively* was pictured with her new helm shelter. In July directors of the O&TSCo.Ltd met with debenture holders of the PPP&STTSCo.Ltd to negotiate sole rights at West Hoe Pier, but on inspection the stone jetty was found in a poor state of repair and the plan was abandoned.

There were changes in directorships of the MS&TCo.Ltd in 1945. John Parson, founder of the MS&TCo.Ltd had died during the war and on 9 June his shares were transferred to Mary Kate Parson of Millbrook who became the permanent Chairman of the company, and to W. T. Crawford who became the permanent Managing Director – having already been running the company for a number of years. The MS&TCo.Ltd offered the first trip to Weir Head aboard the *Western Belle* on 23 June.

Piers Alexander, the fifth Earl of Mount Edgcumbe, died in 1944, ending the direct line of descent. Mount Edgcumbe House lay in ruins until restoration was started in 1958. In June 1945 the Mount Edgcumbe Estate sold the rights of the Cremyll Ferry to the MS&TCo.Ltd, who had been operating it since 1943. A Plymouth Council meeting, reported in the *Western Evening Herald*, reflected the disappointment felt by many that the ferry had not passed to local authority ownership:

> "The Earl of Mount Edgcumbe, I regret, has seen fit to dispose of the Cremyll Ferry to the Millbrook Steamboat Co. instead of giving us the chance," said the Lord Mayor Ald. H. G. Mason, when he moved the minutes of the Special Purposes Committee.
>
> Ald. Mrs Marshall said she was told two months ago that the Steamboat Co. had got it and complained of the Council's slowness. The Lord Mayor said ... they heard several bodies were competing, including Cornwall County. A joint meeting was arranged. The only way out was a joint arrangement and in the meantime it had been disposed of.

Both the *Armadillo* and *Shuttlecock* were still steam powered in1945. Both had gained a reputation for unreliability. The *Armadillo* was still in steam on the Cremyll Ferry in the following year but the *Shuttlecock* suffered bad damage after grounding at Cremyll Quay in 1945 and went into Mashford's Yard at Cremyll to be rebuilt and converted to diesel – Mashfords of Saltash had taken over Rogers' premises in 1936. The *Armadillo* continued on the ferry until she too was converted to diesel power by the MS&TCo.Ltd in the winter of 1946-7.

On the Torpoint Ferry naval manning ended on 30 July 1945 but a shortage of civilian crews and refusal to employ women, meant single ferry operation for a few months.

The O&TSCo.Ltd continued their programme of repairs by ordering a new pontoon for the Gutter landing at Oreston. Record takings of £528. 15s. 0d were recorded on the Cattewater steamer service over the August Bank Holiday weekend in 1945. In December the MoWT informed the O&TSCo.Ltd that the *Lady Beatrice* was up for disposal and could be inspected at Mashfords' Cremyll Yard. But she was in a bad condition and not considered worth repairing. She was seen hulked at Southdown late in the 1940s by Jack Abbot. The *City of Plymouth* was likewise available for purchase late in 1945. She was laid up at Cattedown and offered by MoWT at £430. The O&TSCo.Ltd offered £2,250 if she was repaired to pass a Board of Trade examination. The MoWT reduced the price to £150 but the O&TSCo.Ltd was not interested. The *City of Plymouth* was eventually sold and was moored as a houseboat at Gweek on the River Helford in Cornwall until the 1950s. Late in 1945 both the *Swift* and the *Rapid* were fitted with wheelhouses like the *Lively's*. Having sold their entire excursion fleet to the MoWT the O&TSCo.Ltd decided to order a new motor vessel for use on excursions and the Cattewater. In November 1945 directors of the company went to Dartmouth to brief Philip & Son Ltd on her construction.

The CITY OF PLYMOUTH laid up at Cattedown in 1945. The MoWT offered to sell her back to the O&TSCo.Ltd for just £150, but the company declined.
ALAN KITTRIDGE COLLECTION.

A surprising story was pieced together by Richard Clammer in 1986 and concerns the wartime 'career' of a well known local steamer from the past. We last left the old Calstock market steamer *Empress* during the early 1930s, moored on the River Yealm as a weekend houseboat. During the build-up to D-Day (1943-4) the *Empress*, which was either hulked or still moored on the Yealm, was commandeered and towed to Salcombe for use as a fuel pontoon alongside the old Kingsbridge Estuary paddler *Ilton Castle* (once a fleet sister of the *Whitsand Castle*, ex-*Kenwith Castle*). After the war the *Empress* was purchased by a WRNS officer and once again pressed into service as a houseboat, moored in Waterhead Creek on the Kingsbridge Estuary. The old paddler soon suffered hull damage from continual grounding on each low tide and eventually sank and was abandoned. In the early 1950s, following complaints about her unsightly condition, the *Empress* was patched up, pumped out and made her last voyage. She was towed out of harm's way by the Harbourmaster to her final resting place at the head of Waterhead Creek.

The old Calstock market steamer EMPRESS, pictured by the Plymouth photographer Robert Chapman during the early 1950s at Waterhead Creek on the Kingsbridge Estuary. She was hulked here after being abandoned following her second stint as a houseboat.
ROBERT CHAPMAN.

The SWEET CONTENT *at Cawsand after the Second World War. Note the flimsy gangplank, which children took delight in jumping up and down on.* COURTESY C. R. CLOAD

The Mitchell built launches CONTENT *(inside) and the MS&TCo.Ltd's* ENDEAVOUR *at the Mayflower Steps in the 1950s, embarking for Cawsands – when the boat was full you could go.* COURTESY C. R. CLOAD

POST WAR RIVER CROSSINGS AND EXCURSIONS

The post war years of the 1950s and 1960s saw a massive growth in private car ownership and each weekend 'family saloons' crowded the roads – exploring the surrounding countryside, going for picnics on Dartmoor, or across the Tamar at Saltash and Torpoint to beaches in Cornwall. The terms 'bottleneck' and 'traffic jam' became part of the holiday vocabulary, especially in the summer months when local weekend motorists joined the queues of tourists heading for the westcountry's 'beauty spots'. Few places became more congested than the floating bridges at Saltash and Torpoint where the old fashioned, lumbering steam vessels worked hard to keep pace with burgeoning tide of motor vehicles.

The Sea Front of Plymouth had been developed before the war to cater for increasing numbers of swimmers. During the 1930s Tinside was terraced and in 1935 the 'art deco' style circular lido, known locally as 'Big Pool', was opened. From landing steps adjacent to the site of the Promenade Pier a shuttle of open motor launches ran hundreds to the beaches at Bovisand, Kingsand and Cawsand. It is difficult to convey just how busy the Sea Front once was. Vast crowds of people covered the rocks and grassy slopes. During the summer months, the smell of suntan lotion pervaded the air and the incessant cacophony of thousands of happy voices only died down at sunset. From Sutton Pool yet more passenger boats, including Cload's 'Content' launches, carried trippers to beaches beyond the Breakwater, while from Phoenix Wharf 'steamers' of the O&TSCo.Ltd and MS&TCo.Ltd took day trippers to the River Yealm or up the Tamar to see the 'Dockyard and Warships' and to 'call in' at Calstock.

Meanwhile the Tamar Valley lay silent, its industrial past largely forgotten by Plymothians and unknown to outsiders. The tradition of calling in at Calstock continued but visits to Weir Head became rare occasions. The moribund Tamar Manure Navigation Company was liquidated after the war. Not until 1967, when Frank Booker's classic book *The Industrial Archaeology of the Tamar Valley* was published, followed by a BBC television programme *The Silent Valley*, was interest and tourism in the beautiful Tamar Valley slowly rekindled.

THE DEMISE OF THE TURNCHAPEL & ORESTON STEAMBOAT CO LTD.

The O&TSCo.Ltd's new 31tg, 62 x 14.5 x 5.5 feet, steel motor vessel, the *May Queen*, was launched by Mrs C. C. Elford on the evening of Monday 17 June 1946 at Philip's yard on the River Dart. Costing £5,900 the new boat was powered by a Lister three cylinder diesel engine. The *May Queen* made a trial trip on the Dart on 17 July and gained a certificate for 195 passengers. Her maiden voyage to Calstock and Weir Head on 27 July was a special occasion, with guests including officials from Philip & Son Ltd, O&TSCo.Ltd shareholders and friends.

In spring 1948 the O&TSCo.Ltd purchased Steamer Quay, in Calstock, from the PPP&STTSCo.Ltd for £400. Debenture shareholders of the pier company could hardly believe their good fortune when in 1952 they received compensation from the War Damages Commission for the loss of the pier. The receiver of the pier company subsequently awarded Eglington Bros a contract for the demolition and removal of all metal from the bomb ruined Promenade Pier.

The O&TSCo.Ltd purchased another motor vessel in 1947, intended principally for use on

The Oreston & Turnchapel Steamboat Co Ltd's new motor vessel, the MAY QUEEN *of 1946, pictured at Phoenix Wharf in August 1947, to pick up for an evening Tamar excursion. Despite the frugal economics of the O&TSCo.Ltd, the* MAY QUEEN'*s Lister diesel engine was still operated by an engineer in the engine room, signalled by bell from the skipper in the wheelhouse.*
B. Y. WILLIAMS.

the winter Cattewater service. The *Sweet Marie* was on offer at a Government surplus auction in Sutton Harbour and after inspection and a trial trip the company successfully bid £1,270. The boat had been built by Mashfords at Cremyll in 1939 and acquired by the MoWT during the war. She had a wooden hull measuring 45 x 12 feet and was powered by a Ricardo engine. The O&TSCo.Ltd fitted a cabin and wheelhouse and put her on the Cattewater service in September 1948 with a certificate for 85 passengers. The company soon discovered that both the *Sweet Marie* and the *May Queen* could maintain the Cattewater service for a fraction of the steamers' running costs. The price of coal in 1948 was about £4 per ton – increasing each year. Diesel oil was 1s 8d per gallon but Shell Mex offered it at only 10¼d per gallon direct from their pipeline at Cattedown. In the following month a Lister diesel engine was ordered for the *Swift*. Her steam engine and boiler were removed in November and sold for scrap. The new diesel engine was delivered in December and fitted by company employees during the winter. The *Swift* re-entered service in 1949 as a motor vessel with a wheelhouse fitted on her top deck, forward of her funnel. Meanwhile, in July 1948, the motor launch *Tiger* had been sold locally and in the following year the *Sweet Marie* was sold to P. & A. Campbell Ltd of Bristol for use as a tender to their coastal excursion steamers at Lynmouth and Lundy Island.

Both the *May Queen* and the *Swift* were fitted with refreshment bars for excursions – with crockery and provisions provided by the Manager, H. R. Elford. Some profitable special excursions were run in November 1949 when HMS *Amethyst* returned home from her 'Yangste Incident'. And in 1951, during the Festival of Britain Week, nearly 3000 schoolchildren were carried on Dockyard and Warship trips run in conjunction with British Rail. But that is about as good as it got for the O&TSCo.Ltd after the war and in the early 1950s the company's fortunes fell into terminal decline.

On 21 August 1949 a new bus route was started by Plymouth Joint Services (Plymouth Corporation and Western National) from St Andrews Cross (in the City Centre) to Mount Batten. The Ministry of Transport asked if the O&TSCo.Ltd would object if the bus ran to Turnchapel. The company indignantly replied that 'we certainly should do so' and solicitors Foot & Bowden were instructed to appear on their behalf at an inquiry. Due to coal shortages the Turnchapel railway line was temporarily closed on 14 January 1951 resulting in increased takings on the ferry. The O&TSCo.Ltd expressed a hope that the closure was permanent, as indeed it soon was. Although rail services recommenced on 2 July, so many

The LIVELY *off Phoenix Wharf in the late 1940s. Note her wheelhouse in the bows – fitted in 1945.*
COURTESY JACK KINGSTON

The SWIFT was fitted with a Lister diesel engine in 1949. Her appearance was improved by the erection of a wheelhouse on her top deck with the funnel behind. She is pictured in 1954 following repairs by Fox Haggart of Sutton Harbour after being damaged by fire in January 1954. COURTESY GRAHAME FARR.

The MAY QUEEN (right) and SWIFT at Turnchapel Pier in the '50s. ALAN KITTRIDGE COLLECTION

passengers had transferred to bus and ferry services that permanent closure of passenger train services followed on 10 September 1951. The bus fare to Plymouth City Centre from Mount Batten was increased from 6d to 8d which further increased use of ferry. But neither of these fillips could save the old steamer *Lively*, which was sold in December 1951 to Willoughby Bros Ltd for £250.

Not only were most of their boats and infrastructure ageing but the staff too were looking decidedly wobbly. C. C. Elford, Chairman of the company died in 1950, aged 71. In the same year the board decided to approach W. 'Billy' Phillips regarding retirement as he was 76. He had been with the company since the nineteenth century and the company offered him a £2 pension for life. Harry Tucker, one time skipper of the *City of Plymouth*, and piermaster at Turnchapel, died in August 1952, and G. Meek, who had been with the company for over 30 years, left the company to become the Postmaster at Oreston.

Any hopes regarding the future of the company were severely dashed in 1954 when a catalogue of disasters conspired to close the O&TSCo.Ltd altogether. The *Swift* was badly damaged by fire in January 1954, her engine room, saloon and top deck were all burnt. Fox Haggart in Sutton Harbour carried out her repairs but she was out of service until May. The company's last steamer, the *Rapid*, was put on to the ferry but was badly damaged after going aground and was withdrawn, never to enter service again. In October her machinery was taken out and sold and her hull was advertised for sale at £600. She was eventually sold for conversion to a houseboat in Hooe Lake for just £50. Fortunately the company had re-purchased the *Tiger* in 1953 and she was pressed into use on the ferry and even some excursions in 1954. The company's troubles continued when it was decided that the *May Queen* needed a new engine. The Philip built boat vibrated badly and it was thought that a six cylinder engine would cure the problem. Having only just bought a second-hand Kelvin engine for the *Tiger*, a somewhat dismayed Director, A. H. Davis, suggested that rather than spending any more money on the boats, they should consider selling the company. Both Plymouth Corporation and the MS&TCo.Ltd were approached without success.

The Elfords reduced the O&TSCo.Ltd's rent at Turnchapel Pier and the board were also looking to close Gutter pontoon at Oreston in an

attempt to reduce their rates bill. In the following the year they cut Oreston service completely for the winter.

The origins and 'bread and butter' of the company had always been the year round Cattewater steamer service, but in the mid '50s, having seen off the railway and weathered opposing bus services, the ferry was being undermined by the growth in private car ownership. In 1955 H. R. Elford announced that he wanted to sell his shares and retire and he thought it advisable to sell the company. In March the company was put up for auction but there were no bidders. British Rail expressed an interest in the *May Queen* for use on the Kingswear Ferry but on inspection declined to make an offer. The O&TSCo.Ltd had little choice but to re-engine the *May Queen* and a second-hand six cylinder Thornycroft RL6 engine was purchased and installed by Fox Haggart (this never completely solved her vibration problems, which continued to plague her for the rest of her time at Plymouth). Other repairs were undertaken by the Lucas Yard at Oreston who reported that some of the boat's woodwork was in a very poor condition. Further complications arose when the Board of Trade wanted her fuel tanks repositioned. The final bill to put the *May Queen* back into service totalled a crushing £2,147 (although £675 was recouped by selling her original Lister engine). The only bright spot in 1955 were the August receipts on the ferry and excursions – the best for years. At the end of the year the Elford family sold Turnchapel Pier to the O&TSCo.Ltd company for £100.

In 1956 H. R. Elford reminded the board that he still wanted to retire, so the company advertised for a Manager. Three men were interviewed but the chosen applicant rejected the post. The company then advertised in the *Daily Telegraph* and *Motor Boat* magazine:

> Ferry and river excursion business as going concern. Two diesel boats and valuable waterside and riverside properties. Could be developed. South Coast.

Only one person viewed the property but was not interested. The search for a new manager ended in farce when the Employment Exchange 'phoned enquiring if the company still wanted a manager as they had a retired Major looking for work, the only trouble was he had a bad stammer. The O&TSCo.Ltd politely declined.

Finally, in December 1956, Mr C. A. Partridge of Plymouth expressed an interest in buying the ferry service and the *Swift* but not the *May Queen* or the excursion business. The MS&TCo.Ltd, conversely, did not want the ferry but expressed an interest in buying either the *May Queen* or the *Swift*. In May 1957 the *May Queen* was sold to the MS&TCo.Ltd for £3,500 the Millbrook company also inherited her bookings. Calstock's Steamer Quay was also offered but the two companies could not agree a price. Surprisingly the MS&TCo.Ltd let the old Devon & Cornwall Tamar Steam Packet Co Ltd's quay and stores (and free landing thereafter) slip from their reach when the O&TSCo.Ltd sold it to a private buyer for just £275.

Looking somewhat narrower than memory suggests, Rendel's Iron Bridge at Laira was replaced in 1961 by the current dual-carriageway bridge. Preliminary work on the new bridge is underway.
Behind is the railway bridge which carried trains for the Yealmpton and Turnchapel branch lines
COURTESY KEITH PERKINS

C. A. Partridge could now afford the reduced package and on Saturday 17 August 1957 trading as the Plymouth & Oreston Steamboat Company (P&OSCo), he took over the *Swift*, *Tiger*, Turnchapel Pier and Gutter pontoon for a total of £2,500. The shop, flat and office (old School) at Turnchapel were sold to H. R. Elford for £650 in 1962. In the following year directors of O&TSCo.Ltd met at the company's solicitors, Foot & Bowden, to arrange the liquidation.

Meanwhile the P&OSCo cut the Oreston call to the peak summer months only. A new four lane Laira road bridge, built to replace Rendel's Iron Bridge, was opened in 1961. Whilst not immediately affecting the Cattewater steamer service, it is an indication of the growth of motor traffic to and from the district. In 1962 the accident prone *Swift* suffered her last mishap when she sank at her moorings in a gale. She was beached but subsequently broken. The *Tiger* was assisted by two other motor launches but the 'Turnchapel Ferry', as it had become generally known, was nearing the end and by the time that the O&TSCo.Ltd was finally wound up on 27 May 1965, the P&OSCo had already abandoned the Cattewater service, bringing to a close the collective history of almost all the ferry services that had once plied the Cattewater.

The Philip built Saltash floating bridge No.1 of 1927 at Saltash Passage c1955.
ALAN KITTRIDGE COLLECTION.

The Thornycroft built Saltash floating bridge No.2 of 1933 in the final year of the Saltash Ferry, with the Tamar Bridge taking shape behind the Royal Albert Bridge.
R. C. SAMBOURNE.

CLOSURE OF THE SALTASH FERRY

The end for the Saltash Ferry was signalled with publication of the *Plan for Plymouth* in 1943 – for reconstruction of the city after the war. The plan recommended construction of a high level bridge at Saltash and in 1957 the Tamar Bridge Act authorised Cornwall County Council and Plymouth City Council to construct a suspension bridge across Saltash Passage and nullify the ancient ferry rights. The Tamar Bridge and Torpoint Ferry Joint Committee, comprising five members each of the two councils would henceforth administrate both the Tamar Bridge and the Torpoint Ferry. Saltash Corporation were to be awarded £30,000 compensation for loss of revenue and ferry rights when the bridge was completed – a sum which has subsequently been considered insufficient for the loss of the Borough's ancient rights.

There was only single floating bridge operation at Saltash and twice a year the floating bridges were changed over at night. The retiring bridge was towed onto the gridiron on the Devon shore, immediately upstream of the ferry beach. There was always a danger that the cumbersome bridge might break loose, as happened on one occasion in 1955 when one of the bridges was temporarily washed ashore.

Because there was no further investment in the ferry it fell largely upon resourceful crews and management to keep the floating bridge serviceable until the end. The first ominous sign of their approaching doom was evidenced in 1959 by the demolition of fifty houses and ten shops in Saltash to make way for the suspension bridge.

The last public crossing took place at 11.15pm on Monday 23 October 1961. All day an effigy hung from rigging, holding a placard which offered the ferry staff's parting message 'Farewell to friends and travellers'. At 4.30 in the afternoon on the following day the Mayor of Saltash, Maurice Huggins, and a civic party boarded the ferry for the final crossing. Meanwhile, above them, the roar of traffic indicated that the Tamar Bridge had already opened.

The Thornycroft floating bridge was bought by the King Harry Ferry Company for £2,500 and after a lengthy conversion to diesel engines, entered service on the River Fal on 14 May 1964. The Philip bridge was sold for £1,750 to Haulbowline Industries Ltd of Passage West,

The last, 'ceremonial', crossing of the Saltash floating bridge on Tuesday 24 October 1961, leaving the Saltash landing beach. Below: *The Tamar Bridge opened in October 1961 and replaced the floating bridge of the ancient Saltash Ferry* WESTERN MORNING NEWS

County Cork, for breaking. The bridge set off under tow by a dutch tug, *Loire*, but sank off Falmouth.

The Tamar Bridge and adjacent Royal Albert Bridge create a spectacular scene at the 'gateway to Cornwall' and beneath their towering spans the old ferry beaches are still very much in evidence – reminders of a time when the Celtic county of Cornwall, although only a few hundred yards across the Tamar, felt like a different country.

EXPANSION OF THE TORPOINT FERRY

Writing in 1991 A. R. Warren criticised the design of the three pre-war floating bridges. He considered them obsolete before they were built, being coal fired – rather than oil fired or even diesel engined – and having a capacity for only 16 cars. Following the introduction of double floating bridges in 1932 the Torpoint route into Cornwall became far more popular than the even slower Saltash Ferry. After the Second World War motor traffic increased and rarely could a motorist board the ferry without a

A post-war picture of the Philip built Torpoint floating bridge of 1931. ALAN KITTRIDGE COLLECTION.

The Torpoint landing beach in the late 1940s. ALAN KITTRIDGE COLLECTION.

lengthy queue. On the Torpoint side, especially on weekend evenings, the traffic tailed all the way back through Fore Street. The well practiced motorist could send a passenger ahead on foot to the popular fish and chip shop in Fore Street, and pick their supper up as they crawled past.

From 1950 Cornwall County Council and Plymouth City Council sought to address the ever increasing problem of chronic congestion at the two crossings. The solution for Saltash is described above, but owing to the nature of the Torpoint crossing a bridge was out of the question. In 1959 two new floating bridges were

One of the two Thornycroft built diesel electric floating bridges of 1960-1961 at Devonport. Bicycles, motorbikes and motor scooters waited until the traffic deck was full before being waved on by the ticket collector. The landing prows could take their weight but not other vehicles. WESTERN MORNING NEWS.

ordered from Thornycroft of Southampton. The new vessels had diesel electric engines (diesel generators driving electric motors) and a capacity for around 30 cars. They measured 182ft long overall, inclusive of 40ft landing prows (which were unable to carry traffic) and 54ft wide, with a traffic deck 32ft wide. The first new floating bridge left Southampton in October 1960 but was damaged in a storm *en-route* to Plymouth and didn't enter service until repairs were completed in January 1961. The second bridge arrived in December 1960 and therefore entered service first. The Philip ferry of 1931 was retained in reserve, but the two older bridges were sold for scrapping to Davis & Cann Ltd, near Laira Bridge.

With the opening of the suspension bridge at Saltash in 1961, the Tamar Bridge and Torpoint Ferry Joint Committee set the same tolls on both crossings, and as pedestrians could cross the Tamar Bridge free of charge, the foot passenger tolls on the ferry were also removed.

A third new floating bridge was ordered in 1966 to replace the last steam bridge. Built by Charles Hill & Son Ltd of Bristol she measured 188ft x 57ft. The old Philip floating bridge was sold to Belgian owners, for use as a drilling platform. The familiar queues of traffic through Torpoint vanished in 1967 when marshalling lanes and a control tower were opened just above the ferry beach.

THE TORPOINT FERRY CONTINUES

In 1972 the landing beaches were extended to accommodate a third set of chains and all three floating bridges were put into service. The Western National's bus service on the Rame Peninsula – purchased from the MS&TCo.Ltd in 1968 – was eventually condensed into a single bus route serving Cremyll, Cawsand, Millbrook and Torpoint. In 1979 the route was extended to Plymouth's town centre *via* the Torpoint Ferry. The 'Ferrybus' was given priority over other traffic and passengers could board the bus aboard the ferry.

A. R. Warren, who was appointed Manager of the Tamar Bridge and Torpoint Ferry in

In 1967 the familiar queues of traffic through Torpoint vanished when marshalling lanes, controlled from the tower on the right, were completed. The building on the left, behind the lane lights, is the ferry office. Between the office and the floating bridge is on of the chain pit gantries.
COURTESY KEITH PERKINS.

Rendel Park on the foreshore at Torpoint, adjacent to the ferry was opened in 1978 and commemorates the inventor of the floating bridge – James Meadows Rendel.
COURTESY KEITH PERKINS

The 'stretched' Charles Hill built floating bridge – inappropriately named PLYM *– at Torpoint in 1988.*
ALAN KITTRIDGE

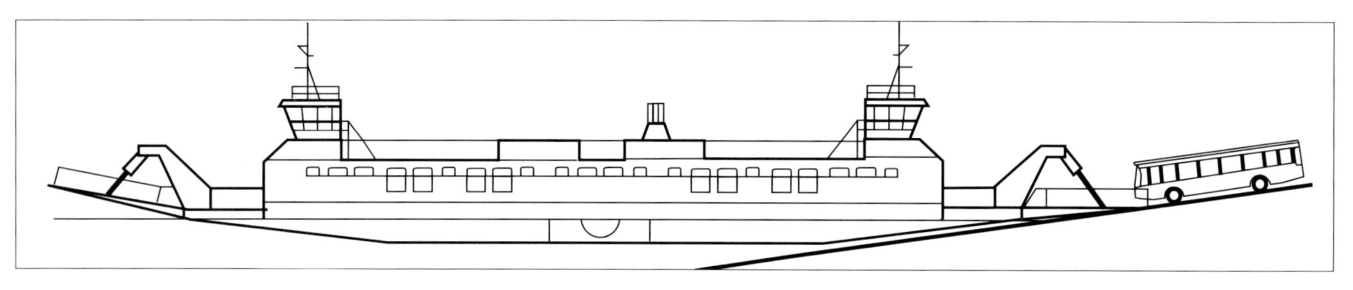

Profile drawing of the projected new generation of floating bridges for the Torpoint Ferry, due to enter service in 2004. ALAN KITTRIDGE

The ex-Cremyll Ferry steamer SHUTTLECOCK *emerged from Mashford's Cremyll Yard in July 1946 as the Millbrook Steamboat & Trading Co Ltd's motor vessel* SOUTHERN BELLE *and rarely could there have been a happier result. For many years the* SOUTHERN BELLE *would reign as the prettiest passenger boat in the Plymouth district, the pride of her owners and crews.* ALAN KITTRIDGE COLLECTION.

1985, was faced with the perennial problem of increasing the ferry's capacity. While the suspension bridge at Saltash had diverted most of the through traffic it was still some 15 miles distant from the population of Torpoint and the Rame Peninsula. Torpoint, although in Cornwall, is a dormitory suburb of Plymouth and since the Second World War it has expanded considerably. The age old ideas of bridges and tunnels were dusted off and promoted once again in the local media. A fourth ferry was discounted on the grounds of space and economics. Mr Warren therefore proposed 'stretching' the existing bridges to carry about 50 cars each. Falmouth Shiprepair Ltd undertook the work of lengthening the bridges by inserting two new sections either side of the engine room. Additional car space was created by changing the prow counterbalance system to independent hydraulic rams, enabling vehicles to be carried on the prows. The first 'stretched' Thornycroft bridge re-entered service in June 1986, followed by her sister in November of the same year. For the first time the floating bridges carried names: *Tamar* and *Lynher* respectively. The stretched Charles Hill bridge re-entered service in 1987 and some 'bright spark' (who could probably be found commanding a desk in Plymouth Civic Centre) decided to christen her *Plym* – the name *Tavy* would have been more appropriate, being a Devon tributary of the Tamar. In 1990 a marshalling area and control tower were built on the Devonport shore, utilising the island of space between Ferry Road and Pottery Road that had once been the Ferry Canal.

The three floating bridges operate a shuttle service between the hours 6.30 am to 11.30 pm, after which a single bridge continues through the night. The ferry provides a continual service every day and night of the year.

In 2001 it was announced that three new floating bridges were to be built – each capable of carrying 73 cars (50 per cent more than the existing bridges). They will also carry lorries of up to 44 tons.

MILLBROOK STEAMBOAT & TRADING CO LTD.

In May 1946 the capital of the MS&TCo.Ltd was increased to £26,000 by the creation of 20,000 £1 shares. New investors in the MS&TCo.Ltd were Sidney Mashford of Mashfords Shipyard, and L. L. J. (Les) Worth of Millbrook – Jack Worth's son. They both joined

The NORTHERN BELLE *(ex-*ARMADILLO*) pictured at Admiral's Hard in 1962.*
B. Y. WILLIAMS

Mary K. Parson and William T. Crawford on the board of directors in the following year.

The *Western Morning News* in July 1946 reported:

> At Messrs Mashford Brothers shipyard at Cremyll the finishing touches are being put to the latest addition to the fleet of vessels owned by the Millbrook Steamboat and Trading Company. Few will recognise in her new guise the well known Cremyll ferry steamer 'Shuttlecock' now to be renamed 'Southern Belle' for she has been entirely rebuilt and converted at the shipyard. The top deck has been strengthened and fitted to accommodate passengers, and the cabin accommodation greatly improved by removing the boiler and steam engines and installing a powerful 72 hp Gleniffer diesel motor, which besides giving increased speed and greater flexibility, occupies much less space...

The Earl and Countess of Mount Edgcumbe, accompanied by their daughter, Lady Margaret McCauseland, were passengers on the maiden voyage of the *Southern Belle* on Friday 5 July. Around sixty other guests, including William T. Crawford, Mary Parson and Sidney Mashford, embarked at Cremyll and Admiral's Hard for a trip to Calstock, calling at Cotehele, where Lady Margaret McCauseland showed the guests around the house.

At the end of the same month the MS&TCo.Ltd acquired the fare stage services and buses of Skinners of Millbrook. For the next twenty years the Millbrook company enjoyed a monopoly of bus services on the Rame Peninsula including access to all the beaches in Whitsand Bay – since the Ministry of Defence had relinquished their sole right of way to the Military Road around the cliff tops.

The Cremyll Ferry steamer *Armadillo* was converted to diesel power in 1947. Although a fleet list drawn up by the MS&TCo.Ltd in 1962 states that she was '...converted from steam to diesel (Kelvin K4) by ourselves in 1947...', some steel reinforcing work was probably undertaken at Mashfords. Renamed the *Northern Belle* she re-entered service in 1947. Unlike the *Southern Belle*, the *Northern Belle* was not fitted with a top deck because it was never intended to use her anywhere else than on the Cremyll Ferry. The company repurchased the *Lady Elizabeth* from MoWT in 1947. She was converted to single screw in 1949 and fitted with the *Tamar Belle's* old Parsons engine.

Ownership of Les Worth's launches, the *White Heather*, *Endeavour* and *Guiding Star* was transferred to the MS&TCo.Ltd in 1947, and they were subsequently used mostly on the Cawsand run from the Sea Front and the Mayflower Steps.

The LADY ELIZABETH *was another Millbrook Steamboat & Trading Co Ltd boat which was transformed after the Second World War. She was converted to single screw in 1949. In 1955 her cabin and boarding steps were altered for her three year charter to British Railways' Kingswear Ferry* (above). *Further changes to her cabin were made when she returned from the River Dart, as pictured at Cawsand in 1962* (opposite). B. Y. WILLIAMS.

The MS&TCo.Ltd's operational fleet in 1947 therefore comprised:

Devon Belle	Millbrook ferry, excursions
Western Belle	Excursions, Millbrook ferry
Tamar Belle	Millbrook and Cremyll ferry
Southern Belle	Excursions
Northern Belle	Cremyll Ferry
Lady Elizabeth	Millbrook and Cremyll Ferry and Cawsand
White Heather	Cawsand and excursions
Endeavour	Cawsand and excursions
Guiding Star	Cawsand and excursions

William James Crawford inherited W. T. Crawfords' shares in 1953 and became the permanent Managing Director with Sidney Mashford as permanent Chairman. Two other Crawfords – Donald and Derek – also became directors.

The *White Heather* was sold to a Torquay owner in 1953. Between 1955 and 1957 the *Lady Elizabeth* was chartered to British Rail to maintain their Dartmouth Kingswear Ferry – following the withdrawal of the long serving ferry steamer, *The Mew*. A major new addition to the fleet in May 1957 was the O&TSCo.Ltd's *May Queen*. She was purchased as an excursion boat and also as a reserve boat on the Cremyll Ferry. She entered service renamed *Eastern*

The EASTERN BELLE *(ex-*MAY QUEEN*) in Plymouth Sound in 1962, with Drake's Island and Mount Edgcumbe in the background.* B. Y. WILLIAMS.

The Mashford built PLYMOUTH BELLE *of 1962 pictured at Cawsand during her second season.*
B. Y. WILLIAMS.

Belle, repainted in the MS&TCo.Ltd's attractive livery of the time – white hull, light blue cabin sides, varnished or scumbled woodwork and a red funnel with a black top. Two years later the *Tamar Belle* was sold to George Pill of Falmouth and in 1960 the *Endeavour* was sold to Torquay.

In 1961 the company took delivery of the *Plymouth Belle* a 65ft long wooden motor vessel, built by Mashfords. She was used on river excursions and the Cawsand run. As built the *Plymouth Belle* had a covered cabin but no top deck. Her appearance and capacity were improved later by the addition of a top deck. The *Plymouth Belle* was powered by a Gardner 6LX (six cylinder) engine which soon became the favoured power unit in the MS&TCo.Ltd fleet, by 1965 the *Southern Belle, Northern Belle, Eastern Belle* and the *Western Belle* had also been fitted with them, while the *Lady Elizabeth* had a Gardner 5LW. The standardisation helped to simplify maintenance and spares. The *Guiding Star* was sold to the Isles of Scilly in 1962.

During the 1950s and 1960s the MS&TCo.Ltd at last enjoyed its very own golden age and monopolised all public transport on the Rame Peninsula. Although Plymouth lay just a mile or so across the water, the contrast between its grey urban landscape and the sunny country lanes of the Rame Peninsula could hardly have been greater. Each summer weekend during this period Plymothians swarmed across the water to enjoy the beaches, parkland and coastline of 'Cornwall's Forgotten Corner'. MS&TCo.Ltd boats crossed to Cawsand, Cremyll and Millbrook and the cream and red 'Millbrook Steamboat' single deck Bedford and Tilling Stephens buses carried locals and visitors around the district. Summer weekends were particularly busy, taking thousands to the beaches in Cawsand and Whitsand bays. The MS&TCo.Ltd were the last independent bus stage service operator in the Plymouth district until, in 1968, their stage and school services were sold to the Western National, which reorganised the network into two routes covering the Rame Peninsula from a base at Torpoint.

The MS&TCo.Ltd also dominated the river excursion business in Plymouth, running mainly from Phoenix Wharf (but only occasionally from the Hamoaze landings after the Second World War). The *Western Belle* ran a daily afternoon Yealm trip and sometimes visited Looe. Evenings would invariably find her at Calstock, she also maintained periodic trips to Morwellham and Weir Head. The *Southern Belle, Devon Belle* and *Eastern Belle* ran Dockyard and Warship trips and were also Calstock regulars. Trips on the Lynher and Tavy rivers were rarely undertaken, but photographs show that occasional visits were made to unusual destinations such as Maristow on the Tavy and Bridgend in Newton Creek. Jack Abbot of the *Western Belle* recalled one occasion in the 1960s going so far up the Yealm that he saw Kitley Quay for the first time, but by the 1970s such

An unusual port of call for the WESTERN BELLE *in the late 1950s or early '60s – Bridgend Quay in Newton Creek on the River Yealm – a location Jack Abbot was unable to identify because in all his years driving the* WESTERN BELLE *on the Yealm, he never went to Bridgend Quay. The presence of press photographer Dermot Fitzgerald suggests a special occasion.* DERMOT FITZGERALD.

Another rare call – the WESTERN BELLE *(inside) and the* DEVON BELLE *at Maristow Quay on the River Tavy. This was possibly a special trip to view Lopwell Dam, which was completed in 1954. Poles in the foreground mark Chucksford, a low tide crossing to the Bere Peninsula.* DERMOT FITZGERALD.

adventurous expeditions were a thing of the past. The only opposition to the MS&TCo.Ltd were the owner operator boats running Dockyard & Warship trips from the Sea Front and beach boats operating from the Sea Front and Mayflower Steps.

The Cremyll Ferry faced a crisis in 1972 when the directors of the MS&TCo.Ltd claimed that they were losing money in providing evening services on the Cremyll and Millbrook ferries. William J. Crawford said 'Personally I am prepared to run the two services if Cornwall County Council is prepared to subsidise them'. Following a public meeting at Millbrook Unionist Hall, Cornwall County Council offered £14 per week to help keep late winter evening services going. But two years later the evening winter departures from Stonehouse at 8.25pm and 9.25pm were cut – the last ferry in future would leave Admiral's Hard at 7.15pm.

During the early 1970s the Millbrook Ferry was still run by the *Lady Elizabeth* or *Devon Belle* but later in the decade only a morning and evening workers boat continued on a casual basis. According to Arthur Grylls and Jack Abbot the Millbrook ferry was eventually run more as a favour to their Millbrook friends than as a regular public service – they could even name the passengers. Researching this once busy crossing has highlighted the fallibility in over dependency of official records. The Millbrook ferry was always run privately so no official documentation or regulation, other than certification of the steamers, was required. Furthermore, there is no neat closure date for the Millbrook ferry – the remnants of the ferry service eventually petered out as the last regular passengers retired.

The W*ESTERN* B*ELLE* *heads for the Tamar while the Eastern Belle performs her daily 'float past' of the Sea Front, advertising her Dockyard and Warships trip.*
B. Y. WILLIAMS

The MS&TCo.Ltd fleet of the early 1970s embodied the history of the district's passenger steamers:

Devon Belle	Bought to replace the MSCo.'s paddle steamer *Hibernia*.
Western Belle	Bought to replace the MSCo.'s paddle steamer *Britannia*.
Southern Belle	Ex Mount Edgcumbe Estate's *Shuttlecock*.
Northern Belle	Ex Mount Edgcumbe Estate's *Armadillo*.
Lady Elizabeth	Ex PPP&STTSCo.Ltd
Eastern Belle	Ex O&TSCo.Ltd
Plymouth Belle	Built for the MS&TCo.Ltd.

The large steel, twin screw, motor vessel *Dartmouth Castle* (81tg, 87 x 20 x 5.8 feet) was

The MS&TCo.Ltd fleet – in the dark blue hull livery adopted in the late 1960s. From left to right: the L*ADY* E*LIZABETH*, N*ORTHERN* B*ELLE*, E*ASTERN* B*ELLE*, W*ESTERN* B*ELLE*, S*OUTHERN* B*ELLE*, D*EVON* B*ELLE and the* P*LYMOUTH* B*ELLE*.
COURTESY ARTHUR GRYLLS.

The EASTERN BELLE *at Morwellham c1980 with skipper Arthur Grylls aboard.* COURTESY ARTHUR GRYLLS.

The SOUTHERN BELLE *off Mashford's Yard, Cremyll in 1983, with her new saloon windows, fitted in the 1970s.* ALAN KITTRIDGE.

The NORTHERN BELLE *at Cremyll in 1981.*
ALAN KITTRIDGE.

purchased from the ailing River Dart Steamboat Co Ltd (RDSCo.Ltd) in 1975 but after just two seasons was sold to the RDSCo.Ltd's competitors, Dart Pleasure Craft Ltd (DPCLtd). In her place the MS&TCo.Ltd bought an even larger, twin screw, motor vessel from the RDSCo.Ltd, the *Cardiff Castle*. Built in 1964 by Bolson of Poole, the steel vessel measured 115tg 100 x 21 x 8.3 feet and was powered by twin Gleniffer engines. In subsequent fleet photographs the Dart boat dwarfed the rest of the Millbrook fleet. Derek Crawford replaced W. J. Crawford on the board of directors of the MS&TCo.Ltd in 1976. In the same year the *Lady Elizabeth* – chartered to a separate company (The Turnchapel & Oreston Steamboat Co Ltd) for reasons which remain obscure – inaugurated a Drake's Island ferry service, which was run in conjunction with the Mayflower Trust. The route was extended to a triangular service from Phoenix Wharf to Drake's Island, Cremyll and back to Phoenix Wharf. The oldest units in the fleet were sold in 1979. After fifty years of service the *Devon Belle* was sold to George Pill of Falmouth and the *Lady Elizabeth* was sold to the Kingsbridge Estuary. They were replaced by the single screw, wooden motor vessel *Humphrey Gilbert* (35 tg, 57.9 x 13.5 x 4.9 feet), an ex-

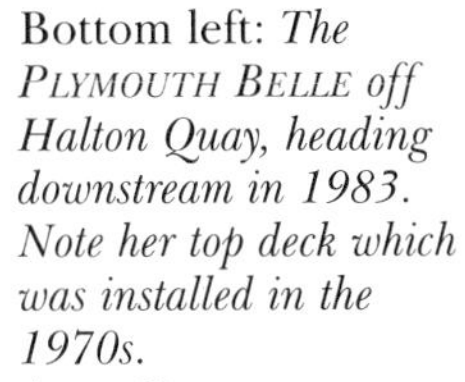

Bottom left: *The* PLYMOUTH BELLE *off Halton Quay, heading downstream in 1983. Note her top deck which was installed in the 1970s.*
ALAN KITTRIDGE.

Bottom Right: *The* DEVON BELLE *in Sutton Harbour in 1975. Excursion information was chalked on the blackboard on her cabin roof.*
KEN ANGUS,COURTESY RICHARD DANIELSON.

The EDGCUMBE BELLE *approaching the Drake's Island landing pier in 1983. Unfortunately this seasonal 'ferry' service is no longer operated and Drake's Island remains a highly visible but difficult to visit landmark in Plymouth Sound.* ALAN KITTRIDGE.

Kingswear Ferry boat built in 1957 by M. W. Blackmore of Bideford. She entered service for the MS&TCo.Ltd renamed the *Edgcumbe Belle* and was used on the Company's Drake's Island Ferry and the Cremyll Ferry.

In 1980 the direct line of descent from the days of the paddle steamers was all but severed when Derek Crawford, Sidney Mashford and Les Worth resigned as directors of the MS&TCo.Ltd, having sold their shares to Robert and Betty Crews and John Padden, directors of Dart Pleasure Craft Ltd. The 'Dart' directors immediately increased the Cremyll Ferry fares by 25% to 20p single with a further increase to 25p in the following year. They also abolished the special workman's 10p fare. Having thus alienated many on the Rame Peninsula the new regime was immediately plunged into a price war with the newly formed, Millbrook based, Plymouth Boat Cruises Ltd (PBCLtd). 'All aboard for a Tamar fares war' read the headline in the *Western Evening Herald*

The CARDIFF CASTLE *off Cotehele in the 1980s.* RICHARD CLAMMER

The WESTERN BELLE *at Looe in 1983, with her new saloon windows, fitted in the 1980s.* ALAN KITTRIDGE.

The 'new order' – PLYMOUTH VENTURER of Plymouth Boat Cruises Ltd, one of the companies that succeeded the Millbrook Steamboat & Trading Co Ltd in 1985.
ALAN KITTRIDGE.

in spring 1982:

> An 83-foot cruiser due to be launched in the Tamar soon is expected to break the river passenger monopoly enjoyed by the Millbrook Steamboat and Trading Company...Plymouth Venturer, now being fitted out at Mashford's boat yard, Cremyll, is expected to leave a fares war in her wake.

A second 'Herald article on 19 April 1982, described the *Plymouth Venturer*:

> The largest boat built by Mashford Brothers at Cremyll since the war is to be launched soon and is expected to be in commission by the end of this month.
>
> She is the 83ft steel-hulled passenger vessel Plymouth Venturer, which has been bought by Plymouth Boat Cruises, of Millbrook. She is destined to become a familiar sight in local waters and will be able to carry 350 passengers.
>
> Power will come from two 170hp diesel engines and Plymouth Venturer will have a cruising speed of 11 knots.
>
> Mr Sidney Mashford, 74-year-old managing director of Mashford Brothers, designed the boat...

The hull of the *Plymouth Venturer* was built at Devoran, in Cornwall, and brought around the coast to be fitted out at Mashford's Yard. She entered service in May 1982, joining the *Plymouth Princess*, which had been in operation since the previous year. Faced with the threat of continued competition with PBCLtd the 'Dart' directors pulled out of the area in 1985 (the centenary of the origins of the Millbrook company) and the MS&TCo.Ltd ceased operating as a passenger boat operator in the Plymouth district. The Cremyll Ferry was sold to Cremyll Ferry skipper, John Knight, trading as Tamar Cruising & Cremyll Ferry (TC&CF) and the fleet was dispersed:

Western Belle	(Dart since 1984) to DPCLtd
Southern Belle	to PBCLtd.
Northern Belle	to TC&CF
Eastern Belle	to PBCLtd
Cardiff Castle	to DPCLtd
Plymouth Belle	to DPCLtd (back to PBCLtd 2003)
Edgcumbe Belle	to DPCLtd
Dartmouth Castle	(which DPCLtd had transferred to the Millbrook fleet) back to DPCLtd
Queen Boadicea II	(bought to maintain Drake's Island ferry) to TC&CF

The event was barely noticed outside Millbrook and it was sad that a company which had given pleasure to hundreds of thousands of Plymothians and visitors for a century and served them faithfully in two world wars should pass without a mention from the local media.

DPCLtd's DARTMOUTH CASTLE, honouring a final charter commitment in the district for the erstwhile MS&TCo.Ltd, with the PLYMOUTH VENTURER astern, at Phoenix Wharf in 1985
ALAN KITTRIDGE.

NORTHERN BELLE at Cremyll Quay in September 2003. She has been plying the Cremyll Ferry exclusively for 76 years. Cremyll Quay offers a good operating base for other boats in the Tamar Cruising & Cremyll Ferry fleet, including their 49tg PLYMOUTH SOUND of 1987, pictured below. ALAN KITTRIDGE

Of all the ferries and steamboat lines that once offered public crossings on the districts' waterways, just two survive: the Cremyll Ferry – which has been maintained for the past three quarters of a century by the *Armadillo / Northern Belle* and the busy, round the clock Torpoint Ferry. Both look set to continue for many years.

The Tamar Valley has enjoyed renewed interest in its industrial past, which in turn has led to the establishment of a maritime museum at the National Trust's Cotehele Quay and development of Morwellham Quay as a living museum. Passenger boats continue to crowd Calstock on weekend evenings, mostly with charter parties – a side of their business that remains strong. Excursions to Weir Head are a rarity. The estuaries of the rivers Tavy and Lynher, and the Yealm upstream of Newton and Noss, have largely returned to peaceful solitude where little seems to have changed in centuries. Their densely wooded shores hide abandoned quays, and largely forgotten ferry crossings and fords – silent reminders of an age when the rivers and lakes of the 'Three Towns' district served its waterside communities as a water highway.

North Corner pontoon, looking forlorn in the 1990s. No longer used as a passenger boat landing, the pontoon and bridge have since been renewed. The two Thornycroft floating bridges of the Torpoint Ferry cross in the background. ALAN KITTRIDGE

Over a quarter of a century after my initial researches into the subject of this book the importance of some personal contacts made at that time is manifest, as many of them, sadly, are no longer with us. Much of their evidence was first hand memory, or in some cases the result of their own earlier conversations with people whose memories went back to the nineteenth century. These recollections breathe life into official records and while further documents and photographs lay waiting to be re-discovered, memory of life on the rivers of the Three Towns district beyond the 1920s is fading away.

The following people have been enthusiastic and generous with their assistance – their contribution is evident throughout the book – I am indebted to all of them: Jack Abbot of Calstock and Millbrook; Sarah Ackrill-Hill; Mary Anthony of Hooe; Ken and Kathleen Badge; J. Behenna; Barry Bridges; Robert Chapman; City of Plymouth Local and Naval Studies Library; City of Plymouth Reference Library; Richard Clammer; Arthur Clamp; C. R. Cload; Richard Danielson; Marjorie Deacon – daughter of photographer Fred. J. Paul of Calstock; John Doddridge – great grandson of photographer Frederick James Johns of Millbrook; Gary Emerson and Morwellham Quay Museum; Grahame Farr; Dermot Fitzgerald; Edgar Foster of Newton Ferrers; Alan Gissing; Geoffrey Grimshaw; Arthur Grylls of Millbrook; Brian Hillsdon of the Steamboat Association; Douglass Hoppins; Ms D. Ide; Tony Kingdom; Jack Kingston of Torpoint; Martin Langley; Fred Lee; Ian Merry; National Maritime Museum; Nigel Overton – Maritime Heritage Officer at Plymouth Museums and Art Gallery; R. T. Paige of Calstock; Eric Payne; Keith Perkins; Chris Robinson; Royal Institution of Cornwall; Ken Saunders; Win Scutt at Plymouth Museums and Art Gallery; Alec J. Short – grandson of George Hodge; Winifred Southey of Calstock; Roy Stribley; Dawn Tapper; Jenny Taylor and the Millbrook Steamboat & Trading Co. Ltd.; E. C. B. Thornton; Douglas Vosper of Saltash; and Bernard Williams – who kept a photographic record of the steamers for half a century until the 1970s.

SOURCES:

The National Archive.

BT31–10 Saltash Watermans Steam Packet Co Ltd company records.
BT31–282 Tamar Steam Navigation Co Ltd company records.
BT31–308 Devon & Cornwall Tamar Steam Packet Co Ltd company records.
BT31–337 Saltash & Saint Germans Steam Packet Co Ltd company records.
BT31–1142 Tamar & Tavy Steam Ship Co Ltd. company records.
BT31–5241 Saltash, Three Towns & District Steamboat Co Ltd company records.

Company Record Office

Millbrook Steamboat & Trading Co. Ltd. company records.

Cornwall Record Office

DC/SG/107 CRO Minutes Calstock Ferry Committee 1945–1967.
Letter from Pole Carew to James Brown 1826.
Notice of opening of Torpoint Ferry 1791.

Plymouth & West Devon Record Office

Plymouth Shipping Registers on microfilm – 1824 to 1876
Agreement between the Plymouth Piers Pavilion & Saltash Three Towns Steamboat Co Ltd and John Parson (1910).
Bills of Sale (1892) for the steamers of William Gilbert to the Saltash, Three Towns & District Steamboat Co Ltd.
Bills of Sale (1910) for steamers of the Saltash, Three Towns & District Steamboat Co Ltd to the Plymouth Promenade Pier & Pavilion Co Ltd.
Letter to Debenture Holders of the Saltash, Three Towns & District Steamboat Co Ltd from the Company Secretary regarding the sale of the *Iolanthe* (1900).

Registry of Shipping & Seamen

Plymouth Shipping Registers 1877 to current

Devon Record Office

Ships' Crew Lists

Plymouth Museums & Art Gallery

Plymouth, Devonport and Stonehouse Carriages and Boats, Regulation Act, Bye-laws & Table of Fares 1847 (?)

Private sources:

Oreston and Turnchapel Steamboat Co. Ltd. minute books 1871–1963 courtesy M. Anthony and D. Elford,
Records courtesy K. S. Perkins:
- Prospectus for the Saltash Bridge c.1822
- Notice of meeting re Saltash Bridge 1830
- Letter to Officers of Duchy of Cornwall regarding intention to apply for a Bill for a floating bridge 1830
- Minutes of Meeting of Directors of Southampton Floating Bridge Company regarding visits to Torpoint and Saltash floating bridges in 1853.

Tape recorded interview with Edward Gill of the Plymouth Piers Pavilion & Saltash Three Towns Steamboat Co Ltd made by D. C. Vosper.
Building specification for *Armadillo* (1926), courtesy Arthur Grylls.

Notes, typescripts etc:

Clark, G. C. notes and lists of Plymouth paddle steamers, compiled c1960s.
Millbrook Steamboat & Trading Co Ltd, typescript notes and fleet list compiled by the company in 1962.
Perkins, K. S. research notes and references relating to J. M. Rendel.
Williams, B. Y. notes of Plymouth passenger steamers compiled in 1935 (including his father's notes dating back to the nineteenth century).
Vosper, D. C. *The Ancient Ferry at Saltash,* typescript (Plymouth Local History Library cat. no. P386.6)

BIBLIOGRAPHY

Anderson, R. C. & Frankis, G. G. A. *A History of the Western National*, David & Charles, Newton Abbot 1979.
Anthony, M. *The Red Funnel Line*, Plymouth 1990.
Booker, F. *Industrial Archaeology of the Tamar Valley*, David & Charles, Newton Abbot 1974.
Burtt, F. *Steamers of the Thames and Medway*, Richard Tilling, London 1949.
Carne, A. J. *Cornwall's Forgotten Corner*, Lodenek Press 1985.
Cheeseman, A. J. *The Plymouth, Devonport & South Western Junction Railway*, Oakwood Press, Blandford Forum 1967.
Colledge, J. J. *Ships of the Royal Navy - an historical index. Vol. 2. Navy-built trawlers, drifters, tugs and requisitioned ships.*
Farr, G. *West Country Passenger Steamers*, T. Stephenson & Sons Ltd., Prescot 1967.
Gill, C. *Plymouth, A New History*, Devon Books, Tiverton 1993.
Grimshaw, G. *British Pleasure Steamers 1920-1939*, Richard Tilling, London 1945.
Hull, P. L. *The History of the Cremyll Ferry*, Truro 1963.
Kingdom, A. R. *The Plymouth and Turnchapel Railway*, ARK Publications, Newton Abbot 1996.
Kingdom, A. R. *The Plymouth to Yealmpton Railway*, ARK Publications, Newton Abbot 1998.
Lane, M. R. *The Rendel Connection*, Quiller Press, London 1989.
Langley, A. F. M. and Small, E. *River & Estuary Ferries of South West England*, Waine Research Publications, Wolverhampton 1984.
Merry, I. *The Shipping and Trade of the River Tamar*, parts 1 and 2, National Maritime Museum, London 1980.
Mingay, G. E. *The Transformation of Britain 1830–1939*, Paladin, London 1987.
Mitchell, P. *A Boatbuilder's Story*, Mevagissey.
Noall, C. *A History of Cornish Mail- and Stage-Coaches*, Bradford Barton, Truro 1963.
O'Brien, F. T. O. *Early Solent Steamers*, David & Charles, Newton Abbot 1973.
Paige, R. T. *The Tamar Valley at Work*, Dartington Amenity Trust, Morwellham 1978.
Patrick, A. *Morwellham Quay, a History*, Morwellham Quay Museum, Tavistock, 1989.
Pearse Chope, R. (Editor) *Early Tours in Devon and Cornwall*, David & Charles, Newton Abbot 1967.
Pengelly, A. *The Inside Story of Calstock*, Calstock 1955.
Porter, P. E. B. *Around and About Saltash.*
Sambourne, R. C. *Plymouth, 100 Years of Street Transport*, Glasney Press, Falmouth.
Stevens, W. *Highways and Byways of Plymouth*, A. C. Brown & Co. Ltd., Plymouth 1943.
Vosper, D. C. *Saltash Remembered* parts 1, 2 and 3, Plymouth (1980–3).
Warren, A. R. *The Torpoint Ferry, A History and Review*, The Tamar Bridge and Torpoint Ferry Joint Committee 1991.

ARTICLES:
Anon. correspondence *Mechanics Magazine* Vol 31 1839.
Anon. 'Floating and Flying Bridges' – *The Penny Magazine* 25 March 1843.
Booker, F. L. 'Tamar Paddle Steamers' *Western Morning News* 20 June 1965.
Clammer, R. 'Search for a Paddler's True Identity' *Paddle Wheels* No 103 1986.
Deayton, A. 'Gresham and her sisters – a story of the L.C.C. paddlers' *Paddle Wheels* Nos 116 and 115 1989.
Gallup, R. 'Weir Quay and Holes Hole' *Tamar Journal* No 13 1991.
Godfrey, J. 'The Paddle Steamer, Sir Francis Drake' *Maritime South West* No 9 1996.
Johnson, G. 'Recollections of early steamboat traffic on the Tamar' *Western Morning News* 10 March 1961.
Kingston, J. 'The History of the Torpoint Ferry' *Old Cornwall* Vol 7.
Kingston, J. 'The River Steamer Era', *Torpoint & District Magazine*.
Kittridge, A. 'Coastal Cruising Out of Plymouth' *Paddle Wheels* Nos 94-96 1983-4.
Patrick, A. 'The Tamar Manure Navigation: A Brief History' *Tamar Journal* No 2 1979–80.
Perkins, K. S. 'Rendel and the Dartmouth Floating Bridge' *Rendel's News* (House magazine for the staff of Rendel, Palmer & Tritton).
Umpleby, G. 'River Knew the Bustle of Commerce' *Western Morning News* 31 January 1951.
Vosper, D. C. 'River Steamers of Saltash' *Tamar Journal* No 4 1982.

GUIDE BOOKS AND DIRECTORIES:
Four Rivers Trip, Three Rivers Trip, Grand Circular Trip guides, published by MS&TCo Ltd and O&TSCo Ltd.
Hearder, G.P. *Guide to the River Tamar*, Plymouth 1841.
Kellys Directories.
Murray's Handbook for Devon and Cornwall (1859), Reprinted by David & Charles, Newton Abbot 1971.
Rowe, C. R. *The Illustrated Western Weekly News Holiday Booklets* (Plym, Tamar, Lynher, Tavy).
Scrine Hill, H. *McBrydes River & Sea Trips.*
The Strangers' Handbook to the Western Metropolis, c1847.

NEWSPAPERS AND MAGAZINES:
Paddle Wheels – magazine of the Paddle Steamer Preservation Society.
Plymouth and Devonport Weekly Journal.
Plymouth, Devonport and Stonehouse Herald.
Tamar – Journal of the Friends of Morwellham.
West Briton.
Western Daily Mercury.
Western Evening Herald.
Western Morning News.

INDEX OF VESSELS

General Index